UNSETTLED

Unsettled

American Jews and the
Movement for Justice
in Palestine

Oren Kroll-Zeldin

NEW YORK UNIVERSITY PRESS
New York

NEW YORK UNIVERSITY PRESS
New York
www.nyupress.org

Library of Congress Cataloging-in-Publication Data
Names: Kroll-Zeldin, Oren, author.
Title: Unsettled : American Jews and the movement for justice in Palestine /
Oren Kroll-Zeldin.
Description: New York : New York University Press, [2024] |
Includes bibliographical references and index.
Identifiers: LCCN 2023028412 (print) | LCCN 2023028413 (ebook) |
ISBN 9781479821457 (hardback) | ISBN 9781479821433 (ebook) |
ISBN 9781479821440 (ebook other)
Subjects: LCSH: Jews—United States—Attitudes toward Israel. | Boycott, divestment, and
sanctions movement—United States. | Israel—Politics and government—Foreign public
opinion, American. | Generation Y—United States—Attitudes. | Palestinian Arabs—United
States—Public opinion. | Zionism—United States—Public opinion. | Public opinion—
United States. | Propaganda, Anti-Israeli—United States.
Classification: LCC E184.355 .K76 2024 (print) | LCC E184.355 (ebook) | DDC
327.1/170973—dc23/eng/20231024
LC record available at https://lccn.loc.gov/2023028412
LC ebook record available at https://lccn.loc.gov/2023028413

This book is printed on acid-free paper, and its binding materials are chosen for strength
and durability. We strive to use environmentally responsible suppliers and materials to the
greatest extent possible in publishing our books.

Manufactured in the United States of America

10 9 8 7 6 5 4 3 2 1

Also available as an ebook

To Stav and Ido
May they help others
draw water from the
wellsprings of liberation

CONTENTS

Introduction

American Jews Challenge the Establishment

Let us begin with two episodes that transpired a few months apart in 2021. As violence erupted in Palestine/Israel in May 2021, many young American Jews watched in horror, feeling angry at and disgusted by the horrifically violent scenes unfolding half a world away.[1] During this violent escalation, Israel and Hamas traded rocket fire and airstrikes, which killed 256 Palestinians in Gaza, including 66 children and 40 women, and 13 Israelis, including 2 children.[2] As is the case with all Israeli military incursions into Gaza, this one, which the Israeli Defense Forces (IDF) called Operation Guardian of the Walls, had catastrophic impacts on the lives of Palestinian civilians. Among the infrastructure of everyday Palestinian life destroyed by Israeli missiles were numerous housing units and several business complexes, including a building that housed the offices of the Associated Press, Al Jazeera, and other news outlets.[3] Between the violent dispossession of Palestinians from their homes in the East Jerusalem neighborhood of Sheikh Jarrah and the wide-scale bombing campaign in Gaza, a growing number of young Jews in the United States were increasingly angry with both the actions of the State of Israel and the American Jewish Establishment's uncritical support of Israeli state violence.[4]

The events of May 2021 had a sobering impact on many young American Jews watching the violence unfold virtually; many considered lending their voices to a growing chorus of Jewish dissenters speaking out in solidarity with Palestinians.[5] In one notable instance, a group of more than a hundred rabbinical students from diverse denominational backgrounds penned an open letter expressing their solidarity with Palestinians. It called on American Jews and their institutions to hold Israel accountable for its "violent suppression of human rights."[6] Using eloquent and forceful language, the letter pointed to the mainstream

American Jewish community's engagement with the racial reckoning concurrently taking place in the United States while remaining conspicuously silent on the ongoing racist violence in Palestine/Israel.

The letter declared, "So many of us ignore the day-to-day indignity that the Israeli military and police forces enact on Palestinians, and sit idly by as Israel upholds two separate legal systems for the same region. And, in the same breath, we are shocked by escalations of violence, as though these things are not a part of the same dehumanizing status quo." The authors cited biblical passages to illustrate their message of demanding justice for all, including Palestinians, thus emphasizing the centrality of Jewishness in their lives. It also made clear that they are the very people who will one day be in positions of power in American Jewish life. To that end, the letter noted, "We are future leaders of the Jewish community. We are training to teach the Torah and lead the rituals that will hold our joy and our sorrow. And we are full of tears. We implore you, our community—our students, teachers, congregations, employers, funders—to find your tears, too. Tap into the empathy that you need to feel and experience the reality on the ground in this place so that we can work to change it." The letter was intensely critical of Israel and even labeled it an apartheid state.[7]

But as is often the case with vocal criticism of Israel within the American Jewish community, those who signed the letter did so at great risk to their professional futures. One signee with whom I spoke admitted to feeling anxious that signing the letter would jeopardize their ability to get a job in a synagogue or another Jewish organization. "I signed the letter," they said, "but I was afraid to do so. I did it because it was the right thing to do, but I don't know if having my name on that letter will make it harder for me to get a job. I already know some people who signed the letter who had job offers rescinded."[8]

Despite the fear of reprisal, these future clergy members chose to publicly express their solidarity with Palestinians while calling on the American Jewish community to consistently apply its liberal and progressive values to Israel. Yet this was not an isolated event; it formed part of a larger shift taking place among younger American Jews. The letter points to the presence of cracks in the previously unbreakable Israel–American Jewish alliance.[9] For many young American Jews, standing in solidarity with Palestinians and acting on personal political beliefs and progressive values are more important than potential employment opportunities. Rather, their political activism and embodiment of Jewish and progressive values are tantamount to how they want to live their lives—personally, professionally, and politically.

* * *

A few months later, in November 2021, at three thirty on a cold Jerusalem morning, six Israeli police officers raided an apartment where four American Jewish activists lived. After banging loudly on the windows, waking up everyone inside, the authorities forced the tenants outside, taking their pictures while shining flashlights directly in their faces.[10] A few days later, eight police officers returned with search warrants and raided the apartment again, knocking down cabinets and emptying drawers.[11] During the raid, two of the activists were summoned to a Jerusalem police station for interrogations, including Oriel Eisner, an active participant in the Palestine solidarity movement as a longtime staffer with the Center for Jewish Nonviolence.[12] After the interrogations, Oriel was told he would be allowed to return home only if he signed a condition of release that included a monthlong ban from Jerusalem. When he refused to sign it, the police arrested him and held him in a cell for six hours until ultimately deciding to drop the conditions and release him.[13]

The police raided the apartment because they suspected that the activists had spray-painted Arabic graffiti in downtown Jerusalem as an act of solidarity with Palestinians. Although the police presented no evidence connecting the activists with the graffiti, there was indeed a widespread campaign at this time to plaster posters around Jerusalem to raise awareness about the current conditions in Masafer Yatta, an area in the South Hebron Hills in the occupied West Bank that is under threat of demolition.[14] Composed of twelve Palestinian villages, Masafer Yatta is home to approximately twenty-eight hundred residents, most of them farmers, whose families have been living there for generations.[15] In the early 1980s the Israeli military declared the area Firing Zone 918, a clear effort to dispossess Palestinians from their land while simultaneously fortifying the Israeli settlements in the area.[16] According to a classified document from the Israeli state archives, the Israeli military has been engaged in this practice for decades, one of several strategies used to

Figure I.1. Oriel Eisner in Masafer Yatta, February 2023. Photo by Emily Glick.

dispossess Palestinians from their homes and increase Israeli settlement throughout the West Bank.[17]

Since the land in Masafer Yatta was declared a Firing Zone some four decades ago, Palestinian residents have lived under constant threat of demolitions and evictions from their land, to say nothing of the daily violence perpetrated by Jewish Israeli settlers living nearby.[18] Although they face harsh conditions, including having little to no access to essential services such as water and electricity, the residents of Masafer Yatta are steadfast in their resistance to the Israeli state and its mechanisms of occupation and apartheid.[19] Among other daily forms of nonviolent resistance, members of this community petitioned the Israeli Supreme Court in hopes of protecting their homes. Following a twenty-two-year legal battle, in May 2022 the Supreme Court made its final ruling on the legality of the Firing Zone, opting to green-light the expulsion of the Palestinians living in Masafer Yatta in what would be the largest mass expulsion of Palestinians from their land since 1967.[20]

In efforts to amplify attention on the situation in Masafer Yatta, Oriel and his comrades, who had already formed deep relationships with Palestinians living there, were participating in awareness-raising campaigns, such as hanging posters in Jerusalem and attending frequent demonstrations against the forced transfer of Palestinians from their homes in the South Hebron Hills. As a result of this activism, Oriel's apartment was raided and he was arrested for a crime he did not commit. Although there is a presence of Jewish Israeli activists working on the campaign, many of the visible and vocal Jewish solidarity activists involved in Masafer Yatta are young Jewish Americans currently living in Palestine/Israel. While some of them are dual American and Israeli citizens, like Oriel, most are solely citizens of the United States. They are strategically using their privilege as American Jews to amplify Palestinian voices and to bring attention to the specific manifestations of occupation and apartheid in the South Hebron Hills.[21]

Oriel reflected on his privileges as a Jew living in Israel:

> Because of my Israeli Jewish identity, I have immense privileges and protections afforded to me by the state, legal and otherwise. I have a right to and am given due process. I can't be held in administrative detention indefinitely, and, as a Jewish citizen, any mistreatment will be more likely to garner public attention and pressure. The vulnerability and lack of control I felt are infinitely more severe for millions of Palestinians who are living under occupation every day. Random arrests and house raids, long arrests without evidence, huge fines and costs for recouping confiscated materials happen to Palestinians all of the time. . . . While the Israeli state works to keep Jews and Palestinians separate, [many of us] commit ourselves together to building a better and shared future.[22]

By leveraging his privilege to bring attention to the communities in the South Hebron Hills, Oriel is exhibiting one of the central roles that young American Jews have been playing to impact the situation on the ground in Palestine/Israel. It is a symbolic expression of solidarity that shows both the Israeli authorities and those who unequivocally support Israel that there is a growing population of Jews who refuse to support Israel's policies of occupation and apartheid. Instead, Oriel and other young Jewish American activists like him are building alliances with Palestinians and participating in the broader Palestine solidarity movement, hoping that it will lead to material changes on the ground as a result of international attention. As Oriel wrote, "We are attacked because we are feared, because we have a fighting chance of stopping the onslaught of violence, suppression and expulsion being carried out by Israel every day."[23]

* * *

Unsettled investigates the myriad ways that young Jewish Americans challenge the American Jewish Establishment's unwavering commitment to Israel and Zionism through their participation in the Palestine solidarity movement. This ethnographically rooted research reflects various ways that twenty- and thirtysomething American Jews are confronting the Israeli government's policies of occupation and apartheid while seeking to transform American Jewish institutional support for Israel. As evidenced by the two stories above, some have chosen to work on the ground in solidarity with Palestinians, while others have labored from the United States, indicating the transnational character of this activism.[24] In this book I ask a series of related questions regarding young Jewish American Palestine solidarity activism: How and why do young American Jews participate in the transnational Palestine solidarity movement? Why is the movement so popular among younger Jews in particular, with a clear generational divide between the activists and their elders? How are the activists themselves contesting dominant understandings of Jewish identity and values?

In seeking answers to these questions, this book argues that young Jewish American Palestine solidarity activists view their activism and commitment to ending the occupation and Israeli apartheid as a Jewish value; it is a necessary response to the changing conditions of Jewish life in the twenty-first century. For them, active participation in this social justice movement is a Jewish ethic. The activists intentionally and strategically infuse their work with Jewish teachings and customs in ways that strengthen and reinforce their Jewish identities, thereby allowing them to articulate this work not only as a reflection of their individualized values but as a distinctly Jewish ethos.[25] The participation of young American Jews in Palestine solidarity activism, consistent with other Jewish social justice initiatives, fosters a connection to Jewish values and identity by associating social justice activism with Jewish traditions and values.[26]

Focusing specifically on the mobilization of young Jewish American activists who challenge Israel's policies of occupation and apartheid and confront mainstream Jewish American support for Israel, this book chronicles the participation of these activists in the Palestine solidarity movement through the lens of three social movement strategies. First, young American Jews target mainstream Jewish institutions that uphold and maintain the status quo regarding uncritical and unwavering "support for Israel." These institutions, which socialized young American Jews with "pro-Israel" politics, are now subject to pressure from young activists because many Jews no longer see supporting Israel and Zionism as consistent with their Jewish identities and values.[27]

Second, they participate in co-resistance activism with Palestinians on the ground in Palestine/Israel. Co-resistance refers to the process through which Palestinians, Israelis, Jews from around the world, and international activists resist policies and structures of occupation and apartheid in collaboration with one another. This type of activism, which usually requires people to travel from their homes to Palestine/Israel, involves leveraging the Jewish activists' privilege with the goal of having a positive material impact on Palestinian communities facing the daily pressures of life under Israeli occupation. Third, young American Jews participate in the Boycott, Divestment, and Sanctions (BDS) movement in order to pressure companies and organizations to not profit directly from the Israeli occupation while isolating Israel in the international arena.

I focus on these three primary activist strategies through the work of four activist groups, each integral to Jewish Palestine solidarity activism in the United States: Jewish Voice for Peace (JVP), IfNotNow (INN), the Center for Jewish Nonviolence (CJNV), and All That's Left: Anti-Occupation Collective (ATL). These groups engage in direct actions in the United States that target the American Jewish Establishment, are deeply immersed in co-resistance, BDS, and solidarity activism with Palestinian communities in Palestine/Israel, and have become the subject of widespread media reporting in Israel and the United States, which has catapulted them and Jewish participation in the Palestine solidarity movement into a contentious transnational debate about Jewish politics and identity.[28] While these groups are part of a broader ecosystem of organizations working in a global context to challenge the occupation, they form the nucleus of Millennial and Gen Z Jewish American Palestine solidarity activism.

This book has two main goals. First, it provides an in-depth examination of the specific ways that young Jewish Americans who are participating in the Palestine solidarity movement show up *as Jews* to support Palestinians. Second, the book explores how the social justice activism of movement participants reflects a larger expression of their global Jewish identities and values.[29] The Jewish anti-occupation and anti-apartheid movement is growing rapidly, which is changing the way Millennial and Gen Z Jews engage with Israel, their families, and their Jewish communities.

In this regard, this book draws on the work of numerous scholars who have made similar arguments, most notably Atalia Omer and David Landy, each of whom published significant books on Jewish Palestine solidarity activism.[30] Omer focuses specifically on American Jews, while Landy's book mostly examines how diaspora Jewish identity in Europe is being constructed in opposition to Israel. My argument builds on and converses with their scholarship by focusing on young adults within this same movement. More specifically, I articulate why younger American Jews engage with and connect to Israel in ways that are different from previous generations, which can help us understand how their participation in the Palestine solidarity movement is impacting the way they are building new and interacting with existent Jewish communal spaces.

Ultimately, my argument is that young American Jews are engaging in Palestine solidarity and anti-occupation activism as a way to demand the consistent application of values in all situations—not to be "progressive except for Palestine," but rather to uphold liberal, progressive, and democratic values across all contexts, even in the case of Israel. In the words of Naomi, one of the activists I interviewed, "I participate in Palestine solidarity activism because I want Judaism to survive. I want it to continue to be relevant, moral, powerful, and vital. I want Judaism and Jewishness to continue being a source for how to live a good life and to build a better world. And in my opinion, it has to change in order to do so."[31] Similar to Naomi's belief that Palestine solidarity activism is essential to transforming Judaism, the activists highlighted in this book mobilize based on the premise that upholding their Jewish identity and their conception of Jewish values obligates them to organize in solidarity with Palestinians and against Zionism.

American Jews and Israel

Despite the large body of scholarship that focuses on the disparate attitudes and connections of American Jews toward Israel as well as the contentious nature of the Israel debate in American Judaism, one thing remains abundantly clear: Israel plays a significant role in American Jewish life, regardless of one's political beliefs or attitudes toward the Jewish state.[32] According to public opinion polls, American Jews have historically offered stronger support for Israel than any other community in the United States.[33] In recent years, as broader American support for Israel has shifted dramatically toward a rift along partisan lines, American Jews as a whole continue to offer strong support for Israel.[34] At the same time, despite widespread support for Israel among American Jews, dramatic cleavages have begun to form along generational lines, with younger American Jews supporting the Jewish state less than older generations.

According to the 2020 Pew Survey on Jewish Americans, which provides the most recent in-depth statistical data on Jewish life in the United States, a few key points are essential to understanding the changing nature of American Jewish attitudes toward Israel. First and foremost, being Jewish is extremely important to American Jews. Second, there are many different core ways that American Jews express the importance of their Jewishness. Third, and most significant to this study, caring for Israel is less significant than other forms of Jewish expression among American Jews. More specifically, younger American Jews show lower levels of attachment to Israel than do older Jews.[35] Data from this survey indicate that the majority of Jews fifty and older say that caring about Israel is essential to what it means to be Jewish (51 percent), in contrast to only 35 percent of Jews under thirty. In fact, 27 percent of Jews under thirty say that Israel is *not* important to what it means to them to be Jewish. Therefore, some Jews feel disconnected from Israel and don't do anything about it; they don't visit the country, give to Israel charities, or engage in any type of Palestine solidarity activism. The young American Jews chronicled in this book don't fall in this latter category, as Israel *is* important to them and their Jewishness in some way, even if that does manifest through Palestine solidarity activism.

Furthermore, these data points are interesting in the context of larger questions on the attitudes and identities of American Jews. For example, the Pew Survey notes that three-quarters of all American Jews say that being Jewish is either very or somewhat important to them, confirming that Jewish identity is an integral component in the lives of American Jews. With regard to specific things that are essential to their Jewish identity, 76 percent of American Jews cite remembering the Holocaust and 72 percent say leading a moral and ethical life. Also of note is the fact that 59 percent say that working for justice and equality in society is essential to their Jewishness.

In contrast, caring for Israel is essential to the Jewish identities of only 45 percent of American Jews, suggesting that it is a more significant element of their Jewishness for American Jews to lead a moral and ethical life and to work for justice and equality than it is to care about Israel. Since the liberal and progressive values that American Jews hold dearly clash with the realities of Israeli state policies, particularly those toward Palestinians, Jewish support for Israel is bound to wane as Jews seek to reconcile their liberal values with the actions of the State of Israel.[36] As such, American Jews are increasingly willing to speak out against Israel in favor of their Jewish values, and no group is doing this more than young American Jews. Pew Survey data demonstrate that young American Jews feel both connected to Israel and deeply critical of it. And yet Israel remains central to the American Jewish experience.

Much of the recent scholarship on American Jews and Israel interprets and analyzes these and other data in order to make sense of these shifting generational trends. While the State of Israel has long been central to American Jewish life, Jews in the United States have never been unified in their relationship to Israel. They have instead endured a complex relationship with the Jewish state.[37] Therefore, although there is undoubtedly a dramatic rift in American Jewish attitudes toward Israel today, this is not a new phenomenon to American Judaism.

Prior to the establishment of the State of Israel, many Jewish groups were ardently anti-Zionist and opposed the formation of a Jewish state in Palestine.[38] The Reform Jewish movement, for example, which is the largest denomination of American Judaism, was vociferously anti-Zionist, arguing instead that the United States was the Zion for American Jews and that it was essential to develop American forms of Jewish life that did not rely on a nation-state in a far-off location.[39] Widespread American Jewish opposition to Zionism dissipated, however, as people learned of the horrors of the Holocaust and the destruction of Jewish life in Europe, pushing them to accept the idea that Jews needed a Jewish-majority state in order to increase their safety and security. After the establishment of the State of Israel in 1948, American Jews began supporting the state in various ways, sometimes enthusiastically and other times reluctantly, all while maintaining support for Zionism as an extension of Jewish values.[40]

American Zionism emerged unevenly but nonetheless over time became synonymous with Jewish values and developed into a central priority for American Jews.[41] Many in the mainstream American Jewish community perceived unconditional Zionism to be central to both their Jewishness and their liberal politics. In the 1940s a cadre of American liberals actively supported the Zionist project of establishing a Jewish state in Palestine, though by no means was it a consensus in left-leaning Jewish American circles. According to scholar Amy Kaplan, "Liberal journalists, activists, and politicians fused humanitarian and political understandings to create an influential and enduring narrative of Zionism as a modern progressive force for universal good."[42] These liberals "crafted narratives that merged the humanitarian idea of a haven for refugees with the political goal of national sovereignty, and they championed Zionism as one among a number of progressive movements for liberation and social justice."[43] Furthermore, American Jewish support for Zionism gave American Jews a particular uniqueness and some visibility, even as it offered them positions of power in the Cold War order.[44] Jews took unprecedented powers in this new political era while gaining both generational wealth and whiteness in the process.[45]

At the same time, many progressive American Jews were enamored with the universal values of liberation that labor Zionism espoused and believed that their support for Israel was aligned with both Jewish and American values.[46] The popularity of Leon Uris's novel *Exodus* (1958) and the subsequent film starring Paul Newman (1960) codified the image of Israel as the underdog and convinced a generation of Americans—both Jews and non-Jews—that support for Zionism as a movement of Jewish liberation and national rebirth was a central American ethos.[47] The national liberation story depicted in *Exodus* rendered the Zionist struggle relatable to American audiences, despite, or perhaps due to, its misleading and myth-filled nature. Following the arc of the narrative produced by *Exodus*, Jews in the United States believed that unconditional Zionism was an extension of their distinctly American Jewish and liberal values because Israel was established in part to keep Jews safe after the Holocaust, which enabled them to see Zionism as solely a liberation movement.

It wasn't until after Israel's astounding military victory in the 1967 War that American Jews began to unequivocally support Israel, a new-found relationship that came to be known as the "pro-Israel" position in American Judaism.[48] For the next decade, support for Israel was the great unifying factor among American Jews.[49] This period was marked by what scholars referred to as the "mobilization model" of American Jewish engagement with Israel.[50] The mobilization model was characterized by a central funding organism that sought to raise money from Jews to give to Israel while simultaneously mobilizing support based on a political consensus that advocated on behalf of the Jewish state. As this model of American Jewish engagement grew in strength and became increasingly normalized in Jewish institutions across the country, it forged a seemingly unbreakable alliance between American Jews and the State of Israel.

Over time, however, the mass mobilization model gave way to one of "direct engagement," in which American Jews related to Israel "directly by advocating their own political views, funding favored causes, visiting frequently or living there part time, consuming Israeli news and entertainment, and expressing a distinctively 'realistic' rather than idealistic orientation toward the Jewish state."[51] Perhaps most significantly, direct engagement with Israel was also characterized by the polarization of the American Jewish community and an increased division between those with left- and right-wing politics.[52] But the more American Jews learned about Israel through this direct engagement and increased access to it, the more willing they were to express a critique of the ways that the actions of the state conflicted with their liberal and progressive Jewish values, which led to a growing generational divide in attachment to and support of Israel.[53]

While a generation ago American Jews were mostly united around public support for Israel, today a growing demographic of Millennial and Gen Z American Jews is speaking out forcefully against the American Jewish Establishment and the government of the State of Israel, adding their voices to a global movement in solidarity with Palestinians. For these mostly young Jews, the unwavering support of Israel by mainstream Jewish institutions conflicts with the Jewish values upon which they were raised—those of freedom, equality, liberation, and liberal democracy—which compels many young Jews to resist Israel's policies toward Palestinians.

The fact that young American Jews are at the forefront of the generational divide over Israel in American Jewish communities has led this demographic to receive widespread attention from scholars as well as mainstream media. Foundations and academic centers have poured resources into studying and publishing reports, articles, and books on young American Jews and their connections with Israel.[54] Based on this research, some scholars fear that young American Jews will lose their attachment to Israel and will continue to distance themselves from the Jewish state.[55] Others argue that even though the dynamics of the relationship are changing, young American Jews will remain connected to Israel.[56]

Even the mainstream media, both Jewish presses and beyond, have started noticing that things are changing in how young American Jews relate to Israel. Recent years have seen articles published in mainstream outlets as disparate as the *New York Times*, *Rolling Stone*, and others speculating on the shifts in the American Jewish community's relationship to Israel.[57] But the conversation has been even more vociferous in the pages of the American Jewish press and media outlets with a focus on Palestine/Israel.[58] Regardless of the varying viewpoints, it is increasingly clear that the American Jewish community is at a tipping point and young American Jews are on the frontiers of the social and communal transformation regarding their relationship to Israel.[59]

This should not be surprising, as young American Jews have been playing a significant role in transforming and reshaping Jewish life in the United States for some time.[60] The actions of the activists that I document in the following chapters bring into sharp focus the overt divergence of American Jewish institutional politics from the Jewish values of a portion of the community they allegedly represent. This divergence has resulted in robust Jewish participation in the Palestine solidarity movement, a trend that challenges the status quo of Jewish American support for Israel and is reshaping the landscape of Jewish social justice activism in the United States.

Palestine Solidarity Activism as a Jewish Value

In his seminal book *The Crisis of Zionism* (2012), Peter Beinart expanded on an essay he penned two years earlier and argued that the Jewish American Establishment's refusal to confront the demise of Israel's democracy and the deepening occupation of the West Bank had the potential to alienate young liberal Jews from Zionism and Israel.[61] He claimed that if American Jews were forced to choose between their liberal values and Zionism the choice would be easy; they would eschew the political ideology that supports the Jewish State: "For several decades, the Jewish establishment has asked American Jews to check their liberalism at Zionism's door, and now, to their horror, they are finding that many young Jews have checked their Zionism instead."[62]

In the years since Beinart wrote these incredibly prescient words, an increasing number of American Jews have abandoned Zionism and their support for Israel because they have come to understand the dissonance between their liberal and progressive values and the actions of the Israeli government. Presenting ethnographic and quantitative data as well as analysis of mainstream and social media, this book provides clear evidence that supports Beinart's thesis that young American Jews would abandon Zionism in favor of liberal values. But I also contend that young Jews are confronting Israel's occupation and policies of apartheid and the American Jewish Establishment that supports it as an important expression of their Jewish values and as a way of performing their Jewish identities.

Beinart's prophetic warning has come to fruition as many young American Jews are indeed alienated from Zionism, Israel, and mainstream Jewish organizations that maintain a close relationship with Israel and Zionism. Instead, they have found new places to engage with Jewish life and have created Jewish communal spaces that reside outside the mainstream. Fed up with the Jewish orthodoxy of communal support for Israel, young American Jews are increasingly turning to alternative ways of engaging with Jewish life by joining or creating organizations or collectives that foster dissenting views on Israel and Zionism. These groups embrace Palestine solidarity activism as one way of expressing one's Jewishness and commitment to liberal and progressive Jewish values.

Beinart's forewarning failed to garner the necessary changes in the American Jewish Establishment, which continuously supports Israel's hawkish policies and demonizes Palestinians, even as the Israeli government has become increasingly right-wing. The young American Jews I interviewed for this book emphasized that as long as the institutions of the American Jewish community continue failing to call for an end to the Israeli occupation and maintain unequivocal support for Israel, they will not participate in Jewish life through those institutional spaces such as synagogues, community centers, federations, and others. The reckoning that Beinart foretold has not only alienated young Jews but also inspired them to engage in a new form of Jewish social justice activism that is rooted in solidarity with Palestinians and is committed to full equality and justice for all people living in Palestine/Israel.

While many young American Jews are clearly "checking their Zionism," this maxim is overly simplistic in today's sociocultural milieu. The research that I present in this book contends that the Jewish activists who participate in the Palestine solidarity movement are instead choosing a different option. They are still entering the door of Jewish politics but are doing so under the mantle of an explicitly Jewish leftist radicalism as opposed to the general American liberalism to which Beinart referred. The activists and their activities documented in the following chapters are mobilizing under the premise not that Zionism clashes with their general political ideals but rather that it clashes with their distinctly Jewish identities and conception of Jewish values.

One way to understand these Jewish values is as a form of critical engagement with Israel and Zionism in ways that invigorate and infuse Jewishness with a renewed and particular sense of social justice and political activism, one rooted in three important pillars: Palestinian liberation, ending the Israeli occupation and policies of apartheid, and liberating Judaism from Zionism. These are the three pillars upon which the participation of young American Jews in Palestine solidarity activism stands. These are the ultimate goals toward which most of the activists are working. In order to achieve these goals, activists engage in three main strategies and tactics: confronting mainstream Jewish American Establishment organizations, co-resistance, and BDS, all of which are explored in greater depth later in this book. Through their Palestine solidarity activism, young Jewish Americans are merging their Jewish and radical values as a form of Jewish political community activism and engagement as an antidote to Zionism's ethnonationalism.

Young Jewish American activists are thus simultaneously pushing back against two parallel strands—Zionism and Israeli occupation/ apartheid. On the one hand, young American Jewish Palestine solidarity activists challenge Zionism's stronghold on American Judaism by resisting the conflation of Zionism and Judaism all while attempting to reclaim their Judaism from Zionism.[63] By challenging Jewish institutional relationships to Zionism and creating alternative Jewish spaces devoid of Zionism as a central ethos, these activists highlight the possibilities for an existence of American Jewish life that is not reliant on a connection to or advocating on behalf of the Jewish state. At the same time, they are actively resisting Israel's occupation in numerous ways, pushing back against the Jewish American Establishment's support for Israel and its occupation of the Palestinian Territories. In opposing the occupation and seeking to end Jewish American support for it, activists are renewing their connections to Judaism in a way that is in line with their universal liberal and progressive values as well as their particular Jewish ones.

In this sense, young American Jewish Palestine solidarity activists are at the forefront of a twenty-first-century political movement of Jewish renewal. For them, Palestine solidarity and anti-occupation activism are significant Jewish values and fundamental ways to perform and express one's Jewishness. By infusing contemporary Jewish practice with Palestine solidarity activism, these young American Jews can be understood as countercultural, going against the grain of mainstream American Jewish life and practice. This is similar to how the denominational Jewish Renewal movement developed in the 1960s as a response to the waning significance of spirituality in Jewish American religious practice, emerging out of the hippie countercultural movement's desire to reconnect with spirituality.[64] In much the same way, this contemporary Jewish renewal of political and social justice activism is challenging the mainstream and creating a whole new way of orienting toward Jewishness, one that is "reimagining Jewishness in solidarity with Palestinians."[65]

This political activism can also be considered a new form of what political scientist Dov Waxman calls "critical engagement" with Israel.[66] Critical engagement refers to the various ways that American Jews engage with Israel today—through questioning, challenging, and criticizing Israel rather than simply accepting or endorsing the state and its policies. This mode of relating to Israel has been on the rise in recent years, particularly among young Jews who see it as a method of joining their complicated connections to Israel with their Jewishly inspired ethical values of social justice and *tikkun olam* (repairing the world).[67] Young American Jews, therefore, use Palestine solidarity activism as a method of making sense of the tension between these values and Jewish communal support for Israel.[68] At the same time, the critical engagement methods of young Jews with Israel have been met with criticism and contempt from many American Jews, especially those of the older generations, which include most of the leaders of mainstream Jewish organizations. This has played a significant role in intensely fragmenting the American Jewish community.

Central to Waxman's theory of critical engagement is the fact that young American Jews are more engaged with Israel than are the previous generations while simultaneously being more critical of Israeli policies than are older Jews in the United States.[69] Drawing on the 2013 Pew Survey of American Jews and other empirical data, Waxman explains why the generational differences between older American Jews and younger ones are so dramatic when it comes to connections with Israel: Millennial and Gen Z Jews have different generational memories of and experiences with Israel than do older Americans.[70]

First, young Jews today are far less proximate to the Holocaust than previous generations were and therefore have a far different understanding of one of Israel's foundational narratives, which intentionally and explicitly links the traumas of the Holocaust to the establishment of the State of Israel.[71] Second, older generations witnessed the birth of Israel and have vivid memories of the perceived imminent destruction of Israel during the wars in 1967 and 1973. On a personal level, I vividly remember having very meaningful conversations with my grandfather, who was born in Brooklyn in 1920, about how the establishment of the State of Israel was the greatest historical moment in his life.[72] For him, it was a living moment recorded in a long and rich life, standing out as symbolically and materially important for improving the living conditions for Jews around the world. Conversely, the watershed years of 1948 and 1967 are moments in recorded history to me and younger generations, not vivid memories that changed or impacted our perceptions of the world. Put simply, younger Jews do not have the same nostalgic memories of Israel's establishment as older generations, which has impacted their view of and engagement with Israel.[73]

Furthermore, most Millennial and Gen Z Jews today are not old enough to remember the hopefulness or the crumbling of the Oslo peace process of the 1990s.[74] Though many encountered a glossy version of Israel through mainstream Jewish institutions, they are also very familiar with Israel as an occupier and likely were exposed to media images or comments from friends that condemned Israel as a constant aggressor and abuser of human rights rather than a righteous victim of anti-Jewish persecution. These Jewish Americans "have grown up during the Second Intifada, Israel's wars against Hamas in the Gaza Strip, wars that have inflicted heavy casualties among Palestinians and generated fierce criticism of Israel around the world."[75] Additionally, young Jews today are far more likely to encounter Palestinian narratives than their parents or grandparents, either from courses they take or by encountering pro-Palestine activism on their university campus, all of which shape the way young Jews relate to Israel.

Young Jewish American Palestine solidarity activism thus represents a new and reimagined mobilized model of critical engagement with Israel. Today's mobilized model looks very different from the way previous generations mobilized Jewish communal support for Israel. While their activism is still based on a group of Jewish Americans engaging with Israel, they are mobilizing in a very different way. Now their actions are rooted in an unequivocal opposition to the occupation and Israeli apartheid while mobilizing to end the mainstream Jewish community's uncritical support for it and the subsequent human rights abuses toward Palestinians. They are mobilizing on social media and challenging mainstream Jewish institutions, are engaging in co-resistance with Palestinians on the ground, and are using BDS campaigns to exemplify Palestine solidarity activism as a Jewish value.

These are all methods and tactics of activism that did not exist or were not widespread a generation ago. Furthermore, social media enables activists to connect with one another quickly and on a deep level, making it possible to mobilize actions and garner widespread support almost instantaneously through posts on Twitter, Facebook, Instagram, and other sites.[76] Today the mobilization is based not on an idealistic perception of Israel but rather on the realistic understanding of the Jewish state's mistreatment of Palestinians and the American Jewish Establishment's enabling and perpetuation of it. Young Jewish American activists involved with the Palestine solidarity movement are pushing back against the efforts of the Jewish institutions that socialized them into caring for Israel while concurrently finding new ways to connect with Jewish life: through anti-occupation and anti-apartheid activism.

In contrast to Waxman's analysis of the new wave of critical engagement with Israel—that younger Jews engage critically with Israel out of a love for Israel and a desire to make it better—the young activists in this study are driven by a commitment to justice and an ethical care for a safe and thriving Jewish future both in Palestine/Israel and globally. Though many of the activists may indeed have a deep love for Israel and a desire to transform Israeli politics and society, the main driving force behind their direct critical engagement with Israel is the ethical imperative of justice that many of the activists were taught to care for in Jewish educational and communal environments.[77] While Waxman argues that critical engagement is rooted in love for Israel and Omer claims that Jewish Palestine solidarity activists are motivated by their dedication to justice, I discovered that this new generation's Israel engagement through Palestine solidarity activism is based on a love for and commitment to the Jewish people, a safe and secure Jewish future, and the consistent application of the Jewish values of freedom, liberation, equality, and justice that they were taught by Jewish institutions. Today's young Jewish activists believe that Israel's human rights abuses of Palestinians harm Jewish life, identity, and culture in both Israel and other places around the world.

They believe that in order to make Jews safer and to ensure Jewish survival, Israel must end its occupation and apartheid policies toward

Palestinians. While many of the activists I interviewed for this project noted that they critically engage with Israel out of the imperative to work for justice, as Omer argues, every single activist engaged in Palestine solidarity activism out of an ethical commitment to the Jewish people. Their activism is not about a love of the State of Israel (*ahavat yisrael*) and the desire to make Israel better, a concept that has been concretized as being intertwined with Zionist goals since 1948.[78] All of their work is instead rooted in a dedication to all forms of justice in service (*avodah*) to ensuring a thriving Jewish identity and culture alongside Jewish safety, security, and survival.[79] The activists whom I interviewed for this book consistently reiterated that they are compelled to work for the end of Israel's occupation and policies of apartheid by the ethical imperative of justice that they were taught in the Jewish educational and communal environments where they were raised.

This is particularly important due to the historically contested notions of Jewish values in American Jewish life and the way that Zionism and support for Israel fit into the framework of Jewish values. As noted above, historically, unconditional American Jewish support for Zionism and Israel was aligned with Jewish values.[80] But Jewish values themselves have long been contested in American Jewish life.[81] As such, while American Jews may tout their *tikkun olam* programming and speak about the importance of social justice, the reality is much more complicated. So when it comes to American Jewish attitudes toward Israel, the contestation of Jewish values comes into very sharp focus.

In previous decades many American Jews successfully merged their liberal values with Zionism and support for Israel. But that started to change after the 1967 War when Israel's occupation and the teachings of Palestinians and African Americans shifted the opinions of American Jewish leftists on Israel.[82] Although the 1967 War led to a new era in mainstream American Jewish relationships to Israel, it also complexified how some left-wing Jews grappled with their support for both Israel and their liberal political leanings. The onset of the Israeli occupation of the Palestinian Territories of the West Bank, Gaza, and East Jerusalem challenged many progressive American Jews to think more critically about Israeli state violence. While they supported anticolonial struggles in other parts of the world, they were reticent to call out Israel as a settler-colonial state, thereby calling into question a consistency of values that remains to this day. According to Eric Alterman, "Israel came to be perceived as more and more a conservative cause, liberals and leftists evinced growing sympathy for the plight of the displaced Palestinians, who, now stateless and oppressed, had come to occupy the underdog role that history had previously assigned to the Jews. Among intellectuals and inside America's universities, their cause was often linked to the cause of Black South Africans against their country's apartheid system."[83]

Through these historical shifts, American Zionism did not fit as neatly into American Jewish values as it once had. Young American Jewish Palestine solidarity activists today are part of a long and thriving tradition of Jews drawing on the teachings of and working in solidarity with anticolonial activists in Black and Palestinian communities in the United States.[84] Conversely, as American Jewish life grew increasingly invested in American Zionism, the community moved away from its authentic commitments to universally held values of freedom, liberation, equality, and justice, as is most evident by the absence of American Jewish Establishment leaders in the fight against South African apartheid.[85] The radical solidarities that the young American Jewish activists chronicled in this book are forming resist a particular notion of Jewish values that are linked to unconditional allegiance to and support for Israel. Young American Jewish participation in the Palestine solidarity movement is therefore a fundamental way to push back against particular long-held Jewish values and to build vibrant new coalitions for justice and as a way of reclaiming Jewish values.

In this regard, young American Jewish Palestine solidarity activists are motivated by and dedicated to an ethic to care for Jewish people, identity, and culture. According to anthropologist Miriam Ticktin, care can be understood as "a form of political warfare: to engage in care is to uphold the right to survive."[86] Rather than a specific set of practices, acts of care can be "a form of political imagination to fuel hope and desire for transformative action. . . . Care in this case unites communities of struggle across and transcending international boundary lines."[87] Jewish Palestine solidarity activism therefore comes from a place of care for Palestinians *and* Jews and the desire to see both communities thrive in the present and future. It is rooted in the fact that both peoples' liberation is inextricably linked.

Young American Jews and Strategies of Palestine Solidarity Activism

This book focuses on Millennial and Gen Z Jewish Americans who participate in Palestine solidarity activism as a Jewish value and as a way of performing their Jewish identities. By "Millennial and Gen Z," I am referring to people born between 1981 and 2003.[88] Although Gen Z typically ends at 2012, I did not interview anyone born after 2003 for this book, therefore I am referring in this book to Millennials and older members of Gen Z. Although precisely defining generations is challenging, this range both is widely agreed upon and represents what scholars understand as being the most progressive generation since the radical youth activism of the 1960s.[89]

Also, though many of the activists I interviewed for this book are the first in their family to challenge the dominant Jewish American attitudes toward Israel and Zionism, they are aware that they are participants in the most recent iteration of a long strand of Jewish resistance to Israel and Zionism as well as Jewish participation in Palestine solidarity activism. As historian Michael Fischbach aptly notes, "Where progressive Americans stand on these issues today . . . stems from the events of decades past."[90] Today's young American Jewish Palestine solidarity activists are standing on the shoulders of a long tradition of Jewish opposition to Zionism in the United States.

For example, founded in 1942, the American Council for Judaism was an ardently anti-Zionist organization that was committed to publicizing the idea that Jews are a religious group rather than a national group, as the Zionist movement claimed.[91] Other groups—such as Breira, New Jewish Agenda, Americans for Peace Now, and *Tikkun* magazine—have in various ways advocated for Palestinian rights within the landscape of American Jewish politics for decades.[92] In addition, progressive Jewish American scholars, journalists, writers, public intellectuals, artists, and others have worked arduously to present a vocal Jewish opposition to Zionism, Israel, and the Palestinian-Israeli conflict.[93] Young American Jews today are aware that they are the newest participants in upholding this legacy of the activists who expressed dissenting views from the American Jewish mainstream, which helped pave the way for them to have a tremendous impact on the Jewish American community's engagement with Israel today. They are taking the lessons from previous generations and applying pressure in ways that are more relevant to the contemporary political, social, and cultural situation, using a particular set of strategies and tactics.

Why does it matter that young American Jews engage in Palestine solidarity activism? Why should Jewish Americans play a role in the Palestine solidarity movement? According to scholar and cultural critic Ariella Azoulay, ending Israeli state violence should not solely be the victim's responsibility but rather should be "the obligations and interests of Israeli Jews and the Jewish community worldwide, of all those who were implicated" in the creation of a state based on maintaining a Jewish majority.[94] Many young American Jews feel implicated in Israeli state violence and are participating in Palestine solidarity activism out of a moral and ethical imperative to declare that this violence should not take place, especially not in their name. In other words, they are boldly rejecting Israeli state violence and claiming that occupation and apartheid are not representative of their Judaism.

The political activism of young American Jews emerges out of a commitment to justice and a dedication to a flourishing Jewish future. While the widespread participation of young Jews in political activism in solidarity with Palestinians may be distinct from older Jews who continue to support Israel, it is not divergent from previous Jewish activists on a range of issues, who have similarly noted Jewish social justice traditions as an impetus for their political engagement.[95] By emphasizing their Jewishness, the activists position themselves to participate in the Palestine solidarity movement as Jews, using tactics to challenge "pro-Israelism" in the Jewish American community and seeking to normalize dissenting views on Israel and Zionism. The activists challenge the emotional and political red lines established by mainstream Jewish communities about what is and what is not acceptable to believe about Israel. By participating in anti-occupation activism in a Jewish context, young American Jewish social justice activists are challenging those red lines and are reimagining a new and meaningful way of engaging in Jewish life.[96]

As scholars note, a social movement needs a diversity of tactics and a quality of participation in order to succeed.[97] In addition to the tactics I describe in this book, there are many other ways that Jewish Israelis and worldwide Jews resist the apparatus of occupation and apartheid alongside Palestinians and others who participate in the Palestine solidarity movement. For example, legal advocacy, nonviolent direct action, conscientious objection, and activist tourism are prominent methods that activists use to combat Israeli state violence.[98] Palestine solidarity activists also lobby politicians in Washington, D.C., organize educational campaigns, and mobilize on social media.[99] All of these strategies, and the ways that young American Jews engage with them, are part of a broader ecosystem of Palestine solidarity activism both in the United States and globally.

As I describe in greater detail in chapter 1, Jewish participation in the Palestine solidarity movement comprises multiple organizations, collectives, and individual activists who are jointly and separately working to end Israel's occupation of the Palestinian Territories, abolish the mainstream Jewish community's support for the occupation, and call attention to the freedom, dignity, and justice that Palestinians demand. Although there are many strategies involved with Palestine solidarity activism, I focus solely on the grassroots activism of young Jewish Americans and on the activists themselves, not on politicians, community leaders, or mainstream institutions.

By focusing on the grassroots level, I examine how Jewish participation in this movement is driving transformative change in the Jewish community regarding Palestine/Israel. Though various organizations and individuals within the broad ecosystem of the movement may have unique or more specific goals to address some of their concerns, the primary goal of this movement is to end the Israeli occupation while eroding American and Jewish American institutional support for it. While it is unlikely that these activists will succeed in ending the occupation, it is not unrealistic for this movement to dramatically impact the way that Jewish Americans think about and engage with Palestine/Israel. In fact, as I argue in the following chapters, pressure from the movement and a changing political and cultural landscape in Jewish American communities shows that the movements' strategies are changing the conversation and impacting people's perceptions of Israel.

Since this research deals predominantly with an internal Jewish conversation on Palestine/Israel, Palestinians and their experiences are largely outside the scope of this book. While Palestinians remain what sociologist Sarah Anne Minkin decisively refers to as "present absentees" from the American Jewish conversation on Palestine/Israel, I do not intend to further invisibilize Palestinians, who ultimately must be the ones to decide the fate of their liberation.[100] My previous writings have focused more intently on the Palestinian experience, highlighting and centering their voices.[101] But in this book my intention is to shed light on the ways that Jews are participating in Palestine solidarity activism as a way of shifting the landscape of unequivocal American Jewish support and American political support for Israel while also challenging Israeli policies of occupation and apartheid on the ground in Palestine/Israel. Although Palestinian voices are not centered in this book, learning about Palestinian experiences of Israeli state violence and dispossession compelled my interlocuters to engage in solidarity activism. Therefore, though Palestinians mostly remain "present absentees" herein, the strong alliances between Palestinians and the young Jewish American activists I interviewed portend a future in which Palestinians and their experiences are not absent but rather are central to the American Jewish conversation about Israel.

A Note on Terminology—"Occupation" and "Apartheid"

In 2018, when I first started my research for this book, I set out to examine the role that young American Jews played in a broader ecosystem of what I understood to be anti-occupation activism. I wanted to learn what this demographic did to challenge Israel's occupation of the Palestinian Territories. But I quickly learned that it was important to qualify the term "occupation." Some of the people I interviewed understood the occupation to refer to the areas that Israel occupied after the 1967 War—Gaza, the West Bank, and East Jerusalem, areas that were not controlled by the Jewish state prior to that military action. Others, including those involved in some of the more radical forms of activism, said that the term "occupation" refers to the entire area of historic Palestine, including the territory that became Israel in 1948. Therefore, following other scholars who have conducted research on similar topics, in this book "anti-occupation activism" refers to multiple things, which change according to particular individuals and/or organizations.[102] That said, most of the people I spoke with are pushing for, at the very least, an immediate withdrawal of Israeli troops from the territories occupied in

1967 in order to establish a Palestinian state there, thus ensuring Palestinian self-determination. They understand this to be a pragmatic goal and a necessary stepping stone to a just, sustainable, and secure peace in the region.

However, over the course of conducting the research, I learned that the rapidly changing conditions on the ground in Palestine/Israel required a rethinking, restructuring, and rearticulation of my inquiry. In the half decade I spent researching and writing this book, the terrain of activism transformed tremendously as Israel's rightward shift intensified and as the international community, led by Palestinians as well as human rights organizations, more forcefully asserted the apartheid nature of Israel's rule over Palestinians. The apartheid framework was once an idea put forward mainly by Palestinian scholars and activists in addition to a small fringe of Israeli academics, which was often dismissed by the international community and by American Jews as an incorrect and inappropriate framing of what they deemed to be a clash of competing nationalist groups.[103]

But as reputable human rights organizations began to articulate the apartheid framework as legitimate for describing the situation in Palestine/Israel, many activists also changed their stance.[104] Additionally, the Jewish organizations and groups I focus on in this book all started using the language of apartheid, some earlier than others, including many whose use of the apartheid framework predated the release of reports from prominent human rights organizations. I stake my claim to the debate on Israeli apartheid in other scholarly work, and this is not the place to relitigate it nor to engage the robust literature on the apartheid system in Palestine/Israel.[105] But as the activists and organizations I focused on in this book began asserting the anti-apartheid drive to their activism rather than merely articulating their work as anti-occupation, it was important to include such language in this project. As such, in this book I use the language of both anti-apartheid and anti-occupation activism to highlight the fact that while some identify as anti-occupation activists, others say they are engaged with anti-apartheid activism.

The multiple articulations of the type of activism are representative of the diversity of political opinions among young American Jewish Palestine solidarity activists. Just like the American Jewish community as a whole is not monolithic, the activists in this movement are also quite diverse in their political opinions. They have a wide spectrum of beliefs regarding the contemporary situation in Palestine/Israel. Some identify as liberal Zionist intent on working toward peace, while others are ardently anti-Zionist who focus more on equality and justice. Some activists are committed to a two-state solution; others are dedicated to the vision of a binational state where Palestinians and Israelis are equals and Palestinians can realize the right of return. Despite the wide range of political beliefs, one thing remains constant: all of the activists are unequivocally opposed to Israeli state violence toward Palestinians and are steadfast in their commitment to ending Israeli policies of occupation and apartheid.

Methodology and Structure of the Book

I write this book from the position of an embedded participant in the movement, albeit one who is rooted in applied, community-driven ethnographic scholarship.[106] Although I have participated in Palestine solidarity activism in various ways over the past decade and a half, I was impressed by how young American Jews impacted their families and communities through their activism. The majority of my activism was on the ground in Palestine/Israel, and although I spoke with my family and friends about what I was doing, nothing I did seemed to have any real impact on how people acted or thought about Palestine/Israel, nor did it make any material impact for Palestinians or Jewish Israelis. As I learned about what young American Jews were doing to challenge the status quo, I decided to commence this research project to discover what they were doing to confront Israel's occupation and American Jewish support for Israel.

I was particularly fascinated by their success in cementing Jewish opposition to and dissenting views of Israel and Zionism as a legitimate and robust Jewish political position in the United States. In many ways I saw the activists as a reflection of myself. While conducting research I often imagined that if I were a little younger, I would likely have been more involved as a participant with the organizations popular with the young American Jews analyzed in this book. As I researched this community of activists, I became involved with some of the organizations they were part of. But more importantly, I developed meaningful friendships with many activists whom I deeply admire and who taught me a lot about what it means to participate in Palestine solidarity activism as a Jew. Throughout this book I insert myself autoethnographically in various ways in an effort to include my own journey with Palestine solidarity activism, my subjectivity, and my own process of questioning the narratives and politics that I learned in my socialization as an American Jew.[107] Born at the tail end of Gen X (sometimes my peers and I are referred to as being in Gen Y), I do not fit neatly into the same generational cohort of the activists I interviewed for this research. But since generation is a key analytical category for this book, and because I highlight many of my own experiences throughout, it is important to note that while my experiences resemble many of those described by activists on the following pages, I do not claim to be part of the same generation of young American Jews who are the focus of my inquiry.

This book involves mixed methods of research, including ethnography and participant observation, in-depth semistructured interviews with activists, and social discourse analyses of online articles and social media posts. The majority of the participant observation conducted for this book took place between 2012–2013 and 2018–2022 both in the United States and on the ground in Palestine/Israel. I interviewed in great detail sixty-three activists, most of whom are young American Jews; I also interviewed some Israeli Jews as well as a few Palestinians and non-Jewish or non-Palestinian activists involved with the Palestine solidarity movement. The heavy majority of the interviewees range in age between nineteen and thirty-nine and identify as either Gen Z or Millennial.

Most of my interlocuters are affiliated with the four main groups discussed in this book—IfNotNow, the Center for Jewish Nonviolence, All That's Left, and Jewish Voice for Peace—but many also have connections with numerous other Jewish activist organizations. My interviewees represent the diversity of Jewish American life regarding geographical location, Jewish denominational affiliation, age, gender and sexual identity, as well as ethnicity, race, and culture. I interviewed students and professionals, some of whom are involved in Palestine solidarity activism as part of their livelihood and others for whom it is an additional element of their otherwise busy lives. While most of the interviewees live in the United States, some are currently residing in Palestine/Israel. Among the interviewees living there, some have chosen to take Israeli citizenship, while others have refused to do so based on ideological and political considerations.

This book traces the process through which young American Jews have become active participants in the broader movement of Palestine solidarity activism. It begins by laying out the terrain of activism and the broad ecosystem of Jewish options for engaging in Palestine solidarity activism. Then it presents the core ways that young Jewish Americans have become integral participants in a social movement of anti-occupation and anti-apartheid activism. The first chapter explains the ecosystem of Jewish anti-occupation activism and lays out the theoretical framework for the book, that social transformation requires harnessing people power rather than relying on community leaders or elected officials to make change.

As participants in a nonviolent grassroots movement, the Jewish Palestine solidarity activists are impacting public opinion through their strategic actions and mobilization, which in turn is shifting the tenor of political engagement regarding U.S. support for Israel among elected officials and a greater segment of the general American population. In addition to laying out a theoretical approach to social movement building, chapter 1 also explains the recent historical episodes that activated young Jews and thus catapulted the social movement into the forefront of Jewish politics in the United States. I show that most people come to anti-occupation organizing through activism on other social issues, which enables them to participate in an intersectional, diverse, and vibrant movement rooted in the understanding that all justice struggles are interconnected.

In chapter 2 I document the process of unlearning Zionism through which young American Jews encounter the contradictions of their Jewish education and their values alongside the realities of Zionism's impacts on Palestinians. I also examine the process through which Jews in the United States are "miseducated" about Palestine/Israel by American Jewish institutions and how activists have started to resist the Jewish educational system and its process of pro-Israel indoctrination. This chapter explores the important role of personal transformation in building the social movement by addressing the ways in which young Jews active in the movement encounter the myths of Zionism and decide to engage in anti-occupation activism. I look at how most young Jews in the United States learn about Israel and what happens to those individuals open to unlearning and challenging the Zionist myths they learned. To frame this discussion, I include an autoethnographic account of my own personal journey with unlearning Zionism and bearing witness to occupation on the ground. In this chapter, I also document some of the personal and political transformations that lead people to become active participants rather than passive supporters of the Palestine solidarity movement. This chapter argues that while the activists in the movement come from diverse Jewish backgrounds and have varied attachments to Zionism, the activists largely perceive Zionism as antithetical to their Jewishness, and thus their engagement with anti-occupation and anti-apartheid activism is in line with their Jewish ethical values of social justice.

In the following three chapters I expound on each of the main methods of young American Jewish involvement in Palestine solidarity activism, beginning with the easiest entry point and moving to the most radical forms of activism, which also have the most severe consequences for participation. Targeting the American Jewish Establishment is the easiest strategy of activism through which one enters the movement, while publicly engaging with BDS is the strategy most likely to lead an activist to be ostracized from their community or even lose a job. These chapters also focus on one or more organizations that play a central role in that particular activist tactic.

Chapter 3 looks at how activists target mainstream Jewish American institutions that are upholding the occupation and strategically omit Palestinian narratives. This chapter examines the "Birthright walk-offs" that took place during the summer of 2018 as a case study to illustrate what it looks like when Jewish activists in the movement target a mainstream Jewish institution. In addition to exploring this protest, chapter 3 also touches on the conversations it started and the questions it raised about the growing movement of Jewish anti-occupation activism in the United States. By focusing mainly on the work of IfNotNow, which largely targets mainstream Jewish American institutions, chapter 3 argues that the activists who walked off their Birthright trips did so not only as a distinct expression of their commitment to social justice and their Jewish identities but also in a highly successful effort to show that targeting mainstream Jewish institutions is a key method of Jewish anti-occupation activism in the United States today.

Chapter 4 focuses on co-resistance activities as a method of nonviolent activism in which Jewish and Palestinian activists resist policies and structures of occupation and apartheid in collaboration with one another. In the co-resistance model, Palestinians set the conditions for action and invite partners to join them based on the shared commitments to bring a just and equitable end to the Israeli occupation. This chapter focuses on how two specific groups, the Center for Jewish Nonviolence and All That's Left, engage in nonviolent direct actions and partnership building. It argues that the co-resistance model presents tangible results to improve the lives of Palestinians on the ground. This chapter also argues that the nature of this organizing model produces a vibrant, intersectional, and powerful anti-occupation movement by building trust and relationships through embodied actions, providing evidence on the ground for what a shared future might look like for Palestinians and Jews in Palestine/Israel.

In chapter 5, I examine young Jews' involvement in the Boycott, Divestment, and Sanctions (BDS) movement. Since participation in BDS activism can have the most severe consequences for individual activists due to the fact that the American Jewish Establishment has made BDS activism the red line for inclusion/exclusion in Jewish spaces in the United States, this form of activism is both the most radical and the least likely for people to openly support. While critics of the BDS movement argue that it both is antisemitic and unfairly demonizes Israel, this chapter examines how BDS has grown to be the largest and most prominent nonviolent movement advocating for Palestinian rights and justice in history and runs counter to these critiques.

By focusing specifically on the work of Jewish Voice for Peace (JVP) and the young Jewish Americans involved with BDS organizing through JVP, this chapter explains how one of the reasons BDS has grown so dramatically over the past decade and a half is because of Jewish participation in and support for the movement. Many young Jews are attracted to this strategy both because it is nonviolent and since it has historical precedent as one of the effective tools that helped end the apartheid system in South Africa, thereby indicating that it may prove successful in ending Israel's occupation of the Palestinian Territories. Activists are engaging in BDS activism on campuses and in their communities because they see it as a tangible method that they can use to make strategic changes. Furthermore, I explore the reasons why Jews who support BDS do not experience it as antisemitic despite the best efforts of detractors to label the entire movement as such. Finally, this chapter engages with the way BDS has been weaponized as a red line within the Jewish community and has thus excluded many young Jewish activists from mainstream institutional Jewish communal life by banning them for their BDS activism.

In the book's conclusion I discuss the internal reckoning over Palestine/Israel that is currently taking place in the American Jewish community. By offering a glimpse into the future of American Jewish communal engagement with Israel, I posit that a different Jewish future lies on the horizon, one in which dissenting Jewish views on Palestine/Israel are not only tolerated but also celebrated as legitimate and significant expressions of Jewish values. In a time of internal Jewish tensions and great despair regarding the possibilities of justice and peace in Palestine/Israel, my conclusion offers a necessary glimmer of hope: that the activism of young American Jews and other Palestine solidarity movement activists is swinging the political pendulum in a new direction, one where the current manifestation of occupation, apartheid, and conflict will end.

1

The Palestine Solidarity Movement

Activism and Resistance among Young Jews

When the 2014 Gaza War between Israel and Hamas began on July 8, Rachel was living in Boston, keeping up to date with the constantly changing events by reading articles online and scrolling through social media.[1] As the violence escalated, she woke up each day to see the death toll rising dramatically. She felt hopeless about the continuous cycles of violence that plagued Palestinian and Israeli communities. Michelle, who was living in Philadelphia, was similarly struggling to comprehend the profound suffering in Gaza that she saw unfolding through Facebook posts and news segments on television. Meanwhile in New York City, Sarah was shocked by the horrors of the war and was angered by Israel's disproportionate response to Hamas rockets. The three women, and many of their friends who had similar experiences during the war, had a common motivation that would eventually bring them together as activists. They were connected not only by their grief in watching the death toll rise but also by their despair over the hawkish response they witnessed coming from mainstream American Jewish institutions.

Rather than let anger and paralysis take hold, Sarah joined a small group of friends in Brooklyn who had decided to hold two private meetings to discuss what they could do that would both be personally meaningful and have an impact on the Jewish community. On July 24, 2014, the group organized a protest outside of the headquarters of the Conference of Presidents of Major American Jewish Organizations (or Presidents' Conference) in Manhattan.[2] Dressed mostly in black, the activists sang Jewish songs and recited the mourner's *Kaddish*, a significant prayer for Jewish rites and rituals of mourning, in memory of the Palestinian and Israeli victims killed during the war. They also read and delivered a letter to Malcolm Hoenlein, who at the time was the executive vice chairman of the Presidents' Conference.[3] The protestors asked the Presidents' Conference to join the activists in their call "to stop the Gaza War, end Israel's occupation, and forge a path forward for freedom and dignity for all people in Israel and Palestine." The Presidents' Conference ignored the activists, prompting further protests. Four days later the activists repeated the same action. This second time, nine protestors were arrested after refusing to vacate the lobby of the headquarters. The activists organized two other events the following week, reciting the Kaddish at Manhattan's Washington Square Park and Brooklyn's Grand Army Plaza.

After the first Kaddish actions in New York, other Jewish activists organized similar demonstrations in numerous other cities across the United States in places as geographically diverse as Philadelphia, Washington, D.C., Chicago, and San Francisco. Coming together under the banner of #IfNotNow, the activists who organized and participated in these actions connected on Facebook and shared organizing strategies on the phone.[4] According to Rachel, "We didn't do a hundred turnout calls to get people to show up to these actions. We just put a Facebook event out with a really compelling idea. It created an incredible spark in a crucial moment and hundreds of people started replicating these actions across the country."[5]

Responding to their own needs as well as to those of their peers, the activists created a framework for young Jews across the country to organize protests to express their disbelief and horror at the war and the Jewish communal response to it. But they also made a compelling link between the outpouring of anguish and a demand for change in those institutions. They were motivated by grief emanating from the significant loss of life as well as the pain they felt witnessing the Jewish community's support for a war that the activists saw as morally reprehensible. By reciting the mourner's Kaddish, they strategically framed the action as rooted in Judaism. Their actions were influenced by the importance of Jewish ritual in their lives.

During the protests, they made it clear that their public resistance to the war was an explicit expression of their Jewish identities and values. Rather than responding to their frustration with the Jewish communal response by distancing themselves from Jewish communities or by taking a stance of shame in relation to their identities, they staked a claim to legitimacy as moral Jewish agents and argued that their interpretation of Jewish ethics should be what moves the American Jewish community forward. What started as a hashtag and a group of friends organizing together soon morphed into the initial structure of IfNotNow, which has, since that time, grown to be one of the most prominent Jewish organizations among young adults active in the Palestine solidarity movement.

The birth of IfNotNow was a watershed moment in the growth of young Jewish participation in anti-occupation and anti-apartheid activism. Unlike Jewish Voice for Peace, which, by 2014, was already fully established and entrenched as a multigenerational player in the movement, IfNotNow was the first intentionally Millennial- and Gen Z-identified anti-occupation Jewish group. In contrast to Jewish Voice for Peace, IfNotNow was founded by Millennials and continues to grow among both Millennial and Gen Z Jews. While this may appear to be a niche within a niche (i.e., young people, anti-occupation activists, leftists, and Jews), IfNotNow is building a broad-based movement in five key ways, leading it to be a central place of Jewish Palestine solidarity organizing.

First, from the outset it capitalized on a military event, using the Gaza War as a political opportunity to mobilize widespread support for the Jewish anti-occupation movement. Second, it highlighted the grassroots nature of their movement with activists mobilizing and planning collective actions with a bottom-up rather than top-down approach, thereby challenging the traditional structure of Jewish institutional organizing. Third, the activists successfully utilized technological tools to foment rapid and active participation in movement activities, using established social networks and social media to spread the word and mobilize support. Fourth, by protesting outside the Presidents' Conference meeting, the activists intentionally targeted one of the most powerful Jewish institutions in the United States, one that represents other organizations that advocate for American Jews to believe that Israel and Zionism must be central to their Jewish identities. Finally, by invoking Jewish prayer and ritual during the *Kaddish* actions, the activists affirmed that their dissenting views are directly connected to their Jewish identities and called out Jewish communal leaders specifically in the latter individuals' departure from Jewish values.

This chapter examines the unexpected, pivotal role young Jews are playing in building momentum and support for Palestine solidarity activism in the United States. How does the movement function to harness the power of people sympathetic to the Palestine solidarity movement? Why is it important to understand how young Jews are building a social movement as a core function of their Jewishness? In order to answer these questions, I lay out a framework for a theory of change upon which much of the movement is based, including an explanation of how activists are implementing these strategies to effect change. Then I discuss the general ecosystem of the movement by introducing the main organizations driving the movement. Pointing to the recent historical episodes that drew young Jews to this type of activism, I show how they have used this attention to catapult their social movement and its activists into the forefront of Jewish politics in the United States. Finally, I discuss how these activists are mobilizing in particular ways that fuse their activism and their Jewish identities by building an intersectional movement rooted in the understanding that all justice struggles are interconnected.

Organizing Is with People

In *Life Is with People: The Culture of the Shtetl*, Mark Zborowski and Elizabeth Herzog emphasize that for small Jewish communities in Europe in the decades prior to the Holocaust the only way to exist Jewishly was to live collectively with others.[6] For the small villages and towns depicted in the book, cultural survival was predicated on the ability to live with others, support each other, and create meaningful Jewish lives together. The book eloquently describes how the strong intracommunal bonds were interwoven into the fabric of everyday life for people living in these *shtetls* through Jewish religious and cultural practices.[7]

Jewish participation in Palestine solidarity activism is similarly shaped by the legacy of living life in community. By organizing collectively, both within and outside of Jewish communal spaces, Jewish Palestine solidarity activists base their work on theories of change that recognize the importance of collective action and grassroots mobilization. This movement does not have one person who speaks on behalf of everyone, nor is it dependent on any single charismatic leader, thus rendering it both non-hierarchical and leaderless.[8] These activists know and understand that the goals they seek to accomplish cannot be achieved by one person alone or through one particular action, organizing campaign, or tactic, but rather require a multiplicity of organizations and individuals that are greater than the sum of its parts.

In a commencement address delivered in June 2015 at College of the Atlantic, climate change activist and author Naomi Klein challenged the graduating students to recognize the importance of collective mobilization to impact social change. She urged the graduates to understand a hard truth regarding social transformation: there is really nothing one individual can do to end social injustices. But rather than leave her audience despondent, she encouraged them to recognize the power that people possess and to channel that power into movements for justice. She told them that power is not about what you do as one person, "but what you [do] as many people, as one part of a large, organized, and focused movement." The only way to encounter the remarkable challenge of social change, she argued, is "together, as part of a massive and organized global movement."[9] Klein, who is Jewish, encouraged attendees to understand that organizing for social change, much like Jewish life itself (in the *shtetl* and outside), is *with* people.[10]

In that same vein, young progressive Jews in the United States are harnessing their power as a collective in challenging the moral legitimacy of Israel's occupation while working to end American Jewish support for Israel's policies toward Palestinians. It is important to understand this Jewish activism as a social movement, as articulated by Atalia Omer, as opposed to existing as a spontaneous generational shift or an advocacy campaign.[11] A social movement is a collective that possesses a common purpose to challenge authority and power by utilizing methods of disruption, confrontation, and collective action.[12] Unlike a generational trend or passing fad, a social movement is marked by agency and strategy. Whereas an advocacy campaign attempts to influence power, a social movement attempts to unsettle or even topple power.[13]

Social movements seek to challenge the status quo. They work toward social change in order to improve peoples' everyday lives.[14] A social movement must begin with the development of a grievance that reflects a social, cultural, or political situation to which people can respond.[15] Thereafter, the group of people must act on that grievance within a social, cultural, or political space that allows for or enables activist mobilization. In the case of the particular social movement at the center of this book's inquiry, the main grievance to which activists are responding is Israel's policies of military occupation and apartheid over Palestinians along with the fact that these policies are supported and maintained by the Jewish American Establishment.[16]

While ending Israel's occupation and policies of apartheid does not necessarily improve the everyday lives of American Jews materially, it impacts their sense of moral identity as well as the political power of the Jewish community. For many American Jewish activists engaged with the Palestine solidarity movement, Israel's policies toward Palestinians are an abomination of progressive Jewish values that must be stopped in order to protect the future of Jewish life. Jewish participation in anti-occupation and anti-apartheid political organizing therefore posits that Israel's policies make the world less safe for Jews (including American Jews) while distorting Jewish values and identity through an ethnic exclusiveness in Israel.

It is not sufficient to have a grievance alone; social movements must also be actively engaged in a struggle to transform a society through a process of contentious politics.[17] According to social movement scholar David Meyer, in order "for large social movements to emerge, people need to believe that participation in a social movement is needed to get some part of what they want and that the movement might be effective, in other words, that protest is both necessary and potentially effective."[18] Social movements therefore seek to move people from being passive supporters of a political idea or particular policy into becoming active participants who work in communion with others for social transformation.[19]

Jewish participation in the Palestine solidarity movement relies on both mobilizing and organizing, two different strategies utilized to build a social movement. Mobilizing is about getting people who already agree with you to take action or move into higher levels of responsibility and leadership within the movement.[20] Organizing, on the other hand, is about building the movement's base by moving people who didn't previously agree with the movement's politics (or who at least didn't think they agreed with them) into the movement's camp.[21] While Jewish anti-occupation and anti-apartheid activism is part of a broader movement for Palestinian liberation that is multidirectional and relies on a multiplicity of strategies, young American Jews, as can be seen by the efforts of IfNotNow, are simultaneously working to move people from passive support to active participation in movement politics.

As evidence of the multiple strategies used by the activists analyzed herein, one of the individuals I interviewed articulated specifically how and why Jewish anti-occupation and anti-apartheid activism should be understood as a social movement. "The anti-occupation movement is not just any one campaign," she said. "It's not just any one organization. It's a variety of strategies and approaches to change. I think that what makes up a movement is that there is not just one way of trying to effect change around a broader issue but that there's a variety of different strategies, a variety of different approaches that are all potentially pushing in a similar direction. It might even have disagreements about specifics like policy or whatever. We certainly have lots of disagreements about tactics and approaches."[22] And yet they are all working toward the same ultimate goal of ending both the occupation and American Jewish support for it.

The history of social movements teaches us that the occupation will end one day, partially because a broad-based and diverse multinational movement exists that is engaging in diverse tactics and strategies to challenge Israeli policies of occupation and apartheid. Although many social movements fail, the more broad-based and diverse a movement is, particularly if it uses nonviolent tactics, the more likely it is to be successful.[23] Even if we consider only social movements over the past century, we see several have directly shaped public opinion and forced social and political transformation.[24]

Mahatma Gandhi's Salt March, Martin Luther King Jr.'s leadership during the civil rights movement, Otpor! in Serbia, the Arab Spring, and Occupy Wall Street, among many others, illustrate how people with seemingly little power to effect change or sway public opinion were able to make dramatic and sweeping social changes to improve and transform their societies.[25] Although all of these were successful movements, to varying degrees, the two movements that resonate most closely with Millennial and Gen Z progressive Jewish activists are Occupy Wall Street and the ongoing Black Lives Matter movement, since Jewish activists are most likely to have direct experience with them.

While some may claim that Occupy was not a successful movement, arguably it led directly to the rise of Senator Bernie Sanders as a mainstream candidate for president of the United States as well as a surge in membership in the Democratic Socialists of America.[26] Similarly, the Black Lives Matter movement has radically transformed the way people understand and view racial issues and identities in the United States; it continues to be a major force in both American culture and electoral politics today.[27] The transformative power of social movements is possible when everyday people join forces to shift the social, cultural, and political conditions, which then forces political leaders to follow suit.[28]

Harnessing collective power is essential to Jewish anti-occupation activism and is a critical component of the theory of changemaking that underlies the Palestine solidarity movement. Much of the framework for organizing emanates from Momentum, a training institute and social movement incubator that teaches people how to use proven strategies and techniques of social protest and direct action.[29] Since its inception in 2017, Momentum has trained hundreds of activists and helped to jumpstart many of the most ambitious organizations driving social justice movements in the United States today, including the founders of IfNotNow.[30]

Momentum's theory of change posits that social transformation requires harnessing the power of the people rather than relying on political leaders or elected officials to make change.[31] Change, they argue, comes from the demands of the people through mobilization and organizing at the grassroots level. In the United States, for example, the successes achieved by the civil rights movement and the LGBTQIA+ community seeking marriage equality came through widespread and coordinated efforts at the grassroots level.[32] Though we often associate collective action with the left, there are also conservative movements that have achieved success in the same way, such as the Tea Party, the anti-abortion-rights movement, and some instances of Evangelical Christian organizing.[33] The focus on collective action is a powerful tool, even when it is not harnessed in service of a wider ideology that values democratic decision making or egalitarianism. Often, regardless of the issue, only after social movement activists successfully bring specific tensions to the surface, concurrently shifting public opinion through protest and direct action, are political leaders able to change public policy to reflect a movement's desires for change.[34]

In this regard, the history of social movements also teaches us that Israeli governmental policies of occupation and apartheid, as well as Jewish American support for them, most likely will not be ended independently by elected leaders. Rather, these systems of oppression will cease when enough people demand that these policies and politics change, thereby forcing elected officials and community leaders to make the changes that the people desire. According to one of the activists I interviewed, "We are learning from social movements, and we understand that at the grassroots level they spring up and change the conditions on the ground. They force the tenor of public opinion that then urges politicians to make policies the movement demands. If they don't make those changes, they are less likely to continue to be in power."[35]

In other words, young Jewish American activists understand and have incorporated into their mobilization efforts one of the most important lessons from social movements: change rarely begins within the political system in isolation but is instead demanded from ordinary people committed to transforming the status quo. Only then will those in power budge on social issues; without being significantly pressured from those outside the political system, this won't happen. As Dr. Martin Luther King Jr. reminds us in his renowned *Letter from a Birmingham Jail*, "We know through painful experience that freedom is never voluntarily given by the oppressor; it must be demanded by the oppressed."[36]

People cannot stand idly by waiting for the world to change. Instead, they must harness people power to mobilize support to demand the changes they desire. Social movements require large collectives to agitate, protest, and disrupt. When they do that, they take the power away from politicians and put it in the hands of public opinion. Once there is enough public support for a given social or political issue, the politicians in power will be forced to respond, thereby acquiescing to the demands of social movements.

Implementing the Theory of Change

After the 2014 Gaza War ended, a group of twenty activists, many of whom had organized the initial *Kaddish* actions, joined the Momentum Training Institute. Unsure how to capitalize on the success of the actions during the war, they wanted to build a long-term strategy for sustaining the movement they hoped to build. During the yearlong program, the activists formed an official nonprofit organization called IfNotNow. More crucially, they designed the DNA of the organization, which was written up into a document that included their foundational narrative alongside a clearly articulated multiyear strategy, guiding principles, and structure that would "allow the movement to grow with both autonomy and unity."[37] Their intention was to create a framework to guide them during the next stage of their growth; their goal was to end Jewish American support for the occupation.

During the incubation period, the activists studied social movement history and strategy. But they were not exclusively focused on the past. Rather, they were taught to build their movement in relationship with other contemporary social movements. It helped that some of the activists learned about direct action and contentious politics during Occupy Wall Street (2011) and in Ferguson, Missouri, with the Movement for Black Lives (2014). Their experiences during those social uprisings provided them with analyses and skills that they further developed within their framework of anti-occupation organizing. Building on lessons from contemporary social justice spaces and encounters with other distinct but sympathetic social movements, they tried to form a broad-based coalition with allies engaged in other justice struggles.

This collaborative attitude was nurtured at the Momentum Institute, where IfNotNow worked alongside Movimiento Cosecha, an organization working to win permanent protection, dignity, and respect for undocumented people in the United States, and Sunrise Movement, a group at the forefront of public advocacy for the Green New Deal who are inspiring young people to make climate change an urgent priority across the country. The activists working across these movements shared ideas, strategies, and lessons regarding their successes and failures, a process that ultimately strengthened each of their distinct projects. Through the work at Momentum, and in conjunction with other social movements led by young, progressive activists eager to impact their communities, IfNotNow developed their theory of change.

Their model for social transformation is best described by one of the activists involved with developing this theory during the incubation process:

IfNotNow's theory of change is that through bold action that involves sacrifice and disruption we can change public opinion in the American Jewish community on the occupation in a very short amount of time. It draws upon a lot of research around civil resistance that says that the job of social movements is, basically, to polarize, in a positive way, people who are neutral on a particular issue. We want to polarize the people who don't have to think about the question or would rather not think about the question or feel like it's too complicated for them to engage. The theory of change says that we can change the world by public disruptions and actions that can move those people to . . . agree with us on our issues and actions, to join the movement and become active supporters. And once we get a critical mass of people to . . . move from the neutral categories into agreeing with us and supporting our movement, then we can effect broad change and other institutions will have to follow public opinion.[38]

While their theory of change clearly defines a method for moving people to action, the activists knew that they had to target the right people in order to enlist them in their cause. To that end, IfNotNow made the strategic decision to publicize their message widely while also focusing their main outreach efforts on Millennial and Gen Z American Jews.[39] This decision was anchored by the belief that they had more social ties to and commonalities with others in their generation and therefore it would be easier to connect with them to bring them into the movement. It was also motivated by the fact that many of the already established progressive Jewish groups working on the Palestine issue, most notably Jewish Voice for Peace, were composed of "older radicals estranged from mainstream Jewish communal life, making it an uncomfortable fit for young Jews raised in the establishment and often just beginning to question its politics."[40]

At the end of the yearlong process, IfNotNow officially launched and began implementing their theory of change in Jewish communities across the United States. One of the members of their core team acknowledged the monumental effort of that moment:

We did beta-tests across the country with different groups. We did them with different constituencies who we knew would be necessary in order to make an impact on the Jewish community. So, we reached out to rabbis; people who were not politically active; Millennials who were not Jewishly affiliated, like high school and college students; people in geographically diverse regions; Ashkenazi Jews; Jews of Color; Sephardic and Mizrahi Jews; all sorts of groups that we wanted to integrate into the movement.[41]

Having studied social movements before the launch, they knew that to succeed they needed to build a broad-based coalition. Thus, they sought to engage as diverse a Jewish population as possible.

After identifying key constituents, IfNotNow created an extensive program to teach people about who they were and to train people in their theory of change. They conducted trainings with young Jews from around the country and, as they did so, found that their ideas resonated with people who had been longing for a Jewishly identified anti-occupation space. IfNotNow filled a need among young, progressive Jewish Americans who were seeking a meaningful Jewish communal space to actively oppose the Israeli occupation. The response to the movement and IfNotNow's organizing principles was profound. According to one activist, "I left the training feeling like I can be Jewish again, that I can be Jewish and powerful and a human being and connected to my ancestors and fight the occupation. I can be a part of a movement that will actually work and I can believe in its vision."[42] This trainee's experience resonates with the initial spark of the *Kaddish* actions, disrupting narratives of what American Jews support and interrupting the power that Zionist communal leaders exercise via the threat of social and religious exclusion.

A key idea that IfNotNow learned from the Momentum Institute, which was incorporated into the organization's DNA, is that it was not merely enough to give people a meaningful Jewish experience through the training sessions. Rather, they needed to mobilize the energized trainees to grow the number of people who actively support the movement's agenda. They needed to increase the interest and commitment level of trainees so that they would be both willing and excited to recruit more people to become involved. Once there are more active participants in the movement, people feel safer and more emboldened to engage in disruptive actions; higher participation leads to increased safety

Figure 1.1. IfNotNow activists attend a vigil in Boston after the Tree of Life synagogue massacre, October 2018. Photo by Emily Glick.

and comfort. In order to continue making gains and to remain relevant, a social movement must grow its base of active supporters.

But the question for social movements is always this: how many people is enough to tip the scales? The answer, according to scholars Erica Chenoweth and Maria J. Stephan, is that social movements and political revolutions must gain the active and sustained participation of 3.5 percent of the population in order to cause mass change.[43] According to the most recent figures, there are approximately 7.5 million Jews in the United States, so 3.5 percent would equal 262,500 people.[44] Therefore, according to this logic, if that number of American Jews became active and sustained participants in the movement to end Jewish American support for the occupation, the movement would be successful. With that number, they would have enough people to mobilize politicians and community leaders to make change through legislation and public policy. And without Jewish American support for the occupation, it would be significantly more challenging for Israel to sustain its policies of occupation and apartheid.[45]

In fact, there is ample evidence to show how IfNotNow's participation in the broader Palestine solidarity movement is succeeding and that this theory of change is working. One technique for mobilizing people power to challenge elected officials in order to shift public policy is to force politicians to take a stand on an issue they would prefer to avoid. Since most politicians will generally not move a progressive political agenda forward on their own, people must force them to take a stand on a particular issue in order to institute social change. IfNotNow activists used this technique during the 2020 presidential campaign, forcing Democratic candidates to take a position regarding whether or not they support the Israeli occupation of the Palestinian Territories.[46] In pressuring candidates to respond to these questions, IfNotNow activists hoped to make support for the occupation one of the main issues of the campaign. They successfully received assurance from most of the Democratic candidates that they would oppose the occupation and work to end it as president. Once Joe Biden became the party's nominee, a consortium of over a hundred progressive groups signed on to a letter to pressure him to support Palestinian rights as a central part of his campaign.[47]

In further efforts to polarize the issue of support for the occupation in Democratic Party politics, activists affiliated with IfNotNow and other groups disrupted the relationship between Democratic politicians and the American Israel Public Affairs Committee (AIPAC), a pro-Israel lobbying group. These organizing efforts caused several progressive members of Congress to turn down an AIPAC-sponsored trip to Israel, shaking the foundation of the lobby's dominance over the Israel conversation in American politics.[48]

Additionally, numerous politicians, including Democratic presidential candidates, refused to attend the annual AIPAC conference in Washington, D.C., fearing that their attendance would alienate the progressive base of the party and jeopardize their chances at a Democratic nomination for the highest political office in the country.[49] While for some this might seem like two minor accomplishments, it shows that the Palestine solidarity movement is forming increasingly significant cracks in unequivocal American support for Israel and that young American Jews are on the vanguard of these shifts. This was arguably the first time AIPAC had been unsettled in such a significant way.

Further, the steady progress emanating from these actions is based on a broader movement strategy of harnessing power to force politicians to take a stand against the occupation. A few short years ago, many thought it impossible for prominent Democratic presidential hopefuls to skip an AIPAC conference. But Jewish participation in the Palestine solidarity movement has changed contemporary understandings of what is possible with regard to American support for Israel's policies.

Implementing this theory of change has already provided some meaningful victories for Jewish involvement in the Palestine solidarity movement. At the same time, sustaining the movement for the Herculean fight that it will take to end the occupation and Jewish American support for it is another matter entirely. In fact, IfNotNow's original road map was to end Jewish American support for the occupation five years from their inception, which was an ambitious goal in its own right. The failure to reach this goal, as well as changes to the organizational structure and the shifting nature of the Palestine solidarity landscape, forced IfNotNow's leadership and members to reevaluate their initial intentions and shift toward more long-term strategies.[50]

As such, some maintain that in order to ensure long-term success, the movement must build on past victories while also finding new ways to bring uninvolved people into the fold, and they must continue engaging in contentious politics. To that end, activists are continuing to intervene on relevant and controversial social, cultural, and political issues or events to drive a wedge to split the Jewish community between those who are anti-occupation and those who are either supportive of or indifferent to it. Young Jewish American activists are continuing to frame the issue as a choice: Are you for justice, peace, and equality? Or are you on the side of exclusive ethnonationalism, violence, and injustice? They act as if every wedge issue is a new opportunity to bring people into the movement, and every person who moves from being a passive supporter to an active participant increases their chance of success by reaching the 3.5 percent threshold.

Mobilizing Moments and Capitalizing on Political Opportunities

Social movements often grow when they capitalize on certain moments that activists can exploit for political gain.[51] According to this idea, often referred to as political opportunity theory, activists and social movements can capitalize on these political opportunities in order to mobilize people to engage in contentious politics.[52] This theory helps explain why social movements either emerge or grow at particular times. Though political opportunities are varied, each one can potentially be utilized to push marginalized political ideas into wider acceptance. It is in these moments that social, cultural, or political issues can be centered, forcing the uninvolved to no longer ignore them.[53]

The all too frequent killings of unarmed Black men prove a particularly painful example of such political opportunism, which mobilizes people within the context of racial justice and police brutality in the United States. This phenomenon was clearly demonstrated by the protests that erupted around the country after the police murders of Michael Brown in Ferguson in 2014, which led to the birth of the Movement for Black Lives, and of George Floyd in Minneapolis, which ignited a push to defund the police. These and other police murders spark protests and anger among certain segments of the population, which enables activists to capitalize on these horrifying events to organize around racial justice issues.[54] Social movements therefore use political opportunities to stake a claim about a particular issue, generally framing it as a moral issue that requires a precise stance. Movements use such moments to mobilize people. They claim that their stance on an issue is the only moral choice to make, something that necessitates action.[55]

The challenge of maintaining active and sustained participation and engagement is one of the major obstacles to success for nonviolent social movements. This highlights the significance of capitalizing on every political opportunity that arises.[56] Each mobilizing moment brings more people into a campaign and broadens the base of those participating in resistance activities. Garnering mass popular support is essential to the success of a social movement because highly engaged activists can burn out, experience fatigue, or face life circumstances that make it harder to be active participants at all times.[57] Therefore, the more people involved in the movement and the more diverse strategies and technologies used, the easier it is to sustain momentum through cycles of increased confrontation, multiple campaigns, and contentious direct actions.[58]

The two most significant events that catalyzed Millennial and Gen Z Jewish American participation in the Palestine solidarity movement were the 2014 Gaza War (Operation Protective Edge) and Donald Trump's victory in the 2016 U.S. presidential election.[59] At the same time, there were many other influential moments that brought smaller numbers of young Jews into the movement as well. For example, for older Millennials, the 2008 Gaza War (Operation Cast Lead) was a major catalyst. Younger Gen Z Jews were motivated to join the movement because of Israel's May 2021 assault on Gaza and the subsequent Unity Intifada, the name for the spring 2021 Palestinian uprising.[60] Some were compelled to action based on Benjamin Netanyahu's right-wing politics and repeated election victories.[61] Others were politicized by the virtual dissolution of a viable political left in Israel alongside the government's increased support of religious Jews and exclusion of secular and liberal Jewish practices.[62] Still others were politicized as a result of their increased awareness and knowledge of the Israeli occupation and exposure to Palestinian narratives, which changed their perception of Israel, rather than any single political event.[63]

By far the most galvanizing moment for young Jewish participation in the Palestine solidarity movement was the 2014 Gaza War, which resulted in the death of 67 Israeli soldiers and 2,251 Palestinians, including 1,462 Palestinian civilians, 551 of whom were children.[64] Many young Jewish Americans consuming social media perceived the devastation in Gaza to be disproportional, which brought into sharp focus a much larger truth: this conflict has always been disproportionate and the dramatic imbalance of power has tilted in Israel's favor for decades.[65] After seeing images and reading reports of the killing of children and the near complete destruction of the Shuja'iya neighborhood in Gaza, such activists became convinced that Israel's actions were morally reprehensible. They simply could not support the Israeli government's military action.[66]

As noted above, the fifty-one-day assault on Gaza was such a catalyst for Jewish participation in the Palestine solidarity movement that it led to the founding of IfNotNow and to the dramatic rise in membership of other Jewish pro-Palestine organizations, most notably Jewish Voice for Peace (JVP). During the war and its immediate aftermath, JVP's online mailing list grew 37 percent and their Facebook posts received more likes than those of any other Jewish group working on the Palestine/Israel issue.[67] Their Twitter following tripled, new chapters formed in eighteen different U.S. cities, and they received more donations in July

2014 than any other month in the organization's history.[68] These statistics quantify just how significant of a political moment the 2014 Gaza War was and how Jewish Palestine solidarity activists capitalized on it by inspiring multitudes to become active participants in the movement.

This was also confirmed through qualitative data. Numerous people I interviewed said that the 2014 Gaza War caused them to think differently about Israel, a process that led them to become active participants in anti-occupation and Palestine solidarity politics. For example, one activist said about the war, "That was the first time I had a definitive opinion about Israel. I remember being with some of my friends, and I remember looking at these headlines and saying, 'This is wrong. This is definitively, morally wrong.' I just remember that was the first time I was able to have a very clear stance on where I stood about Israel."[69] For many activists, the intersection of the war and the proliferation of local and national opportunities to engage with anti-occupation politics through an intentionally Jewish space encouraged them not only to think differently but also to act in new ways. As was the case with the previous Gaza Wars (2008–2009 and 2012), the 2014 Gaza War inspired many people to become newly active participants in the Palestine solidarity movement. As people saw what was happening in Gaza, they were no longer able to ignore the harsh realities of the impacts that Israeli state violence had on Palestinian communities, thereby mobilizing them into action.

Donald Trump's 2016 presidential victory was another political opportunity that inspired young American Jews to make a similar choice. After the election, people all over the political map jumped into action. In the wake of Trump's January 2017 inauguration, millions of people joined Women's Marches all across the United States in what became the largest single-day demonstration of political solidarity in American history.[70] Approximately four million protestors flooded the streets in cities across the country, galvanized by the impending terror and doom that American progressives felt toward the fledgling Trump administration.

In the Jewish American community specifically, Trump's election was also a political earthquake. People were desperately looking for a way to be active on social and political issues they felt were important. Some followed the lead of progressive Jewish groups like Bend the Arc: Jewish Action and Jews for Racial and Economic Justice (JFREJ), two prominent Jewish social justice organizations. Others joined progressive groups championing specific issues threatened by the Trump administration, such as women's reproductive rights and civil liberties.

Perhaps the most outsized Jewish presence came in response to the so-called Muslim Ban, an executive order signed by Trump one week after his inauguration that banned foreign nationals from seven predominantly Muslim countries from visiting the United States.[71] In solidarity with Muslims and immigrants impacted by the travel ban, Jewish activists protested in massive numbers, most prominently at airports nationwide.[72] They participated in the protests with signs that read "Daughter of a Refugee from Nazi Germany. No Ban" and "My People Were Refugees Too." By showing up to these demonstrations not just as protestors but specifically as Jewish protestors, they were rewriting the dominant (and false) narrative that Jews and Muslims should be antagonistic toward each other. Jews also joined these protests as a refusal of a long anti-immigrant and anti-refugee history in the United States, a history in which Jews were habitually targeted and excluded in the same way Muslims were by the executive order.[73]

Trump's electoral victory galvanized the anti-occupation movement and inspired young American Jews to get involved in Palestine solidarity politics in part due to the refusal to acquiesce to uncritical Jewish American support for Israel, thus similarly rewriting a dominant communal narrative. Furthermore, many activists were motivated by their frustration that American Jewish institutions were selling out their values by supporting Trump based on the belief that he would be "good for Israel" and thus also "good for Jews." They made a clear connection between rising authoritarianism and white supremacy in the United States and the occupation in Israel. Already critical of Israeli prime minister Benjamin Netanyahu and his right-wing politics, they feared that Trump would enable Netanyahu to continue Israeli settlement expansion unabated, move the U.S. embassy to Jerusalem, further support Israeli military violence, punish Palestinians in the international political arena, and annex Palestinian land in the West Bank.

Jake, who is now quite active in the anti-occupation movement, articulates how the 2016 election motivated people in his generation, including himself:

[When] Trump got elected . . . I thought, "I need to take action. I need a way to protest and do something." I heard about IfNotNow and it reflected my views and I thought they were doing [interesting] stuff. I . . . signed up for my first IfNotNow training, which was a couple months [after the election]. . . . IfNotNow saw a surge of people getting involved after Trump. I think for one thing, people were looking for a way to take action immediately. We wanted to join a movement, to get organized. I think so many people in my generation were looking for that.[74]

Jake, and others like him, felt motivated to do something in response to both Trump's election and to Israel's policies of occupation and apartheid. The further the Israeli government moved to the right and the more mainstream Jewish institutions were unwilling to speak out against the Trump administration's unequivocal support of Israel, the more they alienated American Jews, in particular young Jews who value equality and inclusion and deeply believe that social justice is integral to their Jewish identities. As the Trump administration increased their support for Israel's policies of exclusion, young Jewish American concerns for these issues increased.

To be clear, while the Gaza Wars and the election of Donald Trump were major catalysts, there was a range of passive supporters who were moved to action after not having had much of an opinion previously. Some had been worried about being ostracized by the Jewish community. Others needed to be engaged in Palestine solidarity work from a Jewish place and felt that their Jewishness might bring unwanted attention or even antisemitism within non-Jewish anti-occupation and pro-Palestine organizing spaces. But regardless of what was holding them back previously, most of the young Jewish American activists I interviewed for this book started to work with the Palestine solidarity movement in self-identified Jewish spaces as a way to connect with their Jewishness in meaningful and comfortable ways.

Building an Intersectional Movement

Most of the groups and activists in the Palestine solidarity movement see the struggle against Israeli occupation and apartheid as part of a broader movement for global justice. As such, they are building their work on the idea of intersectionality, that various forms of oppression, discrimination, and domination intersect, overlap, and influence one another.[75] The theoretical concept, first coined by Kimberlé Crenshaw, has become not only a buzzword in activist communities but also a significant framework for understanding how oppression functions on multiple levels, which creates advantaged and disadvantaged groups.[76] Understanding intersectionality is critical for meaningful participation in the Palestine solidarity movement. New recruits are commonly trained to understand that their social movement organizing exists intersectionally, whether nationally or globally.

At the same time, not all young Jewish activists need to be taught about intersectionality because many get involved in the Palestine solidarity movement through their participation in other justice movements. They are often drawn to anti-occupation and Palestine solidarity activism because of the connections between systems of oppression. For example, it is common for people to have social justice activism experiences through union organizing, climate change campaigns (e.g., fossil fuel divestment), racial justice organizing, and economic justice campaigns. Furthermore, the fact that so many of the activists learned organizing strategies and direct action tactics in addition to studying intersectionality prior to joining the Palestine solidarity movement means that they brought these skills and their critical analyses with them to the Palestine/Israel struggle. Sharing theories, strategies, and tactics across political struggles strengthens the movement and enables certain campaigns to be more impactful, both materially and symbolically.

An intersectional movement means that activists understand the existence of deep connections between the various oppressions and injustices they are working on. Young Jewish Palestine solidarity activists are part of a movement that not only recognizes these links but also actively connects their activism with other struggles for justice, including the fight against white supremacy and the struggles for racial and economic justice, immigrant rights, LGBTQIA+ rights, and climate change, to name just a few. They understand that sexism is linked to racism, which is also connected to heterosexism, homophobia, and transphobia. They know that classism and ableism are also part of a system where certain groups construct the world for their benefit while excluding others. Activists in the movement understand that climate change is linked to immigrant rights, that antisemitism and Islamophobia are connected, and that Christian cultural dominance and white supremacy in the United States are the linchpins that hold it all together. They work to dismantle these forms of oppression in alliance with one another because they are all part of the same struggle for justice, equality, and liberation.

The intersectional nature of the Palestine solidarity movement manifests when activists show up as allies to demonstrations organized by other justice movements, such as Black Lives Matter marches or protests against immigrant detention centers. Palestine solidarity movement activists understand that there is little difference between being an ally to Palestinians and being one to Black and immigrant communities in the United States.[77] An intersectional movement requires consistency with commitments to justice and a steadfast refusal to remain silent in the face of injustice. Whereas most mainstream Jewish American community institutions might be willing to speak out when police brutality causes the death of unarmed Black men in the United States, they remain conspicuously silent when similar acts of Israeli state violence are carried out against unarmed Palestinians.[78] Just as young Jewish participants in the Palestine solidarity movement are reimagining the hegemonic Jewish identity in the United States that promotes Israel advocacy, they are likewise pushing the boundaries of Jewish American participation in other social movement struggles by declaring their solidarity, for example, with the Movement for Black Lives.[79]

Ultimately, allyship is rooted in shared political commitments and a steadfast refusal to acquiesce to injustice in all contexts. To be a true ally in the fight against racial inequality or for the rights of immigrants, these activists understand that they must be willing to stand consistently on the side of justice, leveraging their influence and privilege across movement lines. Similarly, just as Jewish activists show up in the fight for immigrant rights and racial justice, they expect that non-Jewish activists will join them as they combat the rise of antisemitism and white nationalism in the United States. As part of an intersectional movement, the activists work together to build alliances across differences that may ultimately help them all succeed in their quests for justice, freedom, and equality. In the end, collective liberation is bound together.

The Movement Ecosystem

Young Jewish participation in the Palestine solidarity movement draws on both a long tradition of Jewish activism in leftist social movements as well as the anti-occupation activism of previous generations.[80] IfNotNow is just one of many activist collectives participating in the Palestine solidarity movement that includes young American Jews. This book also examines the activism of some other groups, focusing particular attention on the Center for Jewish Nonviolence, All That's Left: Anti-Occupation Collective, and JVP. Each of these four groups focuses on different tactics to achieve the movement's goals.

IfNotNow focuses most of its efforts on targeting mainstream American institutions in its attempt to shift American Jewish sentiment about Israel and to end the American Jewish community's support for the occupation. The Center for Jewish Nonviolence and All That's Left primarily participate in co-resistance organizing by engaging in direct action and protest on the ground in Palestine/Israel, working directly with Palestinians. These two groups work very closely with one another, and both are important to the ongoing growth and success of the other. JVP, which was established in 1996 and is the oldest and most established of these groups, works on numerous campaigns in the United States and is the most prominent Jewish group advocating for BDS.

Some might question why JStreet is not featured prominently in this book since it also plays an important role in the Jewish American anti-occupation movement. JStreet is a lobbying group that works at the nexus of the Jewish community and American politics to advocate for a two-state solution to the Israeli-Palestinian conflict. They are a "pro-Israel, pro-peace" organization that has in recent years challenged AIPAC's grip on influencing American policies that "advance shared U.S. and Israeli interests."[81] JStreet's primary tactic is to engage in electoral politics to end the Israeli occupation, which is an important strategy of anti-occupation activism and one employed by both IfNotNow and JVP as well.[82] But this activity is not a central concern of this book because I have chosen to focus on grassroots social movement strategies of disruption and protest rather than lobbying efforts and engagement with electoral politics. Unlike the other organizations and collectives at the center of this book's inquiry, JStreet is not engaged in the tactics of disruption and confrontation that characterize grassroots social movements.

I do not say this to belittle the role that JStreet plays in the broader Jewish anti-occupation movement, which has in fact been quite considerable. JStreet, and in particular JStreet U, its subunit focusing on college student activism, is a feeder organization into many other anti-occupation political organizations. JStreet is a breeding ground for many people who are grappling with the realities of the occupation, those who are struggling to find a meaningful place for their Israel activism and advocacy. They are what I like to think of as a "gateway drug" for deeper involvement in more robust, radical, and grassroots forms of anti-occupation and Palestine solidarity activism.[83]

According to one activist, "IfNotNow grew out of JStreet among other things. IfNotNow, and many Jewish activists in my generation, are very much inspired by the folks who tried the polite lobbying work. But that wasn't enough. We tried talking to our Jewish communal leaders and they didn't do shit."[84] JStreet is actually quite important for the larger movement since it is often the first Jewish space in which people can explicitly express their anti-occupation politics without fear of reprisal or pushback. It often leads to deeper involvement with and in other Jewish activist spaces and helps activists enter the foray of anti-occupation and anti-apartheid organizing. A lobbying group that doesn't have significant popular support, or loads of money and big industry behind it, isn't going to exercise substantial power. Therefore, as IfNotNow, JVP, and other activist groups continue to grow larger and more influential, JStreet's lobbying efforts are likely to gain more success as well. Though JStreet does not feature prominently in the following pages, it must be understood as a key part of the larger ecosystem of Jewish anti-occupation and anti-apartheid activism in the United States and around the world.

While the four groups focused herein form the core organizational structures through which young American Jews are actively involved with Palestine solidarity movement activities, they are part of a broader constellation of anti-occupation Jewish activist organizations across the political spectrum. In Israel, for example, there are dozens of organizations and groups that compose the Israeli Peace Movement. These range from liberal Zionist organizations working in Israel to more radical groups that engage in co-resistance work centering Palestinians and their concerns.

Outside of Israel and the United States, there are many other Jewish anti-occupation activist groups.[85] For example, Independent Jewish Voices (IJV) is a grassroots organization with chapters all over Canada. It is modeled after JVP and supports the BDS movement in Canada. IJV is "grounded in Jewish tradition that opposes all forms of racism and advocates for justice and peace for all in Israel-Palestine."[86] In the United Kingdom, Na'amod (which means "we stand") was founded by a group of young British Jewish activists who were directly inspired by IfNotNow's growing influence in the United States. In their own words, they are "a movement of British Jews seeking to end our community's support for the occupation, and to mobilise it in the struggle for freedom, equality and justice for all Palestinians and Israelis."[87]

Much like any ecosystem, the Jewish element of the Palestine solidarity movement itself comprises multiple organizations employing numerous methods of resistance across the world. Each organization has its own role to play, as does each method, strategy, and tactic of activism and resistance. While some people in the movement may criticize the work of other organizations and their approach to activism, they are all generally supportive and complementary of each other. These activists also understand that they need as many people involved as possible. Ultimately, they don't care how people approach movement activism, as long as they are involved.

For example, one Tel Aviv–based activist originally from the United States told me, "We basically need everyone in the American Jewish world to join in and honestly, people can join in wherever they feel politically comfortable. I don't care. They want to go JStreet, they want to go to JVP, they want go to IfNotNow? Great! There are ones I agree with more, there are others I agree with less. But join the political mass. Join the conversation. . . . Because let's face it, American Jews have a say in what's going on here."[88]

All individuals who join the movement make their own decisions about what method of activism is best for them. Not everyone will advocate in support of BDS, despite the fact that it is a central component to the overall success of the Palestine solidarity movement as a whole (see chapter 5). Similarly, co-resistance is not for everyone since it requires the ability to travel to Palestine/Israel as well as the physical and psychological fortitude to confront Israeli military and police personnel (see chapter 4). With regard to challenging mainstream American institutions, not all members of the activist community believe that such action is a meaningful form of protest (see chapter 3).

Jamie, an activist living in Jerusalem, is steadfast in her commitment to co-resistance as a strategy. She told me, "I think one of the reasons I stay here is because I know if I go back [to the United States] I'm going to have to join a protest against a Federation, and I never want to do that. I'd so much rather be here doing co-resistance than be outside of some Federation building."[89] Despite the fact that not everyone agrees with what others in the movement are doing, each part of the movement ecosystem is important to advancing its overarching goals. In fact, Jamie clarified that while she herself may not be interested in protesting outside of a mainstream Jewish institution in the United States, "I'm glad they're doing it. It isn't what I choose to do, but I am glad they're doing it because it is important."[90]

The organizations that are the primary focus of this book are only one part of the larger ecosystem through which young American Jews engage in anti-occupation and Palestine solidarity activism. There is also a widespread media landscape through which young American Jews share and express their dissenting views on Israel, fomenting a space where anti-occupation and anti-apartheid politics help create a liberatory Jewish identity. For example, *Jewish Currents* is a magazine of the Jewish left that is committed to the rich tradition of activism and Jewish dissent. Originally established in 1946, the magazine transformed in 2018. With an intentional appeal to Millennials, they rebranded, designing a new website and hiring young staff members.[91] Since 2018 they have firmly planted themselves as the vanguard publication of Millennial and Gen Z Jewish radicals, staking their claim as a place where the sometimes-fragmented Jewish left can unify. Also in the same media space are podcasts, such as *Unsettled*, *The Wedge*, and JVP's *Diaspora!*, all of which are produced by young American Jews and tell stories that focus on peace and justice struggles in Israel.

There are also organizations such as Open Hillel, which started in November 2012 as a way for students to express their frustration with the lack of open debate commanded by Hillel International's firm grip on who was and was not allowed to speak at events sponsored by the organization charged with cultivating Jewish life on college campuses.[92] As of their 2010 guidelines, Hillel International will not sponsor an event with any speaker who does not adhere to the traditional "pro-Israel" formula.[93] As a result, Open Hillel created a new space for Jewish students on campus, particularly for those interested in a more robust and open dialogue and debate about Israel. Since its founding, it has enabled both Jewish and Palestinian anti-occupation activists to speak on American university campuses in a Jewish space, allowing students to learn about differing viewpoints about Israel—as Jews—without fear of retribution for their potentially dissenting politics. In 2020, Open Hillel rebranded under the new name Judaism on Our Own Terms. They remain committed to connecting independent Jewish clubs and building radically inclusive Jewish communities on U.S.-based campuses.[94]

In a more traditional Jewish context, some synagogues actively engage in anti-occupation politics as an integral part of their Jewish ritual expression and engagement, which attracts young Jews.[95] Furthermore, a group of American students studying at the Pardes Institute of Jewish Studies, an inclusive and egalitarian yeshivah in Jerusalem, formed Ya'aseh Mishpat, which, drawing its name from a verse from the Torah, calls Jews to justice. Based in Jerusalem, this community of anti-occupation yeshivah students study Jewish texts as part of their activism. Alongside these study sessions, they also organize educational trips and co-resistance work days with Palestinian communities in the West Bank, explicitly drawing from Torah passages to oppose the occupation. Through their efforts, they are challenging the status quo within the religious communities to which they belong, simultaneously teaching other American Jews studying in Israel to both be more aware of and engage more critically with the occupation.

One of the most important elements of this movement is that the activists are Jewish and the organizations with which they are involved are working within a distinctly Jewish framework. As one activist told me, "This is a movement of Jewish activism that has to leverage its power, privilege, and responsibility" *as Jews* to challenge Israeli policies of occupation and apartheid.[96] In this regard, the activists themselves, as well as the groups through which they organize, are providing alternatives to the landscape of Jewish social justice activism as well as new ways for young Jewish Americans to relate to Israel.

For many of the activists I spoke with, the organizations they are involved with often are the center of their Jewish lives. Their activist work has become one of many ways they perform their Jewish identities and express their Jewish values. They are engaged in this transnational struggle because they find it a meaningful way to be Jewish and, more specifically, to connect to their Jewishness as a new way to mobilize around central concerns of justice. The activism is a way to combat the hegemonic Jewish identity promoted by dominant Jewish organizations in which "advocacy for Israel remains among the most urgent and significant community priorities."[97]

Through this activist work, people are both drawing on existing relationships to recruit new people and building meaningful and long-lasting relationships that extend the boundaries of their Jewish community. In the process of building a broad-based coalition of diverse organizations and individual activists, strong bonds and networks are forming between and among the activists. The feeling of camaraderie is essential to the success of the movement. In a Jewish community that silences dissent on politics critical of Israel, acting alongside others who share similar political and ethical values is deeply empowering.

An important element of this social movement is that people who do not feel welcome in some Jewish spaces find deep personal, spiritual, and cultural fulfillment and satisfaction when engaging with the movement. As emphasized by sociologist David Meyer, "The deep human connections forged in the context of a social movement are long-lasting and important in forging and maintaining an individual's identity."[98] While social movements influence politics, policy, culture, and society, they also impact their participants in deep and meaningful ways.

One of the most important personal impacts that participation in the Palestine solidarity movement has with activists is that it creates a particularly Jewish space for a radical politics of liberation. According to one activist,

In some ways we're doing a massive agitation of the Jewish community, but a really loving one. I think it is inevitable . . . especially with the youngest members of our community which are seen as the focus and priority of the Jewish community and Jewish establishment, that reaction is inevitable. We're pushing against this system that's not set up for us to do [anti-occupation activism], not set up for us to say, "actually we want something different." And in a way that shows that we are really committed to the Jewish community and the Jewish future.[99]

Active participation in the movement has become one of the primary ways that activists perform their Jewish identities and maintain strong connections to Jewish community. For them, pushing against the Jewish institutions where they were first socialized to care about Israel—one that did not also teach them about the occupation—is a way of reclaiming a Jewish identity focused on building a Jewish future that is more deeply reflective of their values. In this way, Jewish participation in the Palestine solidarity movement is attempting to neither maintain nor eschew transnational connections with Israel. Rather, it seeks to transform the way that people understand global Jewish connections to the Jewish state. Young Jewish activists are engaging in activism as a way of performing a new Jewish identity, one that is rooted in the desire for justice for all. They are, as Atalia Omer notes, "reimagining Jewishness in solidarity with Palestinians."[100]

2

Unlearning Zionism

Myths, Miseducation, and Pro-Israel Indoctrination

I begin with a personal story of unlearning Zionism. My story illustrates the process of personal political transformations that are integral to many American Jews becoming active participants in the Palestine solidarity movement. Although I am not part of the demographic explored in this book, my story is deeply similar to those told to me repeatedly by my interlocuters. And though the particulars of my story are unique to me, they are representative of the broader experience of young American Jews today who learn about Israel and Zionism in Jewish day schools, summer camps, youth groups, Israel trips, and many other Jewish educational institutions. Since the experiences of the activists I interviewed were so familiar to my own, I offer the autoethnographic analysis herein to elucidate a comprehensive picture of what unlearning Zionism looks like for a person socialized in a normative Jewish community and in mainstream Jewish educational environments.

I was raised in Los Angeles in a Reform Jewish family with a rich tradition of support for Zionism. My paternal great-grandfather escaped the czar's army in Russia in the early twentieth century, traveling by foot to Germany, where he was able to pay for third-class steerage on a ship headed for New York. He was highly educated, an ardent student of Talmud, and a devoted Zionist. In New York, he became a top Talmud scholar and one of the main Yiddish political orators of his day. Among his contemporaries were such Jewish and Zionist luminaries as Rabbi Stephen S. Wise and U.S. Supreme Court justice Louis Brandeis.[1] In the 1930s and 1940s, my great-grandfather made speeches across the Eastern Seaboard advocating for the establishment of a Jewish state in Palestine.

This legacy was passed down to my grandfather, Isaiah Zeldin, a rabbi who established one of the largest Reform synagogues in the country and built the Jewish day school I attended for thirteen years.[2] Zionism was a founding principle and core value of both the synagogue and the school where I was educated. My grandfather believed that the establishment of the State of Israel was a modern-day miracle and was the single greatest historical moment of his lifetime. Though my father was not a rabbi (he was a professor of Jewish education), he treasured his family's Zionist legacy and passed it down to me.

Zionism was also central to my mother's family. My maternal grandfather idolized President Harry Truman because he was the first head of state to recognize the State of Israel after its establishment in May 1948.[3] As a staunch Zionist, he, too, believed that Israel's establishment was among the most important historical moments of his life. My grandfather's love of the State of Israel was passed down to my mother, a rabbi who helped pioneer the Jewish feminist movement in being among the first women to be ordained as a rabbi in the United States.[4] Even prior to her first trip to Israel on a Zionist youth program in 1969, Israel and Zionism played a major role in her personal and professional life. In short, the ethos of unquestioning Zionism and support for the State of Israel was engrained in me from the beginning of my life.

I received a mainstream Reform Jewish education and was imbued with Zionism in every Jewish educational context I experienced. In addition to attending a Jewish day school, where I studied Hebrew and learned about Israeli history and culture, I spent many summers of my youth at Jewish overnight summer camps. Zionism pervaded the camp educational experience.[5] In one particularly memorable activity, the camp reenacted the process of Jewish refugees fleeing Europe and breaking the British blockade by illegally immigrating to Palestine.[6] In another activity, the counselors organized a program where we campers pretended to be Israeli soldiers during the 1948 War. As a kid I never thought there was anything strange about these programs; I believed they were totally innocuous. I was just having fun, unaware of how these educational programs valorized war and Jewish ethnonationalism.

The most formative Zionist experience of my youth took place during my sophomore year of high school when I spent the spring semester living abroad in Jerusalem as part of the NFTY-EIE program.[7] An integral part of the program was a one-month home stay with a Jewish Israeli family in Jerusalem. My host family lived in the French Hill neighborhood, near the campus of Hebrew University. What I did not know at the time was that French Hill is a Jewish settlement established in 1970 on the north side of the Green Line.[8] No one told me that I was spending a month living in an Israeli settlement, and it wasn't until a decade later that I found out, much to my dismay. French Hill is one of many settlements in Jerusalem built on Palestinian land captured by Israel in the 1967 Arab-Israeli War that is perceived by most Israelis to merely be a Jerusalem "neighborhood" since Israel has so successfully incorporated it into Jewish West Jerusalem.[9] By being placed with a host family in a settlement without knowing and without having the context to even understand what a settlement was, I realized how pervasive the process of Zionist indoctrination is among Jewish American youth. This is one of many ways that Palestinian narratives, or even diverse viewpoints on Israeli politics, were omitted from my education.

Throughout these formative educational experiences, I did not ask questions; like the "simple son" from the Passover Haggadah, I knew neither what nor how to ask. Nearly everyone surrounding me in my youth identified as Zionist, which is not something that I ever thought to question. As I reflect on my upbringing, it is strange that I never questioned Zionism or my family's unequivocal support for Israel because I was always encouraged to question everything else that I learned. I was simply unable to recognize the cognitive dissonance of being taught to ask questions and yet be so unaware that I did not know what questions to ask about Israel. It was not until many years after I left home for college that I started to question Zionism, to uncover its myths, and to reconcile what it meant to me personally and politically. In this chapter I situate both my own experiences as well as those of the activists whom I interviewed within a rich body of academic literature on the myths of Zionism.[10] Here I borrow from Jewish Israeli historian Ilan Pappe, who understands myths to be "distortions and fabrications that can—and must—be refuted through a closer examination of the historical record."[11]

I am sharing my experiences here to exemplify what it looks like to uncover these myths and to unlearn Zionism, paying particular attention to how this is integral to the process for many people becoming active participants in the Palestine solidarity movement. This process is an experience of (1) Jews socialized by dominant Jewish and Zionist narratives, (2) whose learning is challenged and disrupted, who then (3) reorient to this particular topic and (4) make connections between different struggles for justice.[12] Unlearning Zionism is a radical reeducation process that enables individuals to assert an emancipatory Jewish identity, one that reclaims Judaism from Zionism and affirms a serious commitment to social justice rooted in Jewish values.[13]

Unlearning Zionism also recognizes that the implementation of Zionism through a commitment to Jewish supremacy in Israel is at odds with core Jewish values. This commonly leads to a profoundly painful experience, an understanding that prior to this point there existed a cognitive dissonance permitting a double standard within one's own ethical system. By unlearning Zionism, Jewish anti-occupation activists are encouraging the Jewish community to confront this same cognitive dissonance, ideally leading them to a political position regarding Palestine/Israel that is more in line with Jewish values. Simply put, unlearning Zionism is a rupture that leads to a profound process of personal transformation, one that enables activists and allies to envision and work to create a shared future for Palestinians and Jewish Israelis rooted in justice, peace, and equality.

For most, myself included, unlearning Zionism is a long and arduous process. But along the way there are moments that form cracks in the foundations of dominant Jewish communal narratives, thereby acting as a rupture with the past. The more people uncover the myths of Zionism, the larger the cracks grow, until the foundation itself crumbles. One of the most significant moments that began chipping away at the Israel education of my youth occurred when I staffed a Taglit-Birthright Israel trip in July 2006.[14] Prior to starting graduate school, I worked at Berkeley Hillel, where one of my responsibilities was to recruit for and lead the Hillel Birthright trip for UC Berkeley students. Between 2005 and 2007 I led three Birthright trips, including one particularly fateful trip in July 2006.

The bus I was on that summer happened to be Hillel's only Birthright trip in Israel at the time, and we were in the northern Galilee close to the Lebanese border on July 12 when the 2006 war between Israel and Hezbollah broke out.[15] Kayaking down the Jordan River, hiking in the mountains in the Golan Heights, and learning about the modern political history of Israel (all routine elements of a Birthright trip) made us feel far away from the escalation of violence. For the first few days of the trip, we went about our planned itinerary with little distraction. But the feeling of distance did not last long.

Shortly after the war began, our group ate dinner on the terrace outside of our hotel in Tiberius, overlooking the Sea of Galilee with the mystical city of Safed on the opposite hillside. Earlier in the day, we had seen plumes of smoke rising in the distance, a perpetual reminder of the falling rockets and escalating violence between Israel and Hezbollah. At night we witnessed the night sky light up with missile fire. The next day, a Saturday, our group ate lunch together in the hotel. We had just sat down to have a Sabbath meal when we heard a deafening noise that shook the building. Some students stood up, looking around with terror. Thirty seconds later, we heard another sound, similar to the first, this one seemingly closer. It was even louder, causing the building to shake even harder. More students got up and started to shriek and run out of the room. An additional thirty seconds passed and there was a third and final boom, even louder and stronger than the first two. This propelled the majority of the people in the hotel into a state of panic.

Three Katyusha rockets fired by Hezbollah, from southern Lebanon, had landed within three hundred meters of our hotel. Everyone, the Jewish American students I was leading and the Jewish Israeli citizens enjoying the day in the hotel in order to escape the fighting farther north, ran frantically to the closest bomb shelters.[16] Our group spent six hours in the hotel's bomb shelter, waiting for clearance until it was safe to leave. Though we communicated with Birthright and the tour operators consistently, they assured us that we were safe and could continue with our itinerary. They told us that there was no need to abandon our tour and relocate to the center of the country, where we would be out of the rockets' reach.

Even today, I don't fault the tour organizers or Birthright for failing to recognize the danger that we were in by being so close to the fighting. But what I began realizing that day was an issue much larger and more systemic than Birthright specifically or Israel education generally. Immediately, the demonization of "the other" ramped up. Whether it was referring to Hezbollah specifically or Muslims generally, including Palestinian Muslims, a hateful rhetoric spoken by those around me emerged. Never once did anyone mention the larger historical context that led to the renewed fighting between Israel and Hezbollah. For example, one of the Birthright staffers who met up with our trip told us that "Arabs hate Jews and want to destroy Israel." Therefore, she said, Hezbollah must be defeated. Otherwise, they will "throw the Jews into the sea." This justification of a brutally destructive and catastrophic war struck me at the time as being both deeply racist and totally myopic. The sheer inability to see or recognize the human suffering on the other side of the border was deeply troubling to me and was a point of rupture in my process of personal transformation.

Years later, I had a Lebanese student who told me that she was living in Beirut during the 2006 war. She shared that her family was traumatically impacted. She had relatives who died and other family members who had to flee their homes, even needing to leave the country, separating themselves from their loved ones and their community. She told me about her fear that the Israeli military could level her family's house or her school at any time. It was a traumatic summer for her, and the impacts of the trauma are long-lasting. The differences between my experience in Israel in the relative safety of the bomb shelter and that of my Lebanese student during the war are stark. We both had the experience of huddling in fear and hearing bombs drop around us. But the consequences for her and her family in Lebanon were far more severe than those for us on the Birthright trip. (For starters, we planned on leaving a few days later regardless of the war.) The lack of acknowledgment of these different experiences reveals a dramatic imbalance of power in Israel's conflicts with its neighbors. It also makes evident the ways that Jewish educational institutions like Birthright do not engage with the entangled nature of the lives of Jews and the people in the countries adjacent to Israel.

During the Birthright trip that summer, no one talked about the experiences of Lebanese civilians or the possible impacts of war on a society that was rebuilding after a decades-long, violent civil war. Instead, Birthright and prominent Jewish leaders spewed pro-Israel propaganda at the staff and participants. The rhetoric appeared to me to be an attempt to capitalize on a recent trauma when telling participants that Israel truly was a "villa in the jungle." "See," they said. "Arabs and Muslims indeed hate Jews, and therefore Israel needs the support of diaspora Jews in order to survive." After the trip, I began to see this process of invisibilization, demonization, and omission as routine. It required me to unlearn the Israeli and Jewish exceptionalism I was taught in my youth and that I so blatantly witnessed that summer.

Although I didn't recognize it at the time, the failure of Birthright and mainstream Jewish organizations to criticize or even recognize Israel's complicity in the outbreak of the 2006 war or its subsequent military incursions into Lebanon was a turning point for me in my political and personal journey toward transformation and unlearning. This was when I began questioning Israel. I asked those in my American Jewish community, why had the IDF acted so violently in Lebanon during that war? Yet I found only a few people who spoke up about Israel's role in the war. Even when they were so quick to condemn other acts of violence, those carried out by other governments, they didn't do so in the context of Israel. My questions led to confusion: Why would supporters of Israel openly cheer at the violent destruction of cities and towns in Lebanon and be so pleased by the deaths of Lebanese civilians? What did Palestinian refugees living in Lebanon experience during the war?

Confusion led to anger and sadness. When I saw images of the impact of the war in Lebanon, I was so deeply angry that Jewish people could cause such destruction. I was sad that people I loved and trusted—my friends and family—condoned the violence that Israel caused, justifying it completely in the name of self-defense. How could the people who taught me to value peace and respect others tolerate such catastrophic killing and destruction? The anger, confusion, and dissonance I experienced in July 2006 mirror the experience of countless other American Jews who were disillusioned by Israel's wars in Gaza since that time. That summer also inspired me to explore Palestinian identity and narratives of conflict more seriously, which led me to a path of study and activist work that I continue to this day. Witnessing the utter lack of nuance and complete erasure of Palestinian narratives throughout my Jewish education was one of the things that led me to further examine my own understandings of Zionism and to seek out opportunities to learn Palestinian histories. I was taught (and believed) the myth that "there is no such thing as Palestinians."

As part of my unlearning, I also traveled throughout the West Bank and saw firsthand the impacts of occupation and apartheid on everyday life for Palestinians. The word "occupation," which was never once uttered in any educational setting in my youth, entered my lexicon, and I made a point of teaching my friends and family as much as I could about what I was learning. What at first felt like a betrayal of my family and my Jewishness, my process of personal transformation—from an unquestioning Zionist background to one committed to anti-occupation politics—actually helped me reassert an emancipatory Jewish identity based on justice for all people. What was most emancipatory for me was the ability to transcend the cognitive dissonance that Zionist politics required, which also helped me to understand that I could practice a Jewishness that had no relationship to an ethnonational Jewish state.[17]

While I was taught that Zionism was about liberation for Jews, I was unaware that Jewish liberation in Israel was predicated on the oppression and ethnic cleansing of Palestinians.[18] I was horrified when I understood the implementation of Zionist policies in Israel as a form of ethnonationalism and that Israel, as a Jewish state, requires a demographic majority of Jews at the direct expense of the Palestinian population. It was painful to view Israel through the lens of settler colonialism, in which Jews aim to eliminate both the Palestinians and their claims to the land.[19]

The most personally painful and challenging element of learning about Palestine was feeling like I was betrayed by the community that educated me—my teachers, my camp counselors, and, most importantly, my family. They taught me to love and support Israel, but also to champion peace and justice and always act ethically. Learning about Palestine introduced a cognitive dissonance between my values and Israel's actions that I could not reconcile and that introduced a painful feeling rooted in betrayal and sadness. At the time I felt a deep loss of something that was important to me, but I can now understand that the pain was the beginning of a process of realigning my beliefs and politics with the values that most mattered to me.[20]

Integral to my process of unlearning Zionism was meeting and befriending Palestinians. I learned from them about their rich cultural and political identities, which further dispelled the myths of Zionism and Israel with which I was raised. My new Palestinian friends taught me that Palestinians are not monolithic, that they have numerous opinions, political orientations, and approaches to community organizing around their liberation. They showed me that Palestinians have a rich history that is deeply connected to the land and that there are families who have continuously practiced farming and herding for centuries. When I participated in a Palestinian olive harvest in the northern West Bank in the fall of 2012, I saw firsthand how deep Palestinian connections are to the land, which mirrored the significant Jewish and Zionist connections to the land that I was taught as well.[21] I also learned from Palestinians that they have a unique culture, one that is distinct from other Arabic-speaking peoples in the Middle East; they were Palestinian Arabs. Further, I learned about the nuances in regional cultures and dialects even among Palestinians.

The most painful thing I learned from Palestinians was that the fragmentation of their people, and Israel's steadfast refusal to allow Palestinian refugees to return to the houses they fled in 1947–1949 or 1967, meant that many were never able to return home. Learning this further complicated the cognitive dissonance I experienced in my process of unlearning Zionism, when knowing full well that since I am Jewish I can travel to Israel or the West Bank any time I want.[22] Moreover, my Jewishness enables me to become an Israeli citizen as a benefit of Israel's Law of Return, all while Palestinians are systematically denied their right to return. Now, all of these things are glaringly obvious. But I needed to learn them, and unlearn other things, because I was raised with the myth that Palestinians did not exist.

To reiterate, my point in sharing part of my own process of unlearning Zionism and personal transformation is to show that what I experienced is very similar to what many of the activists involved in anti-occupation and anti-apartheid activism today learn. For many, unlearning Zionism is a critical step toward engaging in anti-occupation activism. As I describe below, through my scholarship and work as an educator I challenge the previously held views of my students and facilitate a reflective process that enables them to critically rethink and reimagine their connections to Israel.[23] Unlearning is a commitment to doing the emotional and political labor necessary to work in solidarity with Palestinians in the struggle for justice. In short, unlearning Zionism often manifests as a series of mobilizing moments, similar to those discussed in the previous chapter, that crystallize a moral critique of Zionism and solidify the process of becoming an active participant in the Palestine solidarity movement.

Unlearning as Intervention

A month into my "Social Justice and the Israeli-Palestinian Conflict" course, one of my students, Jasmine, mustered the courage to confront me in the hallway after class. "I am not feeling good about this class," she told me. "I think that what you are teaching is biased and I am concerned that the students in the class will not understand how wonderful Israel is and why it is so important to Jewish people." According to Jasmine, the class was biased because I was integrating Palestinian narratives alongside Jewish ones in a course listed through the university's Jewish Studies program.[24] Jasmine's very legitimate feelings about this class stemmed from the fact that Israel held an important place in her self-understanding of her Jewishness.

By the time Jasmine approached me, we had already covered the Nakba, the Palestinian catastrophe of dispossession that accompanied the establishment of the State of Israel. Part of this subunit of the class includes personal accounts of what happened in Palestine/Israel between 1947 and 1949, such as autobiographical texts that referred to the events as "ethnic cleansing," which made Jasmine deeply uncomfortable.[25] Though she felt challenged sitting in class, Jasmine didn't confront me until after the lecture when we discussed intra-Jewish strife in Israel. She was most notably disturbed by learning about the Yemenite Babies Affair and the rise of the Israeli Black Panther Party.[26]

In my class, students are challenged to reflect on their own multilayered social and political identities in order to gain a deeper understanding of the roles they play in international conflicts. While the course focuses on Palestine/Israel, the academic study of the conflict is a mechanism for understanding larger issues of identity, narrative, diversity, and power. We explore these issues through a social justice lens that encourages students to consider how their own identities and narratives emerge in relation to others. In doing so, students' personal experiences and political commitments emerge as central to our class conversations.

As a Jewish woman from a Moroccan family, raised in a pro-Israel, Zionist family in the San Francisco Bay Area, learning about the kidnapping of Yemenite Jewish babies who were then given to Ashkenazi families and the systematic mistreatment and discrimination of Moroccan Jews in Israel was simply too much to bear. Jasmine felt a strong connection to Israel even as she wrestled with the complexities of supporting a state that engaged in behavior that she felt was contrary to her values. I listened to her carefully as she spoke, knowing from my own personal experiences how painful it can be to encounter stories about a country one loves and to which one feels strongly connected. When she finished speaking, I encouraged her to be patient with the class and invited her to meet with me regularly to discuss what we were learning and process the material.

On the last day of the semester, I asked Jasmine if she still felt that the course was biased. Now that she had completed the fifteen-week course, I wanted to know what she thought. "I do not think that this class was biased," she said. When I encouraged her to elaborate on what shifted during the semester, she replied, "I changed. At the beginning of the semester, I wasn't ready to encounter the Nakba and Palestinian narratives. I wasn't ready to reflect on what I learned about Israel and Zionism as a kid and how that differed from what we discussed this semester. By the end of the class, I felt more open to learning alternative narratives and to question the myths I learned when I was younger."

Growing up, Jasmine received a relatively mainstream Jewish American education. She went to Hebrew school and was active in synagogue life. Her teachers and family taught her that care for the State of Israel was tantamount to being Jewish. Throughout her years of Jewish education, no one ever mentioned the word "Nakba" or taught her about Palestinian narratives; instead, her education either demonized and delegitimized Palestinians or omitted Palestinians and their narratives altogether. When Jasmine first encountered Palestinians and their stories as a university student, the experience caused her to feel fear and defensiveness about these "other" narratives.[27] But since she persevered with her learning, and perhaps because she had the space to actively process the new information with her instructor, she was able to integrate these seemingly disparate narratives with one another. Through this process, she experienced feelings of betrayal, confusion, and rage about the Jewish education she previously received.

Jasmine's story is also illustrative of the experience that many young Jews have of uncovering the myths of Zionism.[28] In this chapter, and throughout the book, Zionism refers to the political movement and ideology that supports the establishment and protection of a Jewish state in the Land of Israel. As is the case with most political ideologies, Zionism is not monolithic; rather there is a range of definitions and understandings of Zionism. For some, particularly hard-line "hawks," their Zionism is about ensuring Jewish safety in Israel at all costs.[29] Others, including liberal Zionists, see their political views on the State of Israel as compatible with universal values of justice, peace, and equality.[30] Like so many others in her generation, Jasmine's Jewish education simply glorified Jewish Israelis and Israel while condemning or omitting Palestinian narratives and Palestine altogether, thereby alienating them from all forms of identification with Zionism.[31] After encountering material in my course that challenged the pro-Israel narratives she encountered in her youth, Jasmine worked hard to reexamine the myths of her Jewish and Zionist education regarding Israel.[32]

Unlearning Zionism requires dismantling dominant narratives and communal truths that are deeply engrained in the enculturation of American Jews. A communal truth "is an operating system of ostensibly historical facts that serves to explain a people's worldview, thereby giving it both credibility and legitimacy."[33] Because communal truths often shape a community's beliefs, practices, and values, Jews who unlearn Zionism not only contest widely held narratives about the "righteous" nature of Israel's national project but also reject a monolithic pro-Israel Jewish identity.

Mirroring what French philosopher Louis Althusser posits with the idea of interpellation, when Jewish American communities are taught the normative understanding of Zionism and what it means to have pro-Israel politics, it is first perceived as innocuous.[34] Interpellation is a theory about how our ideas impact our lives; it is a process through which we encounter our culture's values and internalize them as our own. According to Althusser, someone who has been fully interpellated willingly accepts certain values or their role in society. To this end, many American Jews have been interpellated into accepting Zionism as a value, despite its clash with other Jewish values that American Jews are also interpellated into accepting.

In the remainder of this chapter, I examine the role unlearning Zionism has played in the emergence of young Jewish American participation in the Palestine solidarity movement. I articulate and elaborate on a robust internal conversation among progressive Jews who struggle with the nationalist ideology of Zionism and how it impacts both Jewish identity and everyday life for Palestinians.[35] Uncovering the myths of Zionism is integral to the politicization of young American Jews as anti-occupation activists and is an essential experience that enables them to actively participate in the Palestine solidarity movement. Most of the activists go through this process by first unlearning Zionism educationally and then bearing witness to what occupation on the ground actually looks like.[36]

The process of unlearning Zionism is similar to what white allies of people of color go through in order to unlearn racism. In both situations people learn that they must leverage their privilege in order to dismantle systems of oppression.[37] This is not merely a process of unlearning oppressive beliefs and behaviors but also involves relearning and developing an emancipatory knowledge that enables a radical alignment with one's values and commitments to social justice. By comparing unlearning Zionism and unlearning racism I am not equating Zionism with racism or any other form of structural violence, which is outside the scope of this chapter, even though many scholars and activists do make that claim.[38] Rather, I am pointing to the fact that Zionism is deeply imbricated in the structures of everyday life for many American Jews in the same way that racism and sexism are woven into the fabric of American society writ large. In the same way that unlearning racism encourages us to recognize the structural and institutional ways that people of color have been adversely impacted by racism and white supremacy in the United States, unlearning Zionism forces us to recognize the impacts that Zionism has had on its victims—both Palestinian and Jewish.

Racism is pervasive in American society; it functions in a particular way to organize our attitudes and behaviors. Part of dismantling racism and other systems of oppression requires unlearning this behavior and the unfounded fear behind it. Zionism is as deep-seated into the psyche, emotion, and worldview of many American Jews as racism is in society. Unlearning Zionism means arriving at a point where one can understand the impacts that Zionism has had on others in order to dismantle the systemic violence that it has wrought on Palestinian communities in addition to others who have been adversely impacted by Zionism, such as Mizrahi and Ethiopian Jews.[39] Reconciling Zionism's impacts with the values of justice, equality, freedom, and *tikkun olam* taught to Jews by their elders requires unlearning the nationalist myths of Israel and Zionism and challenging the ethnonationalist supremacy inherent in contemporary Zionist policies.

It is easier to learn things than to unlearn them. But despite its challenges, unlearning Zionism is integral to the process of becoming an ally to Palestinians. One way of understanding unlearning is as "the process of reducing or eliminating preexisting knowledge or habits that would otherwise represent formidable barriers to new learning."[40] Unlearning requires openness. In the beginning, one must identify what one believes to be reality and interrogate why one began believing it in the first place in an honest way. Then, one must be open to the possibility that one's understanding might not align with reality, in which case one needs to change. If one is open to it, one must gather evidence to determine the factual basis of one's belief. In the final stage of unlearning, when moving from belief to action, it is imperative to follow the new belief through practice; one must go through one's daily life by practicing what one believes to be the truth. Unlearning helps one understand that one does not need to have the same understanding of things that one did previously. As one acquires new knowledge, one's understanding of the world might change, which, in turn, might cause shifts in one's value system, beliefs, and, perhaps most importantly, behaviors.[41]

Unlearning Zionism therefore necessitates a shift in both values and actions; it leads Jews to build alliances with Palestinians, to bear witness to the Israeli occupation, and to recognize the contradiction between the commitment to social justice developed in Jewish educational institutions and Israel's human rights abuses toward Palestinians.[42] Furthermore, with regard to changing behaviors, unlearning requires examining one's privilege, sharpening an understanding of how one participates in oppressive practices. It involves becoming more conscious of the ways that our lives are informed by systems of oppression as well as how we perpetuate and uphold them. Through unlearning Zionism, Jews become deeply attentive to how Jewish identities benefit Jews within the context of the State of Israel.[43] This also enables Jews to see ways to leverage that privilege to dismantle oppression and systemic violence in Palestine/Israel.

The unlearning process necessarily centers a different story beyond the mainstream Zionist narrative so often taught to young American

Jews. In Jewish educational and social spaces much of what people learn—perhaps understandably—centers around the Jewish experience and thus Zionism and Israel. Amy Shuman, a folklorist and scholar of narrative theory, argues that people believe certain narratives that are available to them and it is hard to access alternative narratives.[44] While most American Jews are provided with a single narrative about Israel, unlearning helps avoid the "dangers of a single story" and helps people access new, counterhegemonic narratives.[45] Centering Jews in stories about Israel encourages people to think that they may be the only people who matter in the Palestinian-Israeli context.

But Palestinian lives matter as well.[46] The privileging of Jewish narratives and the near total omission of Palestinian narratives in many if not most Jewish educational spaces encourage ethnocentrism and xenophobia toward Palestinians, Arabs, and Muslims. Unlearning Zionism, which decenters Jews to make space for Palestinian narratives, facilitates bearing witness to a different story. To use the words of Palestinian scholar Edward Said, it allows Jews to understand Zionism from the standpoint of its victims.[47] Those willing to fully relinquish the Zionist narrative from their Jewish American identity push boundaries beyond one's own communal ethnocentrism to a more universal, humanistic, and emancipatory social justice activism.

For those young American Jews who change their perspectives on Israel and Zionism, the process of unlearning is at once straightforward and inordinately complex. As was the case with my experience and that of Jasmine, who we encountered earlier in this chapter, unlearning Zionism usually begins with a person being raised in a Jewish home where support for Israel is either implicit by the very nature of being an American Jew or overt through educational experiences in Hebrew school, Jewish summer camps, youth groups, or other organized Jewish educational spaces.[48] Support for Israel can manifest in numerous ways, from active support through pro-Israel advocacy work or through a more tacit approach of blind and uncritical backing of the state and its policies. This approach, which I call the "everybody is doing it" reason, generally emerges because people are raised in a community in which most Jews support Israel, so they don't have a model for dissent.

It is also in these same Jewish institutional spaces that young Jews are drilled with Jewish values that emphasize justice, equality, and peace.

Figure 2.1. Jewish American activists in CJNV's Hineinu program clear land in the West Bank to plant olive trees, April 2023. Photo by Emily Glick.

For example, Jewish children who attend Hebrew school on Sunday mornings might sing one of multiple melodies of the song "Lo Yisa Goy," taken from the book of Isaiah in the Hebrew Bible. The verse teaches that people should "beat swords into plowshares," that "nation should not lift up swords against nation," and that "they shall not learn war anymore." This song deeply embeds the idea of peace as a Jewish value in Jewish youth. Furthermore, other Jewish values such as *tikkun olam* and *tzedek* (justice) are similarly entrenched in Jewish education.[49] Young Jews are taught by their rabbis, teachers, and parents that it is a moral and ethical imperative rooted in Jewish values and history to work for justice and peace, to repair the world, to welcome the stranger, and to value every human life.

Generally speaking, these Jewish values are applied to progressive issues in liberal Reform and Conservative Jewish communities. Young Jews engage in projects to feed the hungry, provide shelter for the unhoused, or clean up a local beach or park. These entry-level community service activities are always framed in a Jewish context—we do this because we are Jews—and rooted back to the teaching of Jewish values.

For example, many synagogues require youth preparing for their bar or bat mitzvah to do a community service project, explicitly linking community service and justice work to becoming a Jewish adult and engaging in Jewish ritual. As they age, many Jewish youth get involved with immigrant rights struggles, become climate change activists, or spend time organizing with labor unions. Interestingly, the more they engage with justice work, many young American Jews progress from direct service volunteer projects to political organizing work that seeks to solve injustice by dismantling systems of oppression, thereby changing their understanding and modes of activism.

The majority of activists I interviewed expressed that their social justice activism is a direct result of their Jewishness and is rooted in the Jewish values they learned from a young age. And yet the same values promoting democracy, justice, peace, and equality and valuing human life were rarely, if ever, applied to Israel with the same vigor. This inconsistency leads to a profound cognitive dissonance between the values and actions of American Jewish communities. When young Jewish Americans begin to experience this cognitive dissonance, they generally respond by either unlearning Zionism and becoming active in the Palestine solidarity movement or ignoring the dissonance and engaging in *hasbara* activism and defense of Israel.[50]

Of course education is an important Jewish value, and many American Jews place a heavy emphasis on learning and asking questions. Jewish history is replete with a rich tradition of learning, from studying Torah and Talmud to contemporary emphasis on Jewish day schools and informal education. Since unlearning is a form of critically engaging with what one has learned and is also about relearning new things, unlearning Zionism is itself important to Jewish life for many Jewish Palestine solidarity activists. In fact, Jewish tradition and its emphasis on education and asking critical questions creates the conditions for unlearning Zionism.

For many, the process of unlearning Zionism coincides with the realization that the teaching of Jewish values felt empty when not applied evenly in all contexts because it strategically excluded Israel's state violence and mistreatment of Palestinians. Regardless of when or how unlearning begins, young Jewish activists eventually encounter Palestinian narratives in classes, through friends, on social media, and through movies and television shows. When they do encounter these narratives, they often realize that many of the things they were taught about Israel either were blatantly false or painted a romanticized picture of a Jewish state that misrepresented the reality.[51] This causes consternation in the individual who might feel anger, betrayal, confusion, guilt, and sometimes even shame about not knowing about the horrors of occupation and apartheid or the impacts of Israeli state violence. The process continues as individuals learn more about the realities on the ground in Palestine/Israel and inspires people to learn more, which also means unlearning a lot of what they were previously taught about Israel and Zionism.

Unlearning Zionism is a critical point of departure for active engagement with Palestine solidarity activism and is a process of countering erasures. By privileging their progressive politics over the Zionism with which they were raised, Jewish activists apply the Jewish values that first informed their politics toward the liberation of all people. For many, the process of unlearning Zionism allows them the space to redefine their values in relation to both Jewish communities and Palestinians. Understanding, and internalizing, the fact that Jewishness is not coterminous with support for Israel enables dissenting Jewish politics and actions that celebrate one's ethnic, cultural, and religious heritage while reclaiming the values of democracy, justice, peace, and equality so often associated with Judaism. All of this is possible, however, only with a deep engagement with a profound process of personal transformation.

Personal Transformation

Radical solidarity begins with an awakening. An important theory in the field of peace studies states that conflict transformation requires personal transformation.[52] According to this idea, individuals must undergo a significant process of personal change before they can join the larger project of conflict transformation. In fact, many Palestinian and Jewish Israeli activists attribute their desire to work with the other toward justice and peace to their own profound process of personal transformation.[53]

I provide two examples of this process to show what it looks like for Palestinian and Jewish Israeli activists. They—those on the ground—are the archetype for Jewish Americans; because the stakes are far higher for Jewish Israelis and Palestinians, American Jews often look to and learn from them. In fact, they serve as a model for Jews and non-Jews around the world. I therefore offer these examples not as a direct point of comparison to unlearning Zionism for American Jews but rather to exemplify the ways that Jewish American activists model their processes of transformation after those of the people most affected by the Palestinian-Israeli conflict.

Robi Damelin is a well-known veteran peace activist in Israel.[54] A Jewish woman born in South Africa, she was very involved with the anti-apartheid movement in her youth. She moved to Israel in 1967, intending to stay for only six months, but has lived there ever since. She got married, had two children, and raised them in a progressive and liberal household. Robi took great pride in telling her children about her anti-apartheid activism in South Africa. When Robi's elder son, David, turned eighteen, he enlisted in the Israeli Defense Forces, as military service is compulsory for Jewish Israelis. As the military experience scarred David, he was relieved when his service ended.

Thereafter, he became a social and political activist, like his mother, and began teaching at Tel Aviv University. When he got called up for reserve duty, a requirement for all former soldiers, he struggled with whether or not he should report for his reserve service.[55] He made it clear to his mother that he didn't want to serve in the Occupied Territories, but nevertheless he decided to go, saying to his mother, "If I don't go someone else will go in my place and will do terrible things." Against his wishes, David spent his reserve duty in the Occupied West Bank.

While he was serving in the reserves, a Palestinian sniper killed David and nine other Israeli soldiers at a military checkpoint near an Israeli settlement in the West Bank. In Robi's words, "It is impossible to describe what it is to lose a child. Your whole life is totally changed forever. It's not that I'm not the same person I was. I'm the same person with a lot of pain. Wherever I go, I carry this with me."[56] Unlike others in her society who experience similar loss and turn it into hate, Robi channeled her pain into a very specific positive project. She joined the Parents Circle Families Forum, a joint Israeli-Palestinian organization of over six hundred families, all of whom have lost an immediate family member to the ongoing conflict.[57] Each individual and family in the Parents Circle is involved because they want to prevent the future bereavement of others; they aim to promote dialogue, tolerance, reconciliation, and peace in both Israeli and Palestinian societies. Motivated by the pain of having lost a loved one to the violence of the conflict, they want to ensure that no mother, father, sister, or brother ever experiences the same loss.

After David's death, in 2002, Robi dedicated her life to reconciliation with Palestinians. She has been a peace activist ever since. Robi has made it clear that no violence should be done in David's name. "You may not kill anybody in the name of my child," she said shortly after David's death, speaking directly to Jewish Israeli political and military leaders. Robi understands the necessity of ending the cycles of violence and spends her life working to do just that. Her work is based on a life commitment to nonviolence and to building alliances across differences. Though Robi was a political activist in South Africa, she did not become a peace activist in Israel until after experiencing a significant personal transformation, which radically changed the trajectory of her life.

Prior to her transformation (and the death of her son), Robi was essentially "progressive except for Palestine," meaning that she held progressive and liberal views on virtually all matters except for the issue of Palestine.[58] Even though she was deeply involved in resisting policies of apartheid and similar modes of oppression in South Africa, she ignored and was able to live with the cognitive dissonance of what was happening in Palestine/Israel until the personal cost to her became too painful. This disjuncture in values and actions around the occupation is very similar to what American Jews experience in their communities.

As increasing numbers of American Jews learn about and come to terms with the realities of Israel's policies toward Palestinians, they are forced to confront their relationship to Zionism and the Jewish state. Conflict transformation addresses the underlying causes that give rise to a conflict, so when personal transformation occurs it enables an individual to challenge communal acts of injustice and help to infuse human relations with an ethical mode of being. Just as personal transformation is about recognizing the shared humanity between groups in conflict, the process of unlearning Zionism supports Jewish Americans' ability to humanize, rather than demonize, the Palestinian other. For this reason, after the initial unlearning begins for American Jews, many choose to bear witness to the occupation in the West Bank in person (which I discuss below).

Palestinian activists have their own stories of personal transformation, especially those who have chosen to work side by side with Israelis and Jews in the anti-occupation and Palestinian liberation movement. Sulaiman Khatib provides another example of the significance of personal transformation in overcoming hate and ignorance to work for justice and peace.[59] Khatib is a Palestinian from the West Bank village of Hizme, just north of Jerusalem. He and his family were deeply impacted by Israel's occupation throughout his youth, which shaped his views of both Israelis and Jews. By age twelve he had joined Fatah, the Palestinian national liberation movement, and believed that militant armed resistance was the only way to fight the occupation. Sulaiman threw stones and Molotov cocktails at Israeli soldiers and settlers, and when he was fourteen, he and a friend stabbed an Israeli soldier. Shortly after the stabbing, he was arrested and sentenced to fifteen years in an Israeli prison.

Three years into his sentence he started working in the prison library, which provided him with the opportunity to read and learn about Jewish history, among other things. One day he watched the film *Schindler's List* with his fellow prisoners. This was the first time in his life that he learned about the horrors that Jews faced during the Holocaust. Everyone watching the film in the prison wept, which turned out to present a complex situation for Sulaiman. He struggled with what he learned about the grandparents of his jailers. All of a sudden he felt great sympathy and solidarity with them. After watching the film, he dedicated the rest of his time in prison to reading and learning as much as he could. He learned Hebrew and became open to meeting with Jewish Israelis. Sulaiman suddenly understood his people's struggle differently, which changed his entire outlook on the world.

Sulaiman's personal transformation led him to work with Israelis after his release from prison. In 2006, he cofounded Combatants for Peace, a binational grassroots organization of former Palestinian and Israeli combatants, all of whom are committed to finding a nonviolent solution to the Palestinian-Israeli conflict.[60] Combatants for Peace is based on the belief that the perpetual cycles of violence in Palestine/Israel can be broken only when Israelis and Palestinians are jointly committed to nonviolence. The organization's members work to both transform and

resolve the conflict by ending Israeli occupation and all forms of violence between the two sides; they want to build a just and peaceful future
for both peoples. Every member of Combatants for Peace has a similarly
profound story of personal transformation that shifted their outlook on
the conflict. Sulaiman's experience watching *Schindler's List*, which led
him to grapple with feeling a sense of solidarity with the ancestors of his
jailers, mirrors the experiences of Jewish Americans who learn about the
Nakba and other painful moments in Palestinian history. His transformation, like Jasmine's when she encountered the Nakba, forced him to
reconsider his preconceived notions about the other, enabling the emergence of a radical solidarity to replace that of demonization.

Often directly influenced by Palestinian and Jewish Israeli activists
who have been impacted by the conflict and use their personally transformative experiences as the impetus to work toward justice and peace,
many diaspora Jews and Palestinians also go through a process of personal transformation that propels them toward activism and uncovering
the myths of Zionism.

The Miseducation of Jewish Youth

Encountering and uncovering the myths that Jews learn about Israel
in their youth is one of the most fundamental elements in the process
of unlearning Zionism. While there is abundant research about Israel
education in American Jewish schools, including how students hold the
tensions between various historical accounts of Israel, not much exists
that explains the one-sided and partial nature of how young American
Jews learn about Israel.[61] Yet anecdotal and ethnographic evidence suggests that mainstream Israel education in American Jewish institutions
is indeed misleading and that when students do encounter Israel in
new and critical ways it disrupts their previously romanticized notions
of Israel. This most commonly either evokes feelings of resentment or
leads to intense defensive posturing.[62]

I refer to the one-sided and incomplete Israel education provided by
Jewish institutions as the "miseducation" of Jewish youth.[63] "Miseducation" is the method by which American Jewish institutions teach only
partial truths about Israel, Palestine, and the Palestinian-Israeli conflict,
a process that omits Palestinian narratives, demonizes Palestinians,

and delegitimizes their claims. This process has a profound effect on how young Jews are socialized to care about Israel. Perhaps more importantly, it constructs a belief within Jewish communities that being Jewish requires a strong attachment and connection to Israel. Jewish anti-occupation activists directly contest this in their work after they unlearn Zionism, which decouples Israel from one's Jewishness.

The impact of miseducation is best represented by IfNotNow's #YouNeverToldMe campaign, which was launched in September 2017.[64] During this campaign, young Jews who learned about Israel in Jewish day schools, overnight camps, synagogues, and other institutions expressed rage, dissatisfaction, and disappointment that the occupation was hidden from them during their educational experiences. In questioning why they never learned about the occupation in their many years of Jewish and Israel educational programming, they called attention to the process of deliberate omission of Palestinian narratives.

The campaign also asked these institutions "to provide Jewish education that advances freedom and dignity for all people."[65] By publishing a robust website replete with testimonials from alumni of a wide array of Jewish educational institutions across the movements, the #YouNeverToldMe campaign revealed how widespread this miseducation is and what a core role it plays in socializing American Jews to a particular pro-Israel narrative. Among other things, the campaign highlighted that these institutions embraced nuanced and complex approaches to multiple issues, including interpretations of the Torah and one's Jewish identity, while forbidding this same questioning when it came to Zionism and Israel. Once these activists reached young adulthood and unlearned Zionism, they expressed their distrust of these organizations.[66] To this end, the process of miseducation may best be summarized by bell hooks, who wrote that "[there is a] difference between education as the practice of freedom and education that merely strives to reinforce domination."[67]

Rather than disengage completely from Jewish life or dismiss the role that Israel plays in their identities completely, most activists in the movement use the omission of Palestinian narratives from their education as an opportunity to learn more, which also requires unlearning. For example, one activist shared, "When I did finally come to learn about the Nakba as an element of both history and present-day reality, my reaction wasn't, 'You never told me,' as the ad campaign goes. My reaction was 'This is something I need to learn.'"[68]

There are numerous ways that young American Jews learn about Palestinians, their narratives, and their history. But many first learn through a college course where they are exposed to new ideas. For example, Adam, who has been an active member of numerous anti-occupation groups for many years, told me something that was echoed by numerous others: "I took a seminar on Zionism that was very thoughtful, very critical, in college," he told me. "We read *The Question of Palestine* by Edward Said, and we read Martin Buber's writing, all of these things that I started stepping into the more general mode of left-wing skepticism."[69] It was in the context of this class that he also met Palestinians for the first time, which also changed his perspective on the situation in Palestine/Israel and further catapulted him into activism.

He continued,

> The experience of having Palestinians my age who are friends, and then even a few of them close friends, was a new experience for me. While that in and of itself is not necessarily transformative, I think it is, in some ways, the basis for any meaningful transformation, because as long as this is all kept hypothetical, you can weigh the Palestinians against the concepts of antisemitism, versus the concepts of history versus the concept of ethnic solidarity versus the concept of the Holocaust, and it's all concepts. But as soon as you start thinking, oh, if [an Israeli soldier is] conducting a raid in Hebron and pushing a family into the corner of their living room, that's just not a conceptual Palestinian family, but that could be my friend Nadia's grandmother.[70]

When Adam and other activists personalize the struggle, they unlearn one of the central tenets of Zionism, that Palestine was "a land without a people for a people without a land." Many Jews are taught that Palestine was a barren wasteland and that when the Zionists came, they "made the desert bloom." For example, after I gave a lecture to a class at a local synagogue about understanding Zionism in the twenty-first century, the rabbi, a Millennial who was raised in Reform educational settings, approached me to ask a question that bothered her during my talk. "I was taught that Palestine was a swampland and that the

Zionists came and drained the swamps. If it was a swamp, how could Palestinians have lived there?" This question came from someone who spent close to twenty years studying in Jewish institutions, a longtime student who had fully internalized the myth that Palestine was a land without a people. She never learned Palestinian narratives, and she told me that throughout her robust Jewish education at prestigious Jewish institutions her education prepared her only to contest Palestinian claims to self-determination and never to understand or accept them as valid and legitimate. Not surprisingly, she never met or befriended any Palestinians in her life.

Orli's experience is also indicative of the importance of meeting Palestinians in order to rewrite the dominant script that invisibilizes them. Her journey of personal transformation started while she was living in Jerusalem. For Orli, Zionist myths began to crumble when she saw Palestinians living their everyday lives. According to her, "On a really simple level, being in Bethlehem, just walking down the street of an entire city of Palestinian people—who are a mix of Muslim and Christian, who were living their life and doing their thing three miles from where I lived in Jerusalem"—was all it took to change her perspective.[71] She continued,

> I had been living in Jerusalem for two years. I had traveled to every major city in Israel and I had never been to Bethlehem and an entire world opened up to me. And this is also where I felt like another myth of Zionism just exploded. These are a real people. They live here. This is not a land without a people for a people without a land. This is real. This is a whole city of people. And maybe I was also by extension able to realize, even though I hadn't seen it yet, that that must mean that Ramallah is a whole city full of Palestinian people. And Hebron is a whole city full of people and Jenin and Jericho. What I remember feeling was that this had been hidden from me and then I got angry. Then I felt like you failed me. I went to Hebrew school. I had my bat mitzvah. I did ongoing Jewish education and Jewish learning and no one had ever told me that an entire city of regular people lived there.[72]

For Orli and Adam, the seemingly mundane act of encountering Palestinians disrupted the omission of Palestinians and their narratives from their Jewish educational experiences. Meeting and befriending Palestinians became a radical act that aided in unlearning the miseducation of their youth, which has enabled them to recognize not only that Palestinians exist but also that they have been living under a harsh Israeli military occupation for more than half a century. By unlearning Zionist myths, they utterly disassembled a statement frequently made by many pro-Israel advocates, one that young Jews often encounter in their education, that "there is no such thing as Palestine." Through this type of unlearning process, Jewish activists resist the systematic erasure of Palestine, which exists both in American Jewish educational settings and in Israeli policy that seeks to make Palestine and the Palestinians disappear.[73]

One of the most common ways that activists discuss what Saree Makdisi refers to as an "architecture of erasure" is from the maps of Israel through which many Jews learn about the state and its boundaries.[74] Maps are not benign artifacts; they have tremendous power to impact the development of communal narratives and, as such, are instrumental in socializing young Jews about Israel.[75] Though there are myriad examples of the process of miseducation and erasure through maps, one moment in particular became prominent in the anti-occupation movement because it was shared widely on social media. During his Birthright trip in 2018, Elon looked at a map of Israel that was distributed to everyone in his group.[76] After a careful examination he noticed that it resembled the maps he saw throughout his Jewish day school education. He immediately recognized a problem with what was on the map and, perhaps more significantly, what didn't appear anywhere on it.

To someone without a background in the complexities of the situation in Palestine/Israel, such as most of the people in his Birthright group and the average young American Jew who learns in mainstream Jewish institutions, the map doesn't appear to be problematic. But a closer look reveals that the entire territory shown on the map between the Jordan River and the Mediterranean Sea is marked as Israel. Not only is the West Bank not labeled, but the map refers to that area as Judea and Samaria, a reference to its ancient biblical names and what the State of Israel often calls that territory.[77] Furthermore, Gaza isn't labeled as a separate territory with any clear boundaries separating it from Israel. In the eyes of the mapmakers, and the Birthright program that liberally distributes maps like this to participants, the message is clear: it is all Israel, "from the river to the Sea," thereby effectively and literally erasing Palestine from the map.

Elon, who by the time he enrolled in Birthright was already deep into his journey of unlearning Zionism, immediately recognized that not clearly marking the West Bank and Gaza on the map contributed to the erasure of Palestine. He also understood that it exemplified the miseducation perpetuated by programs like Birthright and those taking place in Jewish educational spaces more broadly. The map Elon received on his Birthright trip resembled the maps plastered in Jewish schools and classrooms worldwide. When the only map young Jews see of Israel in classrooms includes the Occupied Palestinian Territories but without clearly demarcating them as separate, it is not all that surprising that people are mortified when they finally learn the extent of Israel's occupation. While many people do not even know what to ask when participating on a Birthright trip, Elon had already uncovered many of the myths of Zionism and was thus able to confront the Birthright guide over the misrepresentation of the map they had handed out. Another participant on the trip recorded the confrontation with their cell phone and posted it on Facebook, where the video went viral.

It is worth quoting the confrontation available on video in its entirety:

ELON [HOLDING A MAP ON THE BUS]: These maps, are these the ones that Birthright gives to everyone? Is this the one that all Israel Outdoors groups get? Because I mean, literally, if I hadn't asked anything, how would anyone know where the West Bank was? 'Cause this map doesn't say anything.

BIRTHRIGHT TOUR GUIDE: So, Israel sees the West Bank as part of Israel. And Israel does not put anything on our maps around the West Bank because the West Bank is just like Tel Aviv or Jerusalem.

ELON: I mean, literally, like erasing the fact that Palestine exists though.

TOUR GUIDE: Palestine, if you'll ask anybody in Israel. . . .

ELON: But it's not fair. I think the real issue is that it's inappropriate for all of us to be . . . shown this map as if this is the truth. When only Israel and the Israeli government seems to think that the West Bank is part of Israel, when the entire international community and Palestinians themselves would never say that. And the reason is because the people who live there can't vote. They're under military occupation. Their water is being controlled by somebody else and they can't get enough access to it. And, I mean, their lives are made like a living hell because they can't even see their families in Jerusalem. They can't get to other cities [in the West Bank] because the roads are constantly controlled and they have to go through all of these checkpoints. And they never know when something could be shut down or when their day could be made a living hell by the Israeli military.

TOUR GUIDE: Israel is showing you what they believe. Also, in Israel it's very divided and people believe different stuff. But the West Bank is part of the State of Israel, it's part of Israel and that's what the Israeli government is showing you. The country of Israel.[78]

This exchange reflects some of the deep fissures that emerge when Jews uncover the miseducation that omits Palestinian narratives and seeks to inspire an unconditional support for Israel. Rather than showing a full and complex portrait of Israel that includes its military occupation over Palestinians, Jewish educational institutions provide a carefully curated picture of Israel, which is evidenced by this confrontation over the maps that Birthright distributes. The confrontation exposed the depth to which Birthright miseducates participants about the political realities of the State of Israel. The map does not have the Green Line, which is the internationally recognized border between Israel and the Occupied Palestinian Territory of the West Bank. By neglecting to show the Green Line and failing to demarcate a difference between Israel and the Occupied Territories, Birthright is effectively erasing Palestine as a political reality and obscuring the existence of Israel's military occupation over that territory.

Furthermore, equating the West Bank with Jerusalem or Tel Aviv, as this particular guide did, is not only misleading but also inaccurate. The only way this is not a blatant falsehood is if one is referring only to the Jewish Israeli citizens who live in each place. Jewish Israelis enjoy the numerous privileges of citizenship regardless of where they live, be that Tel Aviv or a settlement in the West Bank. In contrast, Palestinians who live in the West Bank do not have any legal status as citizens and, as such, have no access to the same benefits.[79] When Elon pointed to the fact that Palestinians in the West Bank can't vote, that Israel limits their access to water, and that they are subjected to a regime of military check-points, he is highlighting not only the impacts of military occupation on an entire population but also the differential treatment of Jewish Israelis and Palestinians.

According to someone who was on the same Birthright trip, "One really funny thing, I mean, sad, but also kind of funny, is that our guide was like, 'Yeah, you know, the Palestinians in their schools, when they show maps, the whole thing is Palestine. There's no Israel on there. The whole thing is Palestine.' Then, literally the next day, they give us this map. The whole thing is Israel. There's no demarcation of the Green Line. There's no delineation on there. There's nothing."[80]

The discussion about the map also points to the fact that young Jews are willing to confront both individuals and Jewish institutions if they discover a moral or ethical issue with what is presented to them. In this case, a young Jewish activist confronted a Birthright leader because he detected a clear misrepresentation of information. Elon noticed that what the guides were teaching on the trip obscured the realities of the Palestinian-Israeli conflict. So, he spoke out publicly. The trend of con-fronting Jewish institutions, which I examine in greater depth in the fol-lowing chapter, is bound to continue as young Jews uncover the myths they were taught and unlearn Zionism.

This was reinforced by an activist who said that these confrontations "are compelling to me because the anger is there and I think the more malevolently the [Jewish] community tries to hide the information from people, the more people will seek it out, the more they will find it, learn about it, and realize that it clashes with our values. We don't be-lieve in [occupation]. We trusted you with our education and you failed us. I truly believe that there will continue to be heightened confronta-tions."[81] The more Jews are exposed to Palestinian narratives, the more dissonance is created between what they learned in their former Jew-ish environments, which romanticized Israel, and the morals they were taught—freedom, equality, and dignity for all. The dissonance and dis-satisfaction with what they were instructed provokes what Atalia Omer calls an "ethical outrage."[82]

Righteous Indignation

The emotional responses to unlearning Zionism vary from rage and anger to guilt, shame, and betrayal. They can involve a tremendous amount of pain for those who unlearn things they once held as foundational truths. The pain felt by Alexa was palpable when I spoke to her about her process of personal transformation from Zionist youth group leader to anti-occupation activist. "I think in reflecting on the process . . . I was just so angry, and I was really angry at feeling like I'd been lied to and betrayed by my community and my youth movement," she said.[83] "That youth movement was so important to me. I idolized my image of them, and they just never told me about this ever. Not once. Not a single conversation about what actually happened [in Palestine/ Israel]." The deep loss of a romanticized Israel was difficult to process, leading to tears and heartache.

When people learn about and are exposed to Palestinian narratives for the first time, they often feel immense shame that they did not know these things earlier. This is similar to the reckoning in the United States over the Juneteenth holiday. Following the eruption of protests in May 2020 after the police murder of George Floyd, June 19 or Juneteenth, which has been commemorated in some communities for a century and a half, all of a sudden emerged into the public conscious. The following year President Biden signed legislation declaring it a federal holiday.[84] Numerous people, many white, have expressed shame and guilt over not having heard of Juneteenth until the protests. But how could they be expected to know about something that they were never taught, something that was kept hidden from them, either intentionally or out of complete ignorance? Whether related to Juneteenth, Zionism's impacts on Palestinians, or anything else, when individuals begin to uncover the myths they were taught, reckoning and confrontation with one's teachers and family members emerge.

In this regard, unlearning Zionism also often requires a "coming out" to one's family and friends as anti-occupation, anti-Zionist, and/or an outspoken critic of Israel. For some, revealing such dissenting views may be among the most challenging elements of the unlearning process since it forces a confrontation with the most influential and formative people in one's life. But it is also an opportunity to change the minds and hearts of those closest to them. While it is not uncommon for family members to dismiss young activists as naïve and idealistic or to intentionally avoid the topic so as to prevent family conflict, discussions with family members also present an opportunity for individual and collective transformation.

Interviewees consistently noted that members of their families who unequivocally supported Israel started to shift their views after learning more from the new anti-occupation activist in their lives, whether through discussions around the dinner table about contemporary events in Palestine/Israel or through recounting personal experiences as an activist. Many family members became more tolerant and sympathetic to Palestinians and increasingly critical of Israel as a result. When the young activists' experiences alone are not able to change the minds of their family members, their challenging of family members to reconcile their Jewish values with the increasingly right-wing policies of the Israeli government often assists in causing a crack in their pro-Israel foundation.

Most importantly, by having someone in the family model the acceptability of challenging Israel and the stranglehold that Zionism seems to have on Jewish identity in the United States, it becomes acceptable for others to do the same. For example, in a cowritten op-ed published in *Haaretz*, father and daughter Allen and Katie Weiner discussed how the transformation took place in their family.[85] Allen, the father, a child of Holocaust survivors and "a firm believer in the right of self-determination of both Israelis and Palestinians," admits to learning from his daughter that "the injustice and violence associated with Israel's occupation of the West Bank" were not only eroding American support for Israel but also challenging his own personal willingness to protect Israel's reputation. In the op-ed, he pleaded with Israeli prime minister Benjamin Netanyahu not to annex the West Bank, which he believed would cement apartheid into the fabric of Israel. The hours of conversations he had had with his daughter Katie, a Harvard student who was an active participant in Israel Apartheid Week, and Allen's response to these discussions illustrate the potential impact that young Jewish activists can have on the political views of their families. As this vignette demonstrates, he too became infected with a righteous indignation at the actions of the Israeli government, which led him to publicize his dissenting views. His daughter's perspective had helped make it more acceptable.

My activism and political transformation helped to push the needle in my family and friend networks as well. I frequently bring stories from my experiences in Palestine home with me. Though I never heard the word "occupation" growing up, that is no longer an absent word from our family conversations. I now have open and productive conversations with my family, discussions that have pushed the boundaries of what it means to have a critical relationship with Israel. I have also demonstrated that it is possible to be openly anti-occupation and still accepted as Jewish and a member of the family.

At the same time, despite the political shifts in my family and their willingness to openly criticize certain Israeli policies, for some people it remains difficult to fully unlearn what has been so deeply engrained in them in their youth. For example, in a conversation with someone in our family, my then five-year-old daughter mentioned that she wanted to visit Palestine. The family member with whom my daughter spoke immediately remarked, "There is no such thing as Palestine!" Despite the attempts to unlearn, despite my desire to teach my children different things than what I learned, and despite the need to open a space for new generations to be free of the miseducation of Jewish youth, obstacles remain.

And yet, there is optimism for a different Jewish future. As one of the activists I spoke with said, "I'm really hopeful that we're in a time period where we are doing some collective unlearning, so that we can teach our kids something different, so that they don't have to unlearn what we had to unlearn. I hope that we can do the process of unlearning, so that they can just grow up in a Jewish community that is open to being critical."[86] This is precisely the Jewish future that Gen Z and Millennial anti-occupation activists are tirelessly working to build.

The difficulty and pain in unlearning Zionism largely stem from the fact that people feel betrayed by those they love and trust the most. Furthermore, it is extremely difficult to relinquish something that is so deeply engrained. How do you unlearn something that is drilled into you frequently and unabashedly for years or decades? The process often leaves emotional scars; it is a trauma that takes time to heal. Furthermore, rejecting Zionism means rebuffing a central pillar of one's upbringing. All too often that refusal to support Zionism leads to the community itself rejecting the activist, which only increases the personal agony inherent in unlearning Zionism.

The activists with whom I spoke process this trauma collectively both through their activism and by creating meaningful Jewish communal spaces where it is acceptable to critique Zionism or discuss one's unlearning process. Without others who have had similar experiences, or without organizations such as Jewish Voice for Peace, IfNotNow, and the Center for Jewish Nonviolence, among others, it would be easy to feel as though you are falling off a cliff by yourself, alone in the process of personal transformation. Today, young American Jews who are ready to fully step away from Zionism as an ideological project have multiple options for a spiritual and political home that bridges the gap between their values as Jews and what they believe about Palestine/Israel. These Jewish anti-occupation spaces are often decentralized communities that highlight an emancipatory Jewish identity based on the understanding that the liberation of all people is intimately linked to one another.

An Emancipatory Jewish Identity

Amy, a committed and involved activist to the anti-occupation struggle, was raised in a relatively normative Jewish household and attended multiple Jewish educational institutions throughout her youth. Her family members were unquestioning Zionists and full-fledged supporters of Israel. As was the case for many others, when she began to encounter Palestinian narratives and learned more about the impacts of Israeli state violence, Amy felt alienated from her Jewishness, which was a central part of her identity through that point in her life. During her unlearning she was angry; she felt betrayed by the fact that so much of the brutality of the Israeli state was kept from her. Nonetheless, Amy committed herself to unlearning the Zionism she was taught. For her, unlearning was a mechanism of reclaiming her Jewishness as an identity rooted in liberation and justice. "Unlearning is literally wrestling back our heritage from this violence," Amy said.[87] Unlearning also enabled her to grow an emancipatory Jewish identity through which Palestine solidarity activism became a key method of both asserting and performing her Jewish identity.[88]

Asserting one's Jewishness while unlearning Zionism also reclaims a Jewishness that is separate from the State of Israel. By decoupling Jewish identity from support for Israel, it becomes possible to both imagine and create a way of expressing a Jewishness that eschews nationalist fervor in favor of a more radically inclusive identity based on the notion that the liberation of all social groups is interconnected. This is especially challenging within a mainstream cultural milieu centered around Israel.

According to activist Ilana Cruger-Zaken, Jews with non-Zionist and dissenting views on Israel "are alienated from the mainstream Jewish community [because] the community is often centered around the Israel experience; we relate to one another through shared experiences, and many of those involve Israel, an Israel without Palestinians."[89] When anti-occupation activists question Zionism, they do so in ways that challenge the mainstream Jewish community's grip on a Jewish identity predicated on a connection to Israel. Unlearning Zionism instead asserts the possibility of having a vibrant and meaningful Jewish identity devoid of support for an ethnonational Jewish state.

Many people who unlearn Zionism and experience the personal and political transformations that accompany the unlearning process find that they are not alone. Rather, they often gather together to create intentionally Jewish spaces that enable them to openly express their critiques of Israel and Zionism without fear of reprisal. In addition to the organizations at the center of this book, such as IfNotNow, Jewish Voice for Peace, and the Center for Jewish Nonviolence, some people created organizations on campus such as Open Hillel or Alt-J, a Jewish student group formed at Tufts University that intentionally links Judaism to social justice and creates a place for students "to process their Jewish identities and Israel-Palestine."[90]

Moreover, many young Jews even find their Jewish communities and connect to other Jews through these specifically non- and anti-Zionist spaces and through anti-occupation and anti-apartheid activism. Jamie, an activist who grew up in a suburban area in the Northeast, was ostracized from her Jewish community for her dissenting views on Israel, including her support for the BDS movement. Despite feeling unwelcome in the community where she was raised, Jamie continued to strongly identify with her Jewishness and sought out spaces where she could be both Jewish and open about her anti-occupation politics:

I continue to feel Jewish because it has been so formative for my entire life. But I felt very disconnected from [the] Jewish community, and I would say that didn't really change until I joined Jewish Voice for Peace after college. . . . I feel like over the past seven years, I have been able to find more and more Jewish communities that are primarily among other young Jews, other Millennials and Gen Z Jews who are also engaged in anti-occupation work on some level, and also a lot of queer Jews. I feel like a lot of my queer community and anti-occupation Jewish community overlap very heavily.[91]

Through her work as an activist Jamie found other Jews like her, and she found Jewish community through anti-occupation activism. Together, as activists and as Jews, they are building intentional Jewish spaces that not only allow for open debate and dissent on Israel and Zionism but thrive off of them.

Activists who find support and comfort in these Jewish spaces are attracted to them in part because they reconcile the contradictions that most Zionist and pro-Israel Jewish organizations and communities do not. They "walk the talk" of Jewish ethics by consistently applying the Jewish values to all contexts, especially and including to Israel. While mainstream Jewish organizations continue to claim the importance of *tikkun olam* and the centrality of justice in Jewish life, they all too often fail to apply these values to Israel, rendering them unattractive to young Jewish anti-occupation activists who have decided to form their own Jewish communal spaces through which to express a more liberatory and inclusive Jewish identity. Activist responses to and encounters with mainstream Jewish American institutions are at the heart of the next chapter.

3

#NotJustAFreeTrip

Protest and the "Birthright Walk-Offs"

June 28, 2018, was a warm and sunny day, one week after the official start of summer. For five young women—all IfNotNow activists, ranging in age from twenty-two to twenty-five—it was also the tenth and final day of an intense Taglit-Birthright Israel program. They refused to participate in the final portion of the trip and decided to publicly leave the program, streaming the political act live on Facebook. This marked the first time in Birthright's two-decade history that participants had dared to walk off the program. Almost immediately the video of the walk-off went viral, garnering over a hundred thousand views on Facebook within a day.[1] The act sparked a mixture of criticism and support, generating a buzz about IfNotNow's position in the lives of young Jewish Americans.

By walking off their trip, the activists called attention to the ways that Birthright specifically and mainstream Jewish organizations more generally, which are often referred to as the "American Jewish Establishment," maintain Israel's occupation. They tried to make clear that Birthright renders Palestinian narratives invisible, obscuring the realities of the occupation in order to reinforce unwavering American Jewish support for Israel among its participants. In exposing what they consider to be Birthright's problematic educational process, including glossing over Israeli human rights abuses, the activists highlighted the ways Jewish institutions promote a culture "that omits and denies the legitimacy of Palestinian narratives and rights."[2] By targeting a pillar in Israel education, the activists used support for Birthright as a wedge issue, provoking other young Jewish Americans to rethink their participation in the program and to question how Palestinian narratives have been erased elsewhere in their education.[3] The incident was not a simple flash in the pan. Two weeks after the initial walk-off, eight more activists on two different Birthright trips also walked off their programs in a similar fashion.[4]

This chapter examines the summer 2018 Birthright walk-offs, approaching them as a case study that illustrates how young American Jews have utilized one particular tactic in confronting mainstream Jewish institutions: exposing the ways these organizations support and uphold the occupation through live protests. I argue that the activists participated in this direct action as a way of performing their Jewish identities, which are rooted in a deep commitment to the social justice values they learned from the Jewish communities in which they were raised. The Birthright walk-offs further illustrate the ways in which the participation of Millennial and Gen Z activists in the Palestine solidarity movement represents a new way of critically engaging with Israel.

These walk-offs reflect the broader participation of young American Jews in the Palestine solidarity movement; they are part of a fundamental shift in how young Jews relate to Israel.[5] Their willingness to publicly confront Jewish institutions that invisibilize Palestinian rights and narratives and uphold the occupation illustrates the great lengths to which young Jews are willing to go to hold these institutions accountable to consistently act on the values of human rights, equality, and justice. It is significant to underscore that young Jewish American Palestine solidarity activists are targeting mainstream Jewish institutions in order to transform the Jewish community they so deeply love, not to destroy it, as their critics so often claim.

In this chapter first I discuss why targeting mainstream Jewish institutions is an important tactic for the movement. This contextualizes the importance of the walk-off itself. Second, I provide an in-depth examination of how the Birthright walk-offs have targeted a pillar of the Jewish community. Based on in-depth interviews with ten of the thirteen activists who walked off their trips in the summer of 2018, I explore the walk-offs from their perspective, centering the experiences of the activists in order to make sense of exactly how and why their protest was a meaningful Jewish act in solidarity with Palestinians. The walk-offs were protests carried out by young Jews straddling the line between communal insiders and outsiders; they are simultaneously part of a community they are excluded from due to their anti-occupation activism and their dissenting politics about Israel. I maintain that these demonstrations were a profoundly mature expression of the activists' Jewishness, acts emanating from a history of Jewish social justice activism. In the poignant words of one of the activists, "Walking off that Birthright trip was maybe the most Jewish thing I will ever do in my life."[6]

Confronting the American Jewish Establishment

According to sociologist Sarah Anne Minkin, mainstream Jewish institutions mobilize "American Jews to identify with their version of the Jewish collective, in which strong identification with and advocacy on behalf of the state of Israel are critically important."[7] These institutions range from synagogues, federations, JCCs, and youth groups to political advocacy organizations such as AIPAC and the American Jewish Committee. Generally well-funded, these establishments are united in their objective to defend and enhance Jewish life in the United States and abroad, especially in Israel.[8] Conjuring support for the Jewish state is integral to their respective missions, which seek to cultivate a sense of Jewishness that is deeply connected to Israel.

Many young American Jews are not willing to subscribe to this type of Jewish identity, a worldview that requires an unwavering support for Zionism at the expense of the rights of the Palestinians. On the contrary, as noted earlier, writer Peter Beinart argues that one reason they refuse to accept these institutions is that they "have refused to foster—indeed, have actively opposed—a Zionism that challenges Israel's behavior in the West Bank and Gaza Strip and toward its own Arab citizens. For several decades, the Jewish establishment has asked American Jews to check their liberalism at Zionism's door, and now, to their horror, they are finding that many young Jews have checked their Zionism instead."[9]

Collectively, these mainstream Jewish organizations have played a key role in supporting the occupation, both directly and indirectly, for more than half a century.[10] The establishment is composed of prominent and resource rich institutions that claim a monopoly on the representation of American Jews, despite the fact that the Jewish community is quite diverse and there is no consensus on what the Jewish community actually wants.[11] Furthermore, there is no clear democratic process within these organizations or within the community writ large over who claims the right of representation over the Jewish community. When activists target the American Jewish Establishment, the undemocratic nature of Jewish communal representation is one of the things they bring into sharp focus. It should therefore not be surprising when anti-occupation activists protest an organization that seeks to monopolize the conversation on the connections of young Jews to Israel.

One of the most prominent ways that the American Jewish Establishment seeks to engage Jews is by producing an attachment to Israel that is manifested in outward support for the Jewish state.[12] Support for Israel is an integral element of what it means to be Jewish for many American Jews, and there are ample survey data to support this idea.[13] For example, as discussed (see the introduction), according to the 2020 Pew Research Center study on Jewish Americans, 80 percent of American Jews believe that caring about Israel is either "essential" or "important" to what it means to be Jewish.[14] With such overwhelming Jewish American support for Israel, mainstream Jewish organizations continue to direct massive sums of human and financial resources into maintaining strong ties between the global Jewish population and the Jewish state.[15] Additionally, the Jewish Establishment funnels such incredible resources into nurturing support for Israel that it is largely responsible for generating the very sentiment it uses to justify its continued programming.[16]

Part of the outcome of nurturing support for Israel among American Jews is support for and maintenance of the occupation. In 2018, IfNotNow released "Beyond Talk: Five Ways the American Jewish Establishment Supports the Occupation," a well-researched report that documents five key ways that mainstream American Jewish organizations and institutions maintain and support the occupation.[17] This report, whose findings are detailed below, illuminates the core reasons why young Jewish American Palestine solidarity activists target mainstream Jewish institutions. In short, they believe that by supporting and maintaining the occupation, the American Jewish Establishment is hypocritical because they emphasize the American and Jewish values of justice, equality, and freedom yet do so quite selectively, denying them, for example, to Palestinians. Targeting mainstream organizations is therefore not simply about effective strategy but also about their care for the Jewish community as well as how new generations' Jewish identities are being shaped. This strategy is about calling community institutions and leaders to account, thereby creating a new and distinct vision of what the Jewish future can be.

The report argues that Jewish organizations are deemed complicit in the occupation when they "directly fund institutions that uphold Israel's military, economic, and political control over Palestinians' daily lives."[18] For example, many Jewish organizations, including Jewish Federations in cities across the country, donate money directly to Israeli settlements, in addition to groups in Israel that support these same settlements.[19] Between 2012 and 2015, Jewish federations gave nearly $6 million to fund Israeli settlement projects, including funding projects like the Friends of Ir David in Silwan, a Palestinian neighborhood in East Jerusalem, which is conspicuously over the Green Line.[20] In 2015, the San Francisco Federation donated $275,300 to the Central Fund of Israel, a nonprofit that funds Israeli settlements in the West Bank.[21] Federations not only give money to support Israel's settlement project, which is illegal under international law, but also actively prevent money from donor-advised funds held by the Jewish Federations to go to organizations that support Palestinian rights and/or work to end the occupation, such as IfNotNow and JVP.[22]

In 2018, an investigative report published in the *Forward* revealed that the Helen Diller Foundation, a Jewish philanthropic foundation affiliated with the Jewish Community Federation of San Francisco, was secretly funding the Canary Mission.[23] This organization runs a website that compiles a "blacklist" of Palestinian rights advocates. They also actively engage in vicious public smear campaigns against these individuals, threatening them to cease their Palestine solidarity activities at their peril. The San Francisco Jewish Federation's enabling of the Diller Foundation to support the Canary Mission had widespread effects on the American Jewish community, on Palestine solidarity activists, and on Israeli border control, which used these lists of "blacklisted" scholars and activists to limit travel to Israel.[24]

More specifically, deeper investigative reporting found that Israel's Ministry of Strategic Affairs was using the Canary Mission's blacklist to prevent political activists from entering Israel.[25] In one prominent case, Lara Alqasem, a twenty-two-year-old American of Palestinian descent, was prevented from entering Israel to begin her studies as a registered student at the Hebrew University. Because she was listed on the Canary Mission's site for supporting the BDS movement while a student at the University of Florida, she spent over two weeks in detention at Ben Gurion Airport.[26] Only after international condemnation did the Israeli Supreme Court allow her to enter the country. Once it was revealed that the Hellen Diller Foundation, which holds its money at the San Francisco Federation, was funding the site, young Jewish alumni of Diller Foundation programs engaged in a grassroots campaign to publicly demand that the foundation immediately cease funding the Canary Mission.[27] The Diller Foundation eventually caved to alumni pressure and adjusted its funding priorities accordingly.[28]

By banning progressive anti-occupation organizations from accessing these funds, concurrently funneling money into centrist and conservative organizations, the Jewish Establishment tries to silence dissenting views on Israel. But they have not prevented these groups from growing and doing their work. In fact, every push to eliminate support for these groups has made them only more visible, rendering them more attractive to young American Jews seeking out Jewish spaces to be politically active. As was the case with the mobilization organized against the Diller Foundation and in support of Lara Alqasem, movement activists revealed their discomfort with the impact that funding has had on the silencing of dissenting Jewish views on Israel and demonstrated their power to successfully influence the federation's funding choices.

A second way that mainstream Jewish organizations maintain the occupation is by lobbying American politicians to give unconditional support to Israel, often at the direct expense of Palestinian rights. With the remarkable lobbying power and capacity of national groups such as AIPAC and local ones such as the Jewish Community Relations Council, pressure is placed on politicians to give unconditional support for Israel, often articulated in a way that equates support for Israel with support for the Jewish community writ large.[29] By extension, often when politicians express an opinion contrary to the desires and wishes of the pro-Israel lobby, they are smeared as antisemitic, thus making them a pariah to the Jewish community, as has repeatedly happened to congresswomen Ilhan Omar and Rashida Tlaib, for example.[30] Pro-Israel advocates seek to stifle honest discussions about Israel because they fear that an open debate might cause Americans to question their level of support for Israel. It might even become apparent that their liberal values clash with Israel's policies.[31] By stifling debate, they seek to silence critique of Israel and delegitimize any dissenting politics as antisemitic.[32] The Israel lobby also supports the occupation by funneling massive amounts of money into political campaigns to support pro-Israel candidates who will vote to give Israel a blank check while refraining from condemning Israel's actions on the record.[33]

Yet in recent years, the political power of these lobbying groups has waned, partially in relation to Democrats' slow movement to the left on issues related to Israel.[34] We can also see evidence of the success of the Palestine solidarity movement to oust long-term sitting members of Congress and replace them with more progressive politicians who are both sympathetic to Palestinian rights and more aligned with young Jewish positions on issues such as climate change, racial justice, and immigrant rights. In New York City, for example, a group of activists formed an organization called the Jewish Vote that seeks to leverage the power of Jewish voters to elect leaders willing to implement sweeping progressive changes to local and national politics.[35]

During the June 2020 New York primaries, for example, the Jewish Vote joined a coalition of progressive groups to elect Jamaal Bowman to the fourteenth congressional district and oust Eliot Engel, a sixteen-term member of Congress. Engel, who was endorsed by prominent Democrats like Hillary Clinton and Charles Schumer, was also backed by over $1.5 million provided by Democratic Majority for Israel, a pro-Israel political action committee that sought unsuccessfully to wield its influence on the election.[36] With the support of young Jewish activists, Bowman joined fellow New Yorker congresswoman Alexandria Ocasio-Cortez as a progressive candidate supported by young Jewish activists who were successfully able to confront the strength of the pro-Israel lobby in order to influence American foreign policy on Israel. Bowman's electoral victory demonstrates that progressive Jewish activists can mobilize in many ways, including in challenging the Israel lobby's stranglehold on American foreign policy toward Israel and its attempts to prioritize support for Israel above everything else, including Palestinian rights.

A third way that mainstream Jewish organizations uphold the occupation is by giving a platform to prominent individuals and organizations that advocate for continuing policies of occupation and military and political control over Palestinians. "Beyond Talk" points to three individuals—right-wing Israeli politician Naftali Bennett, former Israeli consul general in New York Dani Dayan, and now-deceased megadonor

Sheldon Adelson—to illustrate the profound impact that the American Jewish Establishment has in supporting right-wing politicians.[37] All three of these individuals, in their own ways, have played distinct roles in ensuring uncritical Jewish American support for Israel, alongside the silencing and policing of dissenting views within the Jewish community and beyond.

Adelson is the most relevant of these three ideologues since he was one of the primary donors to support Birthright. The fact that his money enabled Birthright to become the most significant way that young American Jews visit and learn about Israel is not inconsequential because his radical conservative views are at odds with the political perspectives of the majority of young Jewish Americans. Not only was he a prominent supporter of the Republican Party and a major donor to Donald Trump, but he also supported the expansion of illegal Israeli settlements, opposed the establishment of a Palestinian state, and once said that "the Palestinians are a made-up nation which exists solely to attempt to destroy Israel."[38] This political worldview and revisionist history, one steeped in Israeli exceptionalism and anti-Palestinian racism and which is supported by Jewish organizations that gladly accept his funding, led movement activists to target both Adelson himself and the programs he supported, most notably Birthright.

Fourth, Jewish organizations in the United States often deny the legitimacy of Palestinian narratives, actively omitting these narratives from Jewish educational spaces. This method of supporting the occupation is typified by Birthright, which is what led IfNotNow to target them with the walk-off campaign. As explored in great detail in the previous chapter, the intentional process of miseducating Jewish youth about Palestine/Israel contributes to the socialization process that leads American Jews to love and support Israel without question. By omitting and denying Palestinian rights and narratives, Jewish institutional spaces create a culture in which anti-Palestinian and anti-Arab sentiments flourish alongside a rampant Islamophobia, thereby creating proxy conflicts in the United States between Jews and Palestinians, Jews and Arabs, and Jews and Muslims.

Finally, the American Jewish Establishment puts forth tremendous effort to silence dissenting views on Israel by actively intimidating individuals and organizations that are critical of Israel. Jewish American communities and institutions possess veritable red lines regarding Israel; if organizations or individuals cross those lines with their politics or actions, they might face ostracization from the community, be prohibited from receiving financial support, and even be exposed to vicious individual attacks that sometimes jeopardize relationships and careers.

Support for the BDS movement, which I address in chapter 5, is the most significant red line in the Jewish American community. As such, Jewish Voice for Peace (JVP), the main Jewish organization that supports BDS, has become persona non grata in the mainstream Jewish community. They are seen as so radical that many Jewish organizations have barred JVP from participating in community events. For example, JVP chapters on college and university campuses are not currently permitted to be part of Hillel and must therefore organize outside of a primary mainstream Jewish space on campus.

But the silencing of dissent and exclusion of individuals and organizations from the Jewish community go far beyond those who support BDS and often include any sentiment that can be interpreted as being pro-Palestinian or simply not fully supportive of Israel. For example, JStreet, an organization that does not support BDS but is unequivocally anti-occupation, was not permitted to be part of the Presidents' Conference (see chapter 1), thereby making it clear that the American Jewish Establishment believes that if you speak out against the occupation and vocalize critique of Israeli policies toward Palestinians you will be ostracized from mainstream Jewish spaces.[39] This is to say nothing of the dangerous personal attacks that Jewish (and non-Jewish) critics of Israel regularly experience at the hands of organizations that receive support from mainstream Jewish institutions. The Canary Mission (discussed above) is just one of numerous such groups that attack critics of Israel, and they aren't the only group with a "blacklist." In fact, the AMCHA Initiative, a pro-Israel advocacy organization, published a list of university professors who called for an academic boycott of Israel.[40] Such "blacklists," and the support that hawkish groups receive from mainstream Jewish organizations, silence critique by intimidating scholars and activists who speak out against the occupation.

IfNotNow's "Beyond Talk" report, and the positions it outlines, is integral to understanding why young American Jews are targeting the same mainstream Jewish organizations in which many of them were originally reared. Maintaining the occupation does not require an organization to do all five of these things; an organization need do only one of them, thereby rendering itself vulnerable to protest from young American Jews and the Palestine solidarity movement writ large. Movement activists argue that the Jewish Establishment is completely "out of touch with a growing generation of young Jews and others that demand an end to the status quo."[41] They argue that if the organizations do not change, they will become irrelevant to an entire generation, thereby jeopardizing their future. This substantiates the argument Peter Beinart made about the American Jewish Establishment long before IfNotNow released this report.[42] The willingness to challenge the status quo is one of the hallmarks of the Palestine solidarity movement. As they confront mainstream organizations that maintain the status quo by supporting and upholding the occupation, these activists are demanding that American Jewish communal institutions stand consistently for human rights, dignity, freedom, and justice for both Israeli Jews and Palestinians.[43] Until they do that, these institutions will continue to be a target for protest, as evidenced by the summer 2018 Birthright walk-off.

Confronting a Pillar of Israel Education

Taglit-Birthright Israel is one of the most popular programs teaching young American Jews about Israel.[44] Since its inception, more than seven hundred thousand non-Israeli Jews from around the world have participated in a Birthright trip, making it the single largest organization annually bringing Jews to Israel over the past two decades.[45] According to scholar Shaul Kelner, "Birthright Israel's raison d'être is to ensure the continued existence of vibrant, Israel-oriented Jewish communities abroad."[46] This is significant since Birthright plays a vital role in socializing people into the hegemonic Jewish identity that reinforces an uncritical love of and impetus to care for Israel.

Alongside Taglit-Birthright Israel's developing connection between participants and Israel, they also claim to strengthen the Jewish identities of participants.[47] Various studies have examined the program's impact on issues as diverse as Jewish identity, attachment to Israel, intermarriage, gender, and nationalism, all of which found that Birthright has a significant and positive impact on the Jewish identities of participants.[48] Birthright is now a household name in North American Jewish communities; it has positioned itself as a rite of passage for young adult Jews. Even young Jews who do not have a bar/bat mitzvah, the traditional rite of passage into Jewish young adulthood, are choosing to enroll in Birthright trips as a central initiation into Jewish life.

This widespread communal embrace of Birthright and its firm pro-Israel stance shows one way that Zionism has been substituted for a Jewish religious and cultural identity rooted in shared liturgy, history, or moral frameworks. The Birthright movement is a pervasive example of how today's Jewish institutions are reinforcing this idea. Yet today, young Jewish Americans involved in the Palestine solidarity movement are actively contesting this framework by providing a counternarrative for other like-minded socially conscious Jews. They are showing that there is an alternative Jewish approach to Israel than the one presented by Birthright.

Birthright's success begs an important question: if the program is so effective in connecting Jewish young adults to Israel, why is it the target of protests from the very people the program seeks to serve? Simply put, although many young Jews truly enjoy their Birthright experience and find it to be deeply meaningful, a growing cohort is disillusioned with and dissatisfied by the ways in which many Jewish institutions, including Birthright, "obscure, rationalize, and defend the Israeli occupation."[49] As a result, IfNotNow's 2018 #NotJustAFreeTrip campaign, which began with the walk-offs during the summer, highlighted ways that Birthright invisibilizes the occupation and silences Palestinian voices.

Birthright advertises itself as apolitical, despite it being political in numerous ways.[50] According to Barry Chazan, the main educational architect of Birthright's pedagogical approach to Israel education, no Israel program "that takes pedagogy seriously can remain ideologically neutral."[51] To extend Chazan's admission, by ignoring the occupation and refusing to engage with Palestinian narratives, Birthright is taking a political stance, pedagogically and otherwise. Their leaders and funders are instead making a profound statement as to their ideology pertaining to competing Israeli and Palestinian narratives by highlighting one and ignoring the other. This is to say nothing about how Birthright also fails to meaningfully engage with more complex issues of intra-Jewish strife by skirting around issues such as the systemic racism experienced by Israel's Mizrahi and Ethiopian Jewish communities.

One of the activists who walked off her trip told me, "We know that Birthright is not telling people the truth about the occupation. If you've been on a Birthright trip and you have any sense of what the occupation is and how oppressive it is, you know that they're hiding a lot from you."[52] Not everyone who goes on a Birthright trip is aware of the deep levels of *hasbara* that they are bound to encounter during their ten days in Israel.[53] What one sees on Birthright is clearly only a sliver of a more robust picture of Israeli society and its complex political reality. According to one of the activists who walked off their trip, "I felt pretty confident I was going to see a story told that felt really dishonest and manipulative and I wanted to shed light on that by doing something that was constructive and visible."[54]

Birthright's omission of Palestinian narratives was one of the catalysts that led the activists to walk off their trip. As one activist explained, "We can't keep allowing Jewish institutions to 'miseducate' our generation and our people without saying anything about it. We decided to make that statement and make it clear that we are walking off this trip because [Jewish institutions] intentionally 'miseducated' us."[55] Birthright systematically avoids discussion on topics such as the Nakba, the Separation Wall, and the right of return of Palestinian refugees. At the same time, all Birthright trips are required to visit Yad Vashem, the Holocaust Museum in Jerusalem, and engage in widespread discussions on the impact of the Holocaust on both Israeli and Jewish identity. Similarly, all trips are required to visit the Western Wall in the Old City of Jerusalem, yet generally absent from the discussions is the fact that the Old City remains disputed territory and is illegally occupied by Israel according to international law. And nary is there a mention on Birthright trips of the fact that the Western Wall area where groups gather was created by demolishing the Mughrabi Quarter, a former Palestinian neighborhood, soon after the 1967 War.[56]

Birthright builds a narrative that ignores the injustices required to create and maintain the status quo in Israel while also drawing direct connections with Jewish generational trauma in order to justify and celebrate a national identity. The premise of the protest, therefore, was rather simple. Birthright is a rite of passage for young Jews to explore their Jewish identities and to establish a connection with the State of Israel. But because it does so by strategically omitting histories, identities, and everyday realities of significant portions of the people who live in Palestine/Israel, it needed to be disrupted.

By walking off their trip, the activists asked their peers a fundamental question: Do you think that Birthright should provide a superficial and whitewashed picture of Israel? Or do you think that Birthright participants should learn a more holistic picture of what Israel looks like today, warts and all? To the activists, the answer was clear. As a result, they organized a protest designed to go viral, "knowing that the impact would be much greater if we did a public-facing, really bold and disruptive action, which would reach a lot more people."[57] Through their protest, they successfully highlighted Birthright's process of miseducation, challenging people to recognize how the program's pedagogical approach is political in a way that obscures the realities of Israeli occupation policies and its impacts on Palestinians.

It is important to note, however, that the 2018 protest of Birthright was not the first time that young Jewish activists targeted Birthright for upholding Jewish support for Israel's occupation. In November 2011, during the height of the Occupy Wall Street movement, a group of roughly ten Jewish activists associated with Young, Jewish, and Proud, a group of young Jews organized by JVP, interrupted an event sponsored by the Birthright Israel Alumni Community in New York. While Steven Pease, a venture capitalist and philanthropic supporter of Birthright, was delivering a speech to the crowd, one activist stood up, went to the front of the room, and used the "human microphone" call and response method used by the Occupy movement to deliver a message of dissent and critique of Birthright.[58]

"Mic check!" the activist called out, which was promptly repeated by other protestors present in the audience. "We are the Jewish 99 percent, and we're calling all Jews nationwide to join us in solidarity with Occupy Wall Street and with the Palestinians who live under occupation every day," she continued as each short phrase was repeated by her comrades. Even as the activist was being dragged out of the room by a security officer, she continued proudly and with a smile on her face: "Let's stand up to the one percent of the Jewish community. Birthright doesn't represent us. We will not be fooled by CEOs telling us we are the chosen people."

In a video of the protest circulating on the internet and social media at the time, as the activist is forced out of the room, another activist continues where the first one left off, seemingly without a pause. "And reinforcing Jewish stereotypes. We won't be bribed with free trips to Israel that whitewash the occupation of Palestine. We demand a redistribution of power in the Jewish community. We are Young, Jewish, and Proud! Throughout history Jews have been persecuted as scapegoats for powerful bankers. These memories give us responsibility to speak out against corporate exploitation." After being escorted from the room, the activists can be seen on the video chanting "Occupy Wall Street, not Palestine."[59]

Young, Jewish, and Proud criticized Birthright for being a free propaganda trip "for predominantly middle and upper class American Jews while urgent needs in the United States and Israel go unmet."[60] By linking a protest against Birthright with the Occupy movement, these activists argued that one of the fundamental problems with Birthright was that it was funded by a class of Jewish elites who use their wealth and power not to stand up for human rights but rather to support abuses carried out against Palestinians and, more insidiously, to profit from them. As one of the JVP activists said, "Birthright is a symptom of a larger structural problem in the Jewish institutional world in which our version of the one percent, a handful of wealthy donors including people like the Schustermans or Sheldon Adelson, [are] able to dictate the social and political agenda of the 99 percent. That's because Jewish institutions are so dependent on the one percent for funds."[61]

The Young, Jewish, and Proud activists asserted that during their Birthright trips they were told during official presentations that Palestinians teach their children to hate Jews. In fact, this was the only thing they were taught about Palestinians on the trip, effectively reducing Palestinians to a violent and hateful trope. Birthright's educational approach presented Young, Jewish, and Proud activists with a skewed reality of everyday life in Israel that intentionally erased Palestinians. The Young, Jewish, and Proud protest set the groundwork for future young JVP activists to target Birthright.

In 2017, JVP launched its #ReturnTheBirthright campaign, which called on young American Jews to protest Birthright by refusing to sign up for the trip.[62] Organizing under the motto #ReturnTheBirthright, a group of JVP activists called on their friends to boycott Birthright, urging them to sign a pledge that rejected the free ten-day trip. Those who signed the pledge were agreeing that they "will not go on a Birthright trip because it is fundamentally unjust that we are given a free trip to Israel, while Palestinian refugees are barred from returning to their homes. We refuse to be complicit in a propaganda trip that whitewashes the systemic racism, and the daily violence faced by Palestinians living under endless occupation. Our Judaism is grounded in values of solidarity and liberation, not occupation and apartheid. On these grounds we return the Birthright, and call on other young Jews to do the same."[63]

This was a totally student-driven campaign in which the JVP national organization tapped into local organizing on campuses, specifically places where students had been discussing a Birthright boycott for some time before putting out the call publicly. Some student activists joined the call to boycott Birthright after their personal experiences going on the trip, while others joined the pledge before doing so.[64] What is most significant about this campaign is that, like most other actions by young Jewish activists involved in the Palestine solidarity movement, they articulated it in Jewish terms and rooted it in a Jewish framework. While they centered their concerns over the liberation of Palestinians, they did so by grounding their demands in Jewish values, thereby emphasizing their Jewish identities as significant motivators in their political activism.

The Walk-Off as Radical Protest

As symbolically meaningful as JVP's targeting of Birthright is, one fundamental differentiation between the 2011 Young, Jewish, and Proud protest, the #ReturnTheBirthright campaign, and the IfNotNow #NotJustAFreeTrip campaign is that the viral IfNotNow action in 2018 occurred in Israel rather than in the United States and therefore the activists had the opportunity to walk off their trips and bear witness to the occupation in Palestine. For example, because the protest was conducted in Israel, immediately after walking off their Birthright trip the five activists were able to join the Jewish Israeli NGO Breaking the Silence for a tour of Hebron, the largest city in the occupied West Bank, in order to bear witness to the occupation and its impacts on everyday life for Palestinians.[65]

On the bus to Hebron, the women drafted a letter explaining why they had staged the direct-action protest, also emphasizing the reasons they decided to go to Hebron with another organization to see the impacts of the occupation for themselves. In the letter they confronted Birthright's inability to give them what they called an "honest education" about the occupation, criticizing the program for not "truthfully engaging" with their questions about Israel and Palestinians. The letter also highlighted ways that the program is not ideologically neutral, pointing to how Birthright intentionally obscures the occupation from participants.

It is worth quoting the entire letter since the activists' articulation of their experience with Birthright exemplifies the precise reasons that increasing numbers of young American Jews feel disillusioned by mainstream Jewish organizations, including Birthright:

> Over the past ten days, we have engaged deeply and honestly with our Birthright tour guide and the other participants, who we feel are members of our community. We built strong relationships with them and feel sad to leave them without a proper goodbye, but we could no longer go on with this trip that was so deliberately hiding the truth from all of us. For us, grappling with this important place in our tradition means grappling with it in all of its complexity.
>
> We each came on this trip separately with the hope that—especially in light of the recent killings of more than a 100 [sic] protestors in Gaza and Trump moving the U.S. embassy to Jerusalem—Birthright would trust its participants enough to give us an honest education. We came with questions about what's happening in the occupied territories and wanted to engage with new perspectives, but what became clear over the course of ten days was that Birthright did not want to truthfully engage with our questions. It's clear that young Jews who have critical questions about Israel are not welcome on Birthright. It's shocking that given all the recent violence Birthright would continue to act as if we can't handle the truth.
>
> What we've seen firsthand on this trip is that Birthright is using a political agenda to miseducate tens of thousands of young Jews. We were shocked to see how explicitly Sheldon Adelson—who has given millions

of dollars to Donald Trump and bankrolls right-wing causes in the U.S.—talked about the political imperative for us to "fight the battle against Israel on college campuses" on a trip that repeated over and over again its apolitical nature. As we were getting off the bus this morning a fellow participant said, "The whole point of Birthright is to get you to move to Israel and fall in love with Israel." That felt incredibly telling.

Birthright cynically believes the only way to get us to be in touch with their [sic] Jewish identity is to hide the occupation from us, but we felt compelled precisely by our Jewish values to seek out the truth by meeting Palestinians and confronting the reality here. Our message to the American Jewish community—young Jews who have not yet gone on Birthright and the parents who want to send their children on this trip—is to know that Birthright is not providing the education our generation deserves. It is morally irresponsible to participate in an institution that is not willing to grapple with reality on the other side of the wall. That's why we are on our way to Hebron now.[66]

In this letter, and with their decision to walk off the trip and go directly to the West Bank to bear witness to the occupation, these activists highlighted the growing divide between Birthright as a contemporary pillar of Israel education and the Jewish demographic it seeks to teach, raising questions about the future of American Jewish engagement with Israel.[67] The activists who walked off did so not only as a distinct expression of their commitment to social justice and the integrity of their Jewish identities, as evidenced by this letter, but also as a way to highlight the growth of Jewish participation in Palestine solidarity activism in the United States, which is impacting the way young Jews engage with and relate to both Israel and the Jewish organizations that socialize them to care for the Jewish state. By walking off the trip, the activists called attention to Birthright's omission of Palestinian narratives while also asserting their ability to meaningfully connect with their Jewish identities.

The letter also calls attention to three very important things, all of which illustrate the deeper understanding of how the Birthright walk-off was a radical protest motivated by the Jewish identities and values of the activists. First, it reveals that the activists are deeply concerned with and dissatisfied by Birthright's omission of Palestinian narratives and outright denial of Palestinian rights. This is done through a process that

Shaul Kelner calls "depoliticization," in which "potentially problematic issues are dealt with as unproblematic."[68] Kelner argues that depoliticization most often occurs at the subconscious level, where tour guides and operators aren't necessarily aware of the fact that they are suppressing political issues that present themselves. In their constant questioning of issues regarding Palestinians on their trips, the activists were attempting to bring the process of depoliticization to the surface so that both tour guides and trip participants could become more fully aware of how the program suppresses dissenting voices and criticism of Israel. Put another way, through the walk-off the activists repoliticized a depoliticized trip, marking their refusal to participate in a program that systematically silences dissent and rejects a presentation of Israel in all of its complexity by hiding the occupation from program participants.

Second, the letter highlights the centrality of the Jewish values of social justice activism that compelled their direct action against Birthright. The activists who walked off Birthright understood their activism to be inseparable from their Jewishness and integral to their engagement in broader struggles for justice. It was precisely the connection between their Jewish and activist identities that compelled them to act. One of my interviewees who walked off her trip told me, "When I think of Judaism, I think about standing for the oppressed, standing with the oppressed, and helping others, building a community, social justice. Standing up for what's right isn't necessarily going to feel comfortable. That was a really uncomfortable thing that we did. We put ourselves out there and we stood up to our community. We fought for our community."[69] By framing the walk-off in the context of how their Jewish identity requires them to stand up for others, they were trying to push Jewish leaders to likewise apply their belief in justice consistently, regardless of the cultural or geographic context. More specifically, they were challenging Jewish institutions to break their silence on Israeli abuses toward Palestinians and to end their complicity in the occupation.

The activists stood up to their own community in an effort to transform and improve it. Their drive stems from a hope that future generations of Jews will be able to experience a more holistic, inclusive, and tolerant Jewish education and practice. This was exemplified by one of the activists who said, "We're trying to say that [occupation] is not our Judaism, that is not the kind of Judaism we want to practice. We want to embody a different Judaism. We want a culture that is honest and fights for the justice and freedom and dignity of all people. That was why I walked off Birthright."[70] This was not a protest by some naïve young adults seeking a moment of self-righteousness, a vitriolic critique that the activists often received.[71] Rather, this was a profound expression of their Jewishness, an act emanating from the Jewish social justice discourse of *tikkun olam*. The walk-off was a brave, mature, and radical act rooted in a deep reflection on communal identity and Jewish history.

Third, both the written letter and the public protest demonstrate the strategic and intentional nature of the activists regarding their decision to walk off the trip. They explain that the action was rooted in a morality born out of their Jewish education, a set of values they were taught through the schooling they received in Jewish institutions. All of the activists with whom I spoke articulated that a moral imperative compelled them to make a public statement to confront Birthright's support for the occupation and that the occupation, as a moral issue, required them to take a stand and do a major public facing action. They understood that a strategy calling for widespread change needs to reach the masses. Further evidence of this can be seen from the numerous articles and op-eds that the activists themselves wrote in the days immediately thereafter that explained what may not have been understood through the videos alone.[72]

The activists also expressed concern about the perceived lack of trust that Birthright has in its participants; it seems like Birthright doesn't think students are able to understand the complexities of the political situation in Palestine/Israel. Research shows that even young children are capable of grappling with the complexities of the Palestinian-Israeli conflict. One valuable educational pedagogy to teach young Jews about Israel is to engage with complexity and expose people to multiple viewpoints, including those critical of Israel, its government, and its policies.[73] According to scholar Sivan Zakai, educators and parents alike should not avoid teaching the realities of what is happening in Israel but must devise age-appropriate strategies for making sense of current events.[74]

While Zakai's research focuses on elementary schoolchildren, it is important to consider her findings as applied to college and postgraduate-age participants of Birthright who not only have the social, emotional, and intellectual capabilities to grapple with complexity but are able to draw their own conclusions when presented with multiple viewpoints. The activists targeted Birthright in part due to the fact that Birthright's pedagogy excludes Palestinian narratives out of what the activists believe is an infantilizing approach that participants draw the conclusions that the program wants from them. Birthright strategically focuses on young adults for its program since that is such a formative period in life for exploring one's ethnic, religious, and political identities.[75] Birthright's refusal to trust participants with multiple narratives of Israel stems from their accurate assessment that a nuanced take on Israeli politics and the occupation will lead to increased questioning of Zionist narratives and current political lines.[76]

During numerous interviews with activists, they repeatedly articulated that most participants are unaware of Birthright's political agenda to obscure the occupation. One activist said, "I want people to know that Birthright is just one of many institutions that is upholding the American Jewish community's support for the occupation. . . . It's one of these institutions that plays a really large role in shaping how young American Jews view Israel."[77] They protested in order to demonstrate the fact that this younger generation of Jews will not participate in any institution it deems complicit with taking the wrong moral stance on the question of occupation. One of the activists emphasizes this point:

> My hope is that [the walk-off] makes it clear to our community that the [Jewish] American Establishment needs to reckon with our generation's demands for truth and accountability. I think that what's playing out around Birthright is really a site for a much broader reckoning that's happening and . . . I think it's a really central stage for our community and so I hope people will see it's not just about Birthright. It's about how our generation feels about how our community supports the occupation and that the institutions that raised us and continue to call us in will need to radically shift the way that they engage with Israel if they want us to come with them.[78]

Bearing Witness to Occupation

A key issue the activists contested during the walk-offs is the fact that on their Birthright trip they didn't have an opportunity to visit the West

Bank or engage deeply with Palestinians and their narratives. Though there is a plethora of opportunities for young Jews to go on immersive Israel experiences, in the past twenty years most young people have chosen to go on Birthright because—perhaps above all else—it is a free, all-expenses-paid ten-day trip, including roundtrip travel. Birthright aside, most of the available immersive experiences that provide carefully curated tours of Israel show only certain elements of Israeli society. In virtually none of the myriad Israel programs available to young diaspora Jews do participants visit Palestine or engage deeply in Palestinian narratives.[79]

This is reflective not only of Israel-immersion experiences but also of most mainstream Jewish institutions that generally incorporate pro-Israel and Zionist curricula into their education, thereby eliminating an open exchange of ideas regarding Palestine/Israel. As such, young Jewish activists are often disillusioned by the lack of commitment of these Jewish institutions to engage with critics of Israel's policies; therefore, they seek out ways to get to the West Bank.[80] The walk-off provided these activists with the perfect opportunity to tell Birthright and other mainstream Jewish institutions that they need to change dramatically if they want to continue getting young Jews to participate in their programs.

In other words, the protest revealed a tension in the Jewish community that was important for the activists to highlight, a tension that stems from the fact that the American Jewish Establishment is courting young Jews because of their internalized fears about Jewish continuity. The idea of Jewish continuity refers to the future of the Jewish community with regard to both population size and engagement with Jewish life. According to scholar Aaron Hahn Tapper, "Although older Jews are more likely to speak about [Jewish continuity] than younger ones, the underlying goal is to figure out how to get Jews to stay Jews."[81] As such, Jewish institutions commit incredible resources to ensure this continuity of Jewish identity. Yet, at the same time, they resist giving younger Jews any real power; they don't trust them to be more forthright in their formal Jewish education about Israel and about internal intra-Jewish challenges.[82] These young Jewish American activists have decided that the occupation is the issue that most reveals this tension. They believe that it is such a large-scale moral calamity that it can and should be used as a wedge issue in Jewish communal politics.

One of the main problems for the activists was that they could not trust Birthright to teach them about the occupation or to give them a more nuanced view of Palestine/Israel. Thus, they took matters into their own hands. The fact that they walked off their trips and went straight to Palestine was one of the key factors that made the walk-off so symbolically meaningful for Jewish participation in the Palestine solidarity movement more broadly. Going to the West Bank was intended to give the activists the opportunity to bear witness to the occupation, but in the process of engaging in a public direct action they made a symbolic statement that their generation is determined to end the occupation. One of the activists who walked off the trip explains, "As an American Jew, physically walking away from Israel and going towards Palestinians is such an amazing action because it shows how American Jews are walking away from the Israeli violence, from the Israeli propaganda, from that narrative going towards justice, going towards the people that are being oppressed. Just how much of an impact that can make on an international sphere. It's incredibly powerful."[83]

In an equally public and performative demonstration that included a media campaign and Facebook livestream, a few weeks after the first walk-off a second group of activists walked off their Birthright trip just as the rest of their group was on their way to visit the City of David. Adjacent to Jerusalem's Old City, the City of David, which is managed by Elad, a radical settler organization whose main aim is to take over Palestinian homes and settle Jews in Silwan, has become a major tourist destination.[84] Tour operators bring groups to the City of David to present the dominant narrative of Jewish Israeli settlers, that of a Jewish-ruled Jerusalem in which the Palestinian existence is either ignored or treated as a threat.[85] On a regular basis, thousands of tourists visit the City of David without having any idea that they are crossing the Green Line or that Palestinians were displaced and negatively impacted by its construction.[86]

But instead of visiting this highly contested site, the activists walked off their Birthright trip and went, as an act of solidarity, to meet with a Palestinian family under threat of losing a three-decade-long battle to remain in their home in Silwan. Due to numerous lawsuits filed by Elad, at the time the Sumreen family was facing immediate eviction.[87] The activists walked off their trip and straight into the Sumreen family living room to meet the family and hear about their struggle directly, thereby creating their own opportunities to engage with Palestinian narratives.

While not all of the thirteen activists who walked off Birthright that summer saw the same things or spent the same amount of time in Palestine after their livestreamed protests, all went on a tour of Hebron with Breaking the Silence soon thereafter. This is where they encountered the Israeli military occupation of the West Bank's largest city, with the alleged goal to protect a small settler community of seven hundred Jewish Israelis in the midst of approximately two hundred thousand Palestinians.[88] There, they were shocked to see the stark divide between the Israeli settler population and Palestinians, including a visit to the hauntingly empty Shuhada Street in downtown Hebron, a street that was once the epicenter of a bustling business district for Palestinians but had been closed off for two decades.[89]

In addition to going to Hebron, some of the activists also went to Khan al Ahmar to stand in solidarity with a Palestinian community under threat of demolition. While in the village, they watched the men's FIFA World Cup along with Jewish Israeli and international activists.[90] Visiting this town was significant in that it brought international attention and presence to a community constantly on the verge of being fully demolished by the Israeli military. Despite many of the Jewish American activists being taught in their youth that Palestinians hate Jews and wish violence and death upon them, they sat together joyously watching the World Cup. Through building social ties and friendship, the activists and their Palestinian hosts demonstrated the falsity of propaganda that seeks to keep Jews and Palestinians separated from each other.

Bearing witness to the occupation was a vital element of the walk-off since it enabled the activists to develop a deeper connection with Palestinians on the ground. Though IfNotNow largely targets Jewish institutions in the United States, this moved them into conversation with Palestinians alongside their efforts to pressure their own community. Furthermore, it concretized the complex realities of occupation and enabled them to personalize the conflict they had learned about but never seen firsthand. Their activism was no longer abstract. Being in Palestine reinforced for them that their activism was part of a broader struggle of justice for Palestinians that could have potential ramifications and material impacts on real people. Bearing witness to the occupation also played a profound role in their ongoing process of personal transformation, which also made the walk-off, in retrospect, more personally meaningful and impactful.

Responding to Criticism and Protest Success

Some of the activists took great personal risk in walking off the Birthright trip, which heightened the significance of the protest and everything they experienced in Palestine/Israel. In addition to the vitriolic attacks many of them received on Facebook and other social media sites, they also experienced personal and familial challenges with more severe consequences. Numerous activists had close friends who refused to acknowledge their presence after they walked off the trip. People with whom they had gone to school or had meaningful experiences together in their youth were so angry that they had walked off a Birthright trip that they ended the friendship. In one extreme case, the aunt of an activist broke off all contact with her and her immediate family.

Though they had to respond to a tremendous amount of criticism, the activists were quick to point out that all of the critiques levied against them were either personal attacks or comments that criticized the strategies and tactics of protest. None of the critiques addressed the actual issues the activists raised about the political nature of Birthright trips or how the organization omits Palestinian narratives. One of the activists emphasized this for me in an interview. "What's interesting to me about [our detractors] is that they don't dispute the heart of the issue," she said. "They don't dispute that Birthright is a political trip that is intended to offer a one-sided perspective and through this free trip they manipulate or bribe people into being supportive, uncritical, and unquestioning of Israel and of the occupation. People aren't necessarily calling that into question anymore. They're questioning the tactic we used to make that evident. . . . I'm glad that people can begin to acknowledge themselves that the content of what we're saying is true."[91]

In other words, the protest was a way of setting the terms of engagement for a critical segment of the young Jewish anti-occupation community. The activists were refusing to justify and legitimize the power of mainstream Jewish institutions and their megadonors. While these powerful institutions often dictate what, when, and how young Jews learn about Israel, the critiques of the walk-off sought to reinforce their power by also seeking to delegitimize the means of protest against them. According to an op-ed by Benjy Cannon published in *Jewish Currents* shortly after the walk-offs, "These protesters used their comparably limited power to redirect these dollars, quite literally, from helping to uphold the occupation into a critique of it. Protesting Birthright effectively means protesting the system that created it, and that requires challenging the donors directly, on their own turf."[92] The walk-offs were therefore a way for Jewish activists involved with the Palestine solidarity movement to use a powerful institution as a wedge in the Jewish community and to meaningfully rewrite the rules of critical political and public engagement with Israel and Israel education. This direct action, as is the case with everything associated with Jewish participation in the Palestine solidarity movement, is trying not to destroy Jewish institutions but rather to transform them.

These walk-offs and the broader #NotJustAFreeTrip campaign are markers of the growing divide between the values of young anti-occupation American Jews and mainstream Jewish institutions who uphold the occupation. The activists decided to stand up for their values, refusing to compromise their beliefs in an acquiescence to the miseducation that Birthright provided them. For example, nearly every activist I spoke with mentioned that at least once on their Birthright trip their guide either said "welcome home" or made constant references to Israel as their "home." While referring to Israel as "home" is critical to Birthright's pedagogical underpinnings, it does not match up with the feelings and beliefs of the activists who unanimously consider the United States to be their home. For many of them, Israel is not even a symbolic homeland. This verbal ritual, consciously carried out or not, further fueled their mistrust of Birthright, giving additional weight to the critique that Birthright does not accurately represent these activists' political sentiments and values.

There are both quantitative and qualitative measures that point to the success of the walk-off and public confrontation with Birthright, highlighting the growing divide between the community the activists represent and mainstream American Jewish institutions. According to *Haaretz*, winter 2018 Birthright trips saw a dramatic decline in enrollment, with some tour providers reporting a decrease as high as 50 percent compared to the previous winter.[93] The timing of these data is significant since that was the trip cycle immediately after the summer walk-offs. While the walk-offs likely had an impact on the precipitous decline in program enrollment, they were only part of the reason. As is the case with most high-profile actions like the Birthright walk-offs, they were successful only when seen in conjunction with other contemporaneous mobilization efforts from others involved within the Jewish sphere of the Palestine solidarity movement.

One of the most visible of these other efforts was a widespread call by young Jewish activists to boycott Birthright altogether (as noted earlier). Initially launched by JVP in their 2017 campaign "Return the Birthright," activists on campuses across the country called for a complete Birthright boycott that grew in strength and numbers in fall 2018, immediately after the summer walk-offs. By spring 2019, both IfNotNow and JStreet U also encouraged young Jews to boycott the program.[94] Then, in early April 2019, several hundred IfNotNow activists protested outside the Birthright headquarters in New York City. They demanded that Birthright change their pedagogical stance of eliminating Palestinian narratives from their trips or face a boycott. During the action, Birthright officials asked the police to arrest the activists; fifteen people were detained.[95] In summer 2019, JStreet even launched their own Birthright alternative, which took forty college students on a free trip to Israel that also included a visit to the West Bank.[96]

Another measure of impact that emanated from the summer 2018 protests is that, as a direct result of the walk-offs, Birthright revised the waiver and permission agreement it requires all participants to sign. The leaders of the organization were so repulsed that anyone would have the gall to walk off their free trip—which the program defines as a gift—that they went to great lengths to prevent similar future protests. In effect, the changes to the Code of Conduct section of Birthright's waiver newly indicated that participants who disrupt the program could face disciplinary action, including dismissal.[97]

In response, anti-occupation activists said that this wouldn't deter the movement from targeting Birthright in the future, nor would it prevent curious participants from questioning their guides about Palestinians. In fact, it is entirely feasible, based on current trends, that this attempt to stifle dissent will discourage young Jews from going on the trip at all.

One widely read op-ed from the *Forward* articulated the bind that Birthright finds itself in vis-à-vis anti-occupation activism by arguing that "Birthright is chasing away engaged Jews to please pro-Israel hardliners."[98] This tactic won't bring more people to the program simply because many young Jews in North America today know too much about Israel. Increasingly large segments of today's Jewish youth are not willing to acquiesce to a program that obscures the realities of occupation. Birthright is simply not prepared for the confrontations it brings on itself by refusing to engage with the complex realities of the Palestinian-Israeli conflict.

For example, in December 2018, Birthright thrust itself into the spotlight when the program kicked three participants off of their trip for asking too many questions about Palestinians and the Separation Wall, marking the first time that people were forced off the program in light of the new criteria for participant conduct. Much like the IfNotNow activists who walked off their trips the previous summer, after the three participants were kicked off their trip, they traveled to the West Bank village of Umm al-Khair to bear witness to the occupation.[99] And much like the summer 2018 protest, Jewish media outlets widely published stories about the participants getting kicked off their trips. It was a heated topic of conversation for many friends and families during that year's winter holidays.

Danielle Raskin, one of the first five activists to walk off Birthright, points to the widespread success of the campaign against the program as part of a roundtable published in *Jewish Currents* on the "Ethical Response to Birthright." In her contribution she notes,

> When we walked off, we were able to livestream the whole thing to Facebook and to alert international media. Videos and articles about our action (including in the *New York Times*) went viral, allowing us to reach millions and to challenge the widely accepted notion that Birthright is apolitical. By the end of the summer of 2018, if you were an American Jew between the ages of 18 and 26 googling "Birthright" to sign up for a trip, you would see articles and videos about our actions. The media coverage generated by these actions did far more good than asking questions of our tour guides did.[100]

Now when young Jews look up Birthright in an internet search engine, they not only learn about the walk-off but are also forced to ponder the ethical choice the activists newly introduced into the conversation: Should I go on Birthright or not? If I go on a trip, should I ask questions about the occupation? Should I extend my trip to also visit the West Bank and engage directly with Palestinians living under Israeli occupation? Regardless of people's individual choices, young American Jewish activists have already impacted the decision-making process. Now people are having more robust conversations about alternative ways to visit Israel without going on Birthright.

As part of the #NotJustAFreeTrip campaign, IfNotNow activists went to certain airport departure terminals and passed out material about the occupation to help prepare Birthright participants to better understand the occupation and how the program hides it from them. Furthermore, today there are numerous opportunities for Birthright participants to extend their trip and embed with an alternative program to take them to the West Bank. A program called Extend, for example, specializes in taking American Jews to the West Bank after their Birthright trips so that they can engage more deeply with the Palestinian-Israeli conflict through exposure to Israeli and Palestinian human rights leaders and social justice activists.[101] Similarly, a program called Birthright Unplugged offers alternative travel tours to Palestine/Israel.[102]

Additionally, All That's Left (see chapter 4) started a program called BirthLeft, which organized day trips and walking tours of strategic locations, such as the Palestinian sector of Jaffa and places in East Jerusalem, to give those interested the chance to see what Birthright omits from their itinerary. These Birthright alternatives have become increasingly popular and are of great interest to those Birthright participants who want to engage more deeply with the realities of the Palestinian-Israeli conflict and bear witness to the occupation themselves. As the activists made clear, if Birthright and other mainstream Jewish organizations won't adapt to the demands of their constituents, then new institutions will develop to serve the new values, norms, and needs of young American Jews.

More anecdotally, but nonetheless illustrative of a growing trend among young Jews, is the fact that I have witnessed the impacts of the Birthright walk-offs on my university campus while advising students about various opportunities for them to travel to Palestine/Israel. In my capacity as a professor teaching about the Palestinian-Israeli conflict through a Jewish Studies program at a Jesuit university, Jewish students in particular often consult with me about opportunities to travel to Israel. At the outset of my teaching career a decade ago, Jewish students would frequently ask me specific questions about Birthright, eager to find the right time during their university career when they could take advantage of the free trip to Israel. Those students who had more critical views about Israel, including robust understandings of the occupation, would ask more pressing questions about what kinds of inquiries they should make with their tour guides about the occupation while on Birthright. Nonetheless, most went on Birthright trips.

In recent years, things have changed rather dramatically. I can trace this directly to the rise in popularity of IfNotNow, their successful Birthright walk-offs, and the campaigns encouraging people to boycott Birthright. Students are no longer as eager to register for Birthright, though they are still seeking opportunities to travel to Palestine/Israel. Since the walk-offs, Jewish students are increasingly telling me that they have no interest in going on Birthright. Instead, they want to know what options exist outside of Birthright for young Jews to visit Israel in a way that engages with the complexities and realities of both Israeli and Palestinian societies.

The 2018 summer walk-offs also shifted the discourse about Birthright among many mainstream Jewish institutions. They are now paying greater attention to the changing nature of young Jewish connections to Israel and are concerned over the general unwillingness of young Jews to acquiesce to an uncritical and unquestioning pro-Israel education such as the one provided by Birthright. Over time, Birthright and other Jewish institutions in the United States that uphold or obscure the occupation will be forced to respond to the political and cultural issues that activists promote during their protests. The less they are willing to engage with the demands of Jewish Palestine solidarity activists, and the more they fail to understand that the root of the anti-occupation politics of activists is the desire to uphold the Jewish imperative of justice, the less relevant these institutions will become for Jews. Instead, the Jewish groups and institutions that inspire, foster, and accept anti-occupation politics will become more relevant. Furthermore, they will become the main drivers of Jewish engagement and community for the movement of young Jewish activists and critics of Israel, replacing many of today's normative Jewish institutions.

4

Co-resistance

Palestinian and Jewish Activists in Collective Struggle

On January 2, 2020, for the first time in fifteen years, nonviolent Palestinian activist Kifah Adara drew water from the Ein Albeida spring near her West Bank village of Al-Tuwani.[1] The natural water source had been used by Palestinian communities for generations. But a decade and a half ago, Jewish Israeli settlers living nearby started swimming in the spring and using it as a *mikveh*, a ritual bath, which dirtied the water and made it unsuitable for drinking. Since that time, because of settler violence and intimidation tactics, Palestinians couldn't access the spring at all.

But that was about to change. In a massive nonviolent direct action involving over one hundred fifty Palestinian, Jewish Israeli, and diaspora Jewish activists, Adara reclaimed and rehabilitated Ein Albeida. Alongside supporters and allies, she walked from her village to the spring to fill up water buckets for the first time since her youth.[2]

"I remember coming to this spring with women from my village to collect water for our families," Adara said after the action. "We would travel 1.5 kilometers on our donkeys, just like we did today. Once Israeli settlers began swimming in this spring, it was no longer safe for us to drink. For many years, we could not access the spring at all. I am so happy to be back at this spring. I hope that, through the work we started today, the people of this region can use this water again."[3]

Ein Albeida, which is Arabic for "White Spring," is the only natural water source for people living in Al-Tuwani and other nearby villages in the South Hebron Hills. The spring is also near Avigayil, an illegitimate Israeli outpost established in 2001.[4] Settlers living in Avigayil have access to electricity, running water, and other services provided by the Israeli government, even though the outpost is considered illegal under Israeli law. While the Palestinian village of Al-Tuwani has access to some of

Figure 4.1. Palestinian activist Kifah Adara brings her donkey to Ein Albeida, January 2020. Photo by Emily Glick.

these services, it is denied other resources, such as garbage collection.[5] Meanwhile the Palestinian villages of Rakeez and Mufagara, which are just outside of Al-Tuwani and also once used Ein Albeida as a water source, are denied access to water and electricity. This is representative of one of the many structural inequalities of the Israeli occupation in the West Bank, where the Israeli government systematically withholds services to Palestinians while regularly supplying them to Israeli settlers.[6]

The coalition of activists who participated in the action with Adara joined her to show their solidarity with the Palestinian struggle against occupation and to assert their commitment to justice in the region. Adara and other activists from her village invited the Israeli and diaspora Jewish members of this coalition to demonstrate their commitment to Palestinian solidarity by leveraging their privilege, as Jews, to protect her and other Palestinian activists from settler and state violence. I participated in the action through a delegation organized by the Center for Jewish Nonviolence (CJNV), a group that brings Jews from around the world to engage in nonviolent direct action and co-resistance projects alongside Palestinian and Jewish Israeli partners. My involvement was motivated by my political commitments to the goals of the action but also as a central component of my research for this book.

Though this was not my first experience with joint Palestinian-Jewish resistance enacted in Palestine/Israel, the Ein Albeida action reinforced what I already knew: although there are many methods and tactics used to resist the occupation, the co-resistance model is one of the most impactful in showing tangible results to improve the lives of Palestinians while also shifting Jewish relationships to Israeli state violence. The nature of this organizing model also builds a vibrant, intersectional, and powerful anti-occupation movement by establishing trust and relationships through embodied actions.

Co-resistance activism is a form of civil disobedience performed collectively by Palestinians and Jews to oppose Israeli policies of military occupation and state violence. This type of direct action often takes the form of Jews joining Palestinians in construction and agricultural projects that reclaim stolen land. Other times it involves Jews helping Palestinians maintain their livelihoods on land that is threatened by settlers by accompanying Palestinian shepherds in the fields or participating in an olive harvest.

Political activism rooted in this framework also takes the form of political education (e.g., bringing media attention), such as by lobbying politicians in their home countries or raising money for Palestinian activists facing legal battles and Palestinian families facing eviction orders. Because their aim is to dismantle systems of violence in Palestine/Israel, these strategies are inevitably contentious and confrontational. While many groups of Palestinians, Israelis, and diaspora Jews work on dismantling the institutions of occupation from their own sphere of influence, co-resistance is remarkable in that diverse groups of activists are able to resist in collaboration with one another.[7] Through co-resistance, these distinct communities are able to build alliances across their differences, enabling them to defy the state apparatus in relationship to each other. This approach is rooted in the tacit understanding that the liberation of one is deeply intertwined with the liberation of the other, or, as explained by Paulo Freire in his renowned book *Pedagogy of the Oppressed*, "We cannot say that in the process of revolution someone liberates someone else, nor yet that someone liberates himself, but rather that human beings in communion liberate each other."[8]

Through a co-resistance model, Palestinians set the conditions for action and invite Jewish partners with whom they have previously established relationships to join them. These relationships are based on years of Palestinian and Israeli activists organizing together to end the occupation through collectives such as Anarchists Against the Wall, Ta'ayush, Combatants for Peace, and numerous other peace and justice groups active throughout Palestine/Israel. Participation in co-resistance actions is therefore predicated on genuine commitments to dismantling the connected systems of oppression that harm communities in Palestine/Israel.

As I explain in greater detail below, CJNV was established as a result of an act of co-resistance. More specifically, it emerged after Daoud Nassar, a Palestinian farmer and the founder of Tent of Nations, reached out to veteran Jewish activist Ilana Sumka, with whom he was acquainted through previous visits to Tent of Nations, to bring a group of diaspora Jews to help him replant olive trees that had been uprooted by the Israeli military. Daoud's preexisting trust in Ilana led him to invite her to join in co-resistance work. Similarly, CJNV was able to participate in the Ein Albeida action because they had already built a network of trust and intersecting relationships through previous partnerships with Palestinian villagers, activists, and families in Hebron, the South Hebron Hills, and East Jerusalem.

Each group of diaspora Jews who join a CJNV delegation in turn help to recruit and screen the next group of participants, thus continuing to forge new relationships of trust, which are necessary for co-resistance. Co-resistance is collaborative and is based on Jews (both Israeli and diaspora) becoming allies to Palestinians in the struggle for justice.[9] As noted, co-resistance is always led by Palestinians and centers Palestinian experiences, needs, and desires in the direct actions. Without the leadership of Palestinians, collaborative resistance projects would merely replicate the power imbalance that allows the occupation to continue. The leadership of Palestinians is integral to the collaborative process as the necessary conditions of all co-resistance activities are "the leading role of the [Palestinian] partner and the necessary transformation of [Israeli society]."[10]

Since the Second Intifada, scholars have examined the role and impacts of joint Palestinian-Israeli on-the-ground activism, primarily focusing on co-resistance activism regarding Israel's Separation Wall.[11]

Scholarship has generally examined joint Israeli-Palestinian NGOs, the role of women in peace activism, or the peace movement more broadly.[12] Yet few scholars have looked critically at the role that diaspora Jews play in this type of activism in Palestine/Israel, even fewer still at the participation of young Jewish Americans in co-resistance activities.[13]

This chapter explores co-resistance involving young American Jews and Palestinians as a method of anti-occupation activism in Palestine/Israel. By looking at this specific demographic, through two groups in particular, All That's Left: Anti-Occupation Collective (ATL) and the Center for Jewish Nonviolence (CJNV), this chapter argues that the co-resistance model has tangibly improved the lives of Palestinians while providing evidence of the symbolic importance of Jews resisting Israeli occupation and apartheid alongside Palestinians. These co-resistance activities are largely driven and organized by Millennial and Gen Z Jewish American activists who, as a result of their privilege, have a freedom of movement that is denied to Palestinians, and due to their youth, have a greater ability to engage in physically taxing labor than their older peers. Although it was not the case originally, these younger Jews are currently the leaders of CJNV and ATL. As such, they are able to reach a broad and diverse spectrum of other younger activists, in contrast to organizations such as IfNotNow, Jewish Voice for Peace, and JStreet.

Additionally, co-resistance activism not only contrasts with but actually complements the work of these other organizations, as well as other methods of Palestine solidarity activism highlighted in this book, because it is aimed at changing the material conditions for Palestinian communities rather than seeking to shift Jewish American communal opinion (IfNotNow) or U.S. foreign policy (JStreet and JVP). Looking specifically at the involvement of younger American Jews in co-resistance enables a holistic view of the landscape of Jewish-Palestinian solidarity activism, placing it within a broader strategy of building alliances across differences, something deeply important to younger Jews (which was not necessarily true for previous generations). In presenting both material and symbolic possibilities, co-resistance challenges Israeli state violence and American Jewish communal support for the occupation by exhibiting a different path forward for Jews and Palestinians, one based on solidarity and alliance building.

From Coexistence to Co-resistance

As a direct result of the perceived failure of "coexistence" projects, the term "co-resistance" emerged in popular activist discourse after the Second Intifada of the early 2000s.[14] "Coexistence" most commonly refers to Israeli Jews and Palestinians living and existing together in relative peace. As a result of the 1990s Oslo Peace Process, coexistence programs were established in an attempt to bring Palestinians and Israelis together to learn about and meet one another.[15] The basic premise of coexistence was one rooted in contact theory, the notion that if people representing groups in conflict have the chance to meet each other and connect, such contact could potentially lead to a reduction in the negative attitudes toward the enemy other.[16]

But scholars have proven that contact theory is often insufficient as a form of conflict resolution and transformation, in part because, as applied to Palestinians and Israelis, such efforts reproduce rather than ameliorate the dynamics of power that exist in Palestine/Israel.[17] The main focus of the coexistence model is interpersonal similarities and interactions, which emphasize the notion that "we are all human beings," and therefore we should be able to get along (i.e., we just need to see each other as people who also like movies, music, or other such human interests). This idea fails because, according to Ifat Maoz, an Israeli social psychologist, the coexistence model "does not tend to confront issues such as the conflict between Israeli Jews and Palestinians, dilemmas of national identity, and claims concerning discrimination toward Palestinian citizens of Israel. Consequently, the coexistence model can be seen as supporting the status quo of the existing structural relations between Jews and Palestinian-Arabs in Israel rather than seeking social and political change."[18]

One of the many problems with coexistence activities is that they invisibilize asymmetric dynamics of power—in this case, the power that exists in Palestine/Israel—thereby giving a false sense of equality between participants.[19] Though it did virtually nothing to address the myriad issues related to conflict and power imbalances, coexistence may very well have been a necessary precursor to the rise and development of the co-resistance model for two reasons. First, coexistence organizing gave Palestinians and Israelis an opportunity to meet and learn about each other on a personal level, devoid of outside pressure points such as the media, family, or general societal enmity toward the "other." This was an important step in alliance building since prior to coexistence programs there were few institutional or programmatic opportunities for Palestinians and Israelis to engage with one another on such a level.

Second, coexistence is a model based on managing conflict within the existing conditions on the ground. Though it may have been valuable at a particular moment in history (e.g., during the Oslo era), activists who engaged in coexistence programs and activities often realized that equality is the end goal and there is no means to achieve it in the current structure of Israeli-Palestinian relations. As activists became aware of the inherent problems with coexistence strategies, they developed a new organizing model that rejected the imbalance of power and instead relied on radical solidarity and shared political commitments toward justice, freedom, and equality for all.

For example, activist and organizer Ilana Sumka founded CJNV on the co-resistance model after years of working within the coexistence framework with the organization Encounter.[20] She witnessed that the coexistence framework simply did not make a sufficient impact; sometimes it even exacerbated on-the-ground realities. However, the relationships Ilana developed with Palestinians through Encounter enabled CJNV to join more radical and impactful co-resistance activities with Palestinians. Since their founding, CJNV has taken a much more active role in resisting the occupation than Encounter, among other things by publicly acknowledging the inherent power imbalances in Palestine/Israel.

Co-resistance advocates often accuse the coexistence model of being a form of "normalization," meaning that coexistence activities make the relationships between conflicting sides normal, as if there is some sense of parity between them.[21] According to Palestinian activist Omar Rahman, the problem with creating this false sense of parity is that "when we seek to normalize this relationship by giving each other equal standing and equal voice, we project an image of symmetry. Joint sports teams and theatre groups, hosting an Israeli orchestra in Ramallah or Nablus, all these things create a false sense of normality, like the issue is only a problem of recognizing each other as human beings. This, however, ignores the ongoing oppression, colonization, and denial of rights, committed by one side against the other."[22]

Co-resistance activists thus seek to eradicate normality by showing that Palestinians and Jews must first end Israeli occupation and its systems of exclusion and Jewish supremacy before there can be a shared society based on equality where Palestinians and Israelis "coexist." According to Renad Uri, a Palestinian activist from Ramallah, "Co-resistance requires a commitment to ending the occupation, to the right of return, as well as constantly advocating for equal rights for all. It allows for constructive dialogue that is devoted to collective liberation. . . . We do not waste our time on emotional dialogue that empties peace of its definition. Instead, we are focused on eliminating systems of oppression from the bottom up, predominantly Israel's occupation of Palestinians, and the apartheid state it has transformed into."[23]

Some maintain that the Second Intifada emerged as a direct reaction to policy failures caused by the Oslo Accords, which led to the increased construction of illegal Israeli settlements and the further entrenchment of the occupation.[24] Concurrently, during the Oslo era there was a proliferation of coexistence activities in Palestine/Israel in which Palestinian and Israeli activists joined "dialogue groups," created partnerships through civil society, and participated in Track II diplomatic efforts intended to create the conditions for peace on the ground without input from politicians.[25] But as Oslo crumbled and the despair of the Second Intifada took hold, coexistence efforts subsided; activists began to recognize that "traditional coexistence efforts had merely served to normalize the occupation and calcify the status quo."[26] Furthermore, the Great Recession of 2008 "attenuated the European Union's fiscal support for joint initiatives."[27] Emerging within this context, activists committed to nonviolent resistance turned to a new form of collective activism and joint struggle, one rooted in shared political commitments to end the Israeli occupation. Hence, the birth of co-resistance activities.

Some of the earliest strands of co-resistance work took place in West Bank villages during weekly demonstrations against the construction of Israel's Separation Wall.[28] In 2002, Israel began constructing a wall to separate the Palestinian West Bank from Israel. Officially, the government aimed to secure Israeli citizens from the violence of Palestinian suicide bombers.[29] While the wall was built under the pretext of security, its construction also led to the annexation of additional Palestinian land while incorporating Israeli settlements into Israel.[30] The impacts were catastrophic for Palestinians, as the route of the wall wound deep into Palestinian Territories, cutting Palestinians off from their schools, health care facilities, and farmland and from other Palestinians.[31] But Palestinians refused to remain silent and passive in the face of these latest forms of occupation. In response to the new omnipresence of the wall, Palestinians throughout the West Bank organized weekly nonviolent demonstrations.[32]

At first, the demonstrations were attended almost exclusively by Palestinians. But soon thereafter, Palestinians invited Jewish Israeli activists to join in the protests against the wall, and thus birthed co-resistance as a prominent form of nonviolent struggle against the Israeli occupation. In addition to international activists affiliated with the International Solidarity Movement, Jewish Israeli groups, such as Ta'ayush and Anarchists Against the Wall, participated in demonstrations against the wall in West Bank villages like Budrus, Bil'in, Nil'in, and Nabi Saleh, among others.[33] The presence of these non-Palestinian activists, including diaspora Jews, was important because it provided the opportunity to achieve both material and symbolic goals with each direct action.

In fact, achieving both material and symbolic goals is a hallmark of all co-resistance direct action activism. On a material level, the presence of Jewish Israeli and diaspora Jewish activists at anti-occupation demonstrations has the potential to change soldiers' interpretations of the orders given to them.[34] The Israeli feminist activist group Machsom Watch discovered that when they monitored soldiers at checkpoints the soldiers were less violent toward Palestinians. Those in the military were less inclined to behave violently when being watched by their fellow Jewish Israeli citizens.[35] Thus one of the potential material impacts of co-resistance is that it offers the possibility of reducing physical violence perpetrated by soldiers against Palestinians.

Symbolically, the presence of Jewish Israelis and diaspora Jews at these direct actions challenges the narrative of the "'Other' as 'Enemy'" while simultaneously showing the world that a significant number of Jews are willing to put their bodies on the line in solidarity with Palestinians in order to end Israeli injustices committed in Jews' names. Both materially and symbolically, the participation of Jewish activists in co-resistance direct actions challenges power, seeks to disrupt the status quo, and rejects the forced separation between Jewish Israelis and Palestinians. Most activists who engage with co-resistance are concerned with the material gains of improving the conditions of everyday life for Palestinians as well as the symbolic notion that Israelis, Jews, and Palestinians can resist the occupation together.

As is the case with all co-resistance activities, it is important to note that Jewish Israeli activists showed up to these demonstrations only when Palestinians asked them to, thereby taking the lead from individuals in the marginalized community itself. This demonstrates the importance of establishing relationships between Jews and Palestinians prior to these types of events. Though coexistence programs seek to increase empathy and build relationships, they do not lead to immediate results. They will not radically end the occupation or change the status quo overnight. In fact, they are not predicated on shared political commitments in the same way as the co-resistance model.

Shared political commitments create a unique form of trust, which is different from what emerges from sharing a meal together, for example. The more Jewish Israeli activists participated in these demonstrations, the deeper partnerships developed between the Palestinian and Jewish Israeli activists. These relationships were built not merely on good feeling or deep empathy but rather on shared political commitments to ending Israel's occupation and building a shared society based on equal rights and equitable access to resources.[36] The frequent participation of Jewish Israeli activists in co-resistance activities laid the groundwork for diaspora Jews to join.

Impacts of Young American Jews in Co-resistance

Co-resistance starts with Palestinians and Israeli Jews but must also include international activists, including and especially diaspora Jews, because the institutional support from the Jewish diaspora is a key pillar upholding the occupation. As such, when diaspora Jews challenge the occupation on the ground directly, especially in collaboration with Palestinians, they destabilize the perception of widespread and unequivocal Jewish support for Israel and its policies toward Palestinians. Diaspora Jews are invited to participate in co-resistance activities, but since they are not the ones primarily impacted by the institutionalized separation of Palestinians and Jewish Israelis and the systematic

Figure 4.2. Jewish American and Palestinian activists are harassed by the Israeli military, shortly before being tear-gassed, at a direct action in Masafer Yatta, May 2022. Photo by Emily Glick.

violence of the occupation, they often act as corollaries to the Palestinian and Israeli activists.

That is not to diminish the significance of diaspora Jewish participation in co-resistance activities. On the contrary, their participation is paramount to the success of co-resistance activities. From a symbolic perspective, co-resistance activists find it extremely powerful when non-Israeli Jews participate; their participation shows that Jews with dissenting views are willing to use their bodies in the struggle for justice in Palestine/Israel. This is significant because Israel's existence as an ethnonational Jewish state that excludes and mistreats Palestinians is predicated on the myth that Israel is a state for all Jews. Such a fairy tale is partially able to continue because Israel shields itself from criticism by labeling its critics antisemitic while also demonizing Palestinians as violent. Israel perceives diaspora Jews as essential participants in perpetuating the falsehood of unequivocal support from all Jews worldwide. Thus, this participation of diaspora Jews contradicts and destabilizes such narratives.

When young American Jews participate in co-resistance actions, they do so both to combat the Israeli occupation and to encourage other diaspora Jewish communities to join the struggle for justice in Palestine/Israel. The role of American Jews in these movements is based on a care and love for their own communities as much as it rooted in the desire to work toward justice and peace in Palestine/Israel. The two main Jewish American groups that facilitate co-resistance activism in this way are ATL and CJNV. While each group developed independently of the other, they now work in deep partnership on the ground in Palestine/Israel.

Co-resistance work is not for everyone. It requires time, money, passion, the physical ability to endure long days in difficult conditions, and the emotional stamina to withstand the possibility of Israeli military and/or settler violence. Many young Jewish Americans in particular are often able to engage in co-resistance work more than others because the particular point where they are in their lives is more conducive to this type of activism. Being in their twenties and thirties, they are more likely to be physically fit enough for co-resistance activism, have jobs that allow them to travel (i.e., they just need an internet connection), and do not have children or families to care for.

There are four key motivations for young Jews engaging in co-resistance activism. First, for many young Jews co-resistance provides the opportunity to directly experience what they have largely only read about. This experience changes the way they understand the situation on the ground and impacts how they speak about Palestine/Israel upon their return to the United States. Second, because co-resistance work is always led by Palestinians, the common leftist critique of liberation movements being led by white folks is avoided altogether. Instead, young American Jews experience what it means to take part in a liberation struggle as participants and not leaders.

Third, co-resistance is part of a moral and spiritual reckoning for many young Jews. In the renowned words of twentieth-century Jewish American spiritual activist Rabbi Abraham Joshua Heschel, it provides an opportunity to "pray with their feet." Finally, co-resistance offers young American Jews the chance to spend time in Palestine/Israel in a way that is different from how Zionist trips would otherwise demand them to be. In particular contrast to Birthright (see chapter 3), co-resistance challenges the dominant ways that young American Jews travel to and experience Palestine/Israel by introducing them to Palestine and Palestinians where they are otherwise invisibilized and erased. All four of these motivations are exemplified in the co-resistance activism organized by ATL and CJNV.

All That's Left (ATL)

One night in the fall of 2012, Yoni, a veteran Jewish Israeli activist, was sitting with his friend Ezra at a bar in central Jerusalem. Per the norm, they were talking about how to fight the occupation. "Listen, man," Yoni said, "I have this idea that there needs to be some kind of left-wing American Jewish and diaspora Jewish collective that would somehow gather all the anti-occupation folks in one place."[37] They both knew that every year, thousands of young Jews visit Israel from around the world, and many of them spend some ten months living or studying in the country.[38] Yoni thought out loud, "How can we connect the people who are coming to Israel to the various organizations doing anti-occupation and Palestine solidarity activism? How do we make it easier and more accessible for people coming to Israel to participate in activism?"

The two were veteran activists who had spent years participating in various forms of activism with Palestinians and Jewish Israelis. They had connections with Palestinian and Jewish Israeli activist networks and knew that there was an opportunity to connect others to important work happening on the ground. Ezra agreed that Yoni had a good idea. He approached a few of his friends, other diaspora Jews who had been living in Israel, to discuss it further.

According to Ezra, this small group "started planning and immediately realized there was a lot of resonance, and there really was the potential to fill the need. We didn't know exactly what it would be, but it felt like there was a gap to be filled in that there were a lot of really rad Israeli Jewish movements that we were part of . . . and there were also a lot of good organizations doing work on the ground in the diaspora. It felt like there was a lack of aggregating folks who wanted to engage in left-wing activism."[39]

Another activist at these initial meetings, Jeremiah, further elaborated on Ezra's recollections:

There was this big question about how we can help get diaspora hubs who aren't from here to have an easier time entering [activist work] on the ground. From my vantage point, there were these two big questions. One of them was helping to be the mortar between the bricks of the movement by making contact and connections with people on the ground from people who have already been interacting with others in multiple different movement spheres and organizations. The other thing was creating a conduit for people to easily hit the ground running. You don't know Hebrew, you don't know Arabic, you don't know folks on the ground. You're here for a week or a year and want to get involved in organizing campaigns . . . and want to figure out your life around the movement. This is the access point for that.[40]

ATL's founders understood the significance of connecting diaspora Jews to opportunities on the ground in Palestine/Israel. They knew the strategic importance of involving these activists in building a broader movement against the occupation.

They formed a collective intended to provide easy entry points into anti-occupation activism for people with the interest but not the skills or the trusted relationships to engage in meaningful activism on their own. After a few meetings, this group invited more friends to join them in exploring ways to create new opportunities to connect people to activism on the ground. I was living in Jerusalem at the time conducting dissertation fieldwork and was already in touch with a few Jewish Israeli and Palestinian activist groups. One night at a party, Ezra approached me and told me about the new group that was forming; he invited me to join them at their next meeting.

As I was intrigued by the possibility of ATL's goal of connecting American Jews with opportunities to engage in Palestine solidarity activism on the ground, I decided to attend. At the time, my experience was that, as an American Jew, it was sometimes difficult to find activist spaces in Palestine/Israel in which I felt comfortable participating. In particular, I was wary of seeming as if I was simply parachuting in from the outside.[41] But this group attracted me because it appeared to be approaching Jewish activism in solidarity with Palestinians in a way that was both deeply reflexive and also aware of the power dynamics at play.

When I arrived at the meeting of the yet-to-be-named group in the apartment of an activist who lived in the Nachlaot neighborhood of West Jerusalem, I was pleasantly surprised to see so many like-minded people—other young North American anti-occupation Jewish activists living in Jerusalem. I remember passionate discussions about what to name the group at my first meeting. The result of the discussions, which spilled into subsequent meetings the following months, was that the group decided to call itself All That's Left: Anti-Occupation Collective, a nod to the left-wing political commitments of the group, the rapidly dissipating peace camp in Israel, and the alarming rightward trend of diaspora communities. By claiming that they were "All That's Left," the group boldly cemented their place on the left-wing political spectrum, where they also decided to create an inclusive space, which was no small thing.

As the group was formed in late 2012, the founders of ATL were deeply influenced by both the 2011 Occupy movement and Israel's 2011 social protests, which were fresh in their minds.[42] Whereas the Jewish Americans in the group had cut their teeth in social movement organizing at Occupy campaigns in locations across the United States and Canada, the Jewish Israelis among them had done the same but through Israel's social protests on Rothschild Boulevard in Tel Aviv. As a result, they were deeply inspired and shaped by the non-hierarchical and leaderless organizing structures of these movements and sought to replicate them in ATL.

This was mentioned by numerous activists whom I interviewed. "ATL started just a year and a bit after Occupy and the social protests in Israel," said Leah, a forming member of ATL. "So, I think there was definitely an influence and an emphasis on wanting to be a collective rather than forming an organization. We wanted to recognize that hierarchies are inherently present but not to give any kind of official feel to those hierarchies. There will be no spokesperson, there will be no leader, there will be no board or president."[43] In other words, in replicating many of the Occupy movement's strategies, the activists also decided not to form an organization to add to the plethora of existing organizations on the ground but instead aimed to create a collective open to anyone interested in anti-occupation organizing.[44]

A principal topic of many of the early ATL meetings was forming a one-sentence description of the group. They wanted to pen a concise articulation of their work without committing to a nonprofit organizational structure. After painstaking discussions in meetings alternating between Tel Aviv and Jerusalem, the activists decided on the following: "All That's Left is a collective unequivocally opposed to the occupation and committed to building the diaspora angle of resistance."[45] Their tagline became a calling card for the movement; if someone wanted to know what ATL stood for, members could now cite the same line. This sentence became a pseudo-manifesto for the group, ensuring that everyone involved in the collective shared a clear political commitment— unequivocal opposition to the occupation—alongside a common position that diaspora Jews should be involved in the process of ending the occupation.

Young American Jews participating in co-resistance activities now had a central hub that could connect them with various things happening on the ground. While Jews from the diaspora had numerous opportunities to participate in co-resistance prior to 2012, the creation of ATL produced a concentrated organizing space where young diaspora Jews living in or visiting Palestine/Israel could more easily tap into co-resistance activities with multiple groups and spaces. But ATL didn't start out engaging solely in co-resistance activities. In fact, it took them a few years to recognize the potential value that they, as diaspora Jews, could bring to the co-resistance model. In the beginning, ATL activists planned low-stakes direct actions, which were largely symbolic acts by diaspora Jews acting on their own rather than direct actions performed with Palestinians.

In May 2013, the collective organized young activists from the diaspora to disrupt a speech by Naftali Bennett, who was then Israel's minister of the diaspora.[46] Just as Bennett took the stage during an event put on by MASA—an organization that seeks to "inspire the next generation of Jewish leaders and strengthen their connection to the Jewish people and to Israel"—a group of some thirty ATL-affiliated activists chanted, "Diaspora Jews say no to occupation; Diaspora Jews say no to annexation; Diaspora Jews say *dai la'kibush*" ("no to occupation" in Hebrew).[47] ATL targeted MASA because it is one of the main groups that plays an outsized role in influencing how young diaspora Jews understand and experience Israel.

The protest was aimed at making the attendees, young diaspora Jews, aware of Bennett's right-wing political positions, which included a plan to annex the West Bank, something problematic for both diaspora Jews and Israel. By disrupting a speech given by the minister of the diaspora, the activists sought to bring to the fore the overwhelmingly liberal politics of Jewish communities around the world as opposed to the rightward shift in Israeli politics. Though the stakes for this action were relatively low, it highlighted ATL's insistence on building a diaspora angle of resistance.

Another direct action took place on June 5, 2013, a deeply symbolic date, marking the forty-sixth anniversary of the start of the 1967 Arab-Israeli War, known to Jewish Israelis as the Six-Day War and to Palestinians as al Naksa (the Setback). In this demonstration, a dozen young Jewish activists from the diaspora gathered in central Jerusalem dressed in green. There, near the Jerusalem Municipality light rail station, they placed a lengthy piece of butcher paper and started painting a long green line.[48] Their goal was to make "what can be found only on maps and is forgotten in everyday life" visual, to take "the initiative to materially represent the 1949 Green Line by painting a small section of it on butcher kraft paper."[49] In addition to creating this renegade art installation, activists distributed leaflets explaining the action as a way of highlighting Israel's systematic erasure of the Green Line; by including their new organizational logo, the leaflets also introduced the group to the public.

The Green Line—the 1949 Armistice Lines, marking the internationally recognized borders of Israel—is an integral element of Israel's attempts to Judaize Jerusalem and exert control over the West Bank.[50] In painting the Green Line in a busy section of central Jerusalem, the activists hoped to draw attention to how Israel's policies of occupation and settlement construction have systematically erased what the international community considers to be the border with a future Palestinian state. According to ATL's prepared leaflet, the erasure of the Green Line obscures the reality of the daily horrors of military occupation.

Thereafter, ATL began organizing and engaging in more radical direct actions, those run in partnership with Palestinians on the ground. For example, in June 2015, ATL arranged a two-day work trip to Susya, a Palestinian village in the South Hebron Hills that was under threat of demolition for, according to the IDF, "illegal construction and zoning."[51] As the Palestinian residents of the village prepared for an imminent forced relocation, seventy Jewish activists from the diaspora came to the village at the invitation of the village residents who requested their solidarity.[52] Many ATL activists had already established relationships with these same villagers through their previous work with organizations like B'Tselem, Rabbis for Human Rights, Ta'ayush, and Breaking the Silence.

During the two days, activists helped flatten a road in the village, planted za'atar (an herb) in the fields, and attended presentations delivered by villagers about their situation. According to one participant, "The atmosphere was energetic—reminiscent of something between a Habitat for Humanity project and foreign Zionist volunteers in the 1950s coming to help 'reclaim the land,' albeit this time for Palestinians."[53] By working and reclaiming the land, but doing it in solidarity with Palestinians, the activists made both a material difference, by improving ever so slightly the conditions of everyday life, and a symbolic one, by subverting the Zionist paradigm of Jews working to reclaim the land in the service of building an exclusive Jewish state. This action therefore embodied the central ethos of co-resistance.

The two days in Susya also illustrated the appeal of on-the-ground nonviolent activism for many young diaspora Jews, the simultaneous observing and destabilizing of the Jewish dominant Zionist interaction with the land. Through this experience, young diaspora Jews understood that co-resistance is a way of connecting with the Jewish past while rejecting the harm of Jewish violence carried out on Palestinians in Palestine/Israel. By participating in co-resistance activism, these young Jews were affirming and reclaiming their Jewish values and identities rather than rejecting them.

While ATL has had tremendous success in connecting people with co-resistance activism in Palestine/Israel and is now a significant player in joint nonviolent resistance activities, there remains a major tension in the collective around leadership and sustainability. This begs an important question about movement organizing and ATL's role in this ecosystem: how do you sustain the work of the collective with a transitory population? Inevitably tensions arise between diaspora Jews who live long term in Palestine/Israel and have a sustained presence in activist spaces and those who drop in for a week, month, or year. On the one hand, ATL claims to be a non-hierarchical collective of activists. But on the other hand, many of the same people tend to organize most of the meetings and run point on communicating with their constituency.

According to Marla, an activist who lives in Tel Aviv and is a constant presence in ATL, "One of the things I think is so important about movement building is not keeping knowledge in the hands of a few people. That's really hard, especially in a group like ATL, where some people are coming in and out and some people are here. We say there's no hierarchy in the movement, but how do you actually make sure that's true?"[54]

Though the group identifies as an activist collective and is strong enough to withstand the ebbs and flows of transnational participation, it still struggles to embody its ethos as non-hierarchical. According to Ezra, who was a sustained presence in the collective's early years but has since left Palestine/Israel, ATL "doesn't need any of us. None of us are so important. The collective is not a cult of personality. None of us are an irreplaceable visionary, which so often happens in these movements. Someone comes up with a great idea, and there are two or three people who are pushing it forward, and then they get tired or they burn out or they have kids and they move [away] or whatever and then the whole thing crumbles. That's not what is happening with ATL."[55]

The sustained presence of some activists who live in the region long term enhances ATL's ability to build the diaspora angle of resistance in Palestine/Israel. They are the individuals who have formed the strongest bonds with Palestinian communities. Therefore, when there is a spike in Israeli state or settler violence against a Palestinian community, the activists with the most long-standing and established relationships— those who have shown up time and again for years—receive the calls from their Palestinian counterparts. The trust built by resisting occupation together enables stronger movement alliances, those best formed by standing side by side in front of an Israeli bulldozer attempting to demolish a Palestinian home or rebuilding a Palestinian community center destroyed by Israeli settlers. This trust is also what enables ATL to be a primary hub connecting diaspora Jews with co-resistance activism on the ground.

One of the successes and contributions that ATL has made to the anti-occupation movement is in forging deeply strong and sustained partnerships between young American Jews and Palestinian communities and activists. They have also played a significant role in strengthening the relationships that these activists had already built with leftist Jewish Israeli and international groups, such as Ta'ayush, Anarchists Against the Wall,

Breaking the Silence, Rabbis for Human Rights, and others. By having a sustained presence on the ground, ATL has cemented itself as a central hub to connect diaspora Jews with co-resistance work on the ground. Another group providing opportunities for Jews from around the world to engage in meaningful and deep co-resistance solidarity with Palestinians is CJNV.

The Center for Jewish Nonviolence (CJNV)

In May 2014, Ilana Sumka received a call from a Palestinian friend, Daoud Nassar, a farmer living in the West Bank. Earlier that year, on May 19, the Israeli military uprooted approximately fifteen hundred trees on his land; they claimed it was state land from which the Nassar family needed to be evacuated.[56] Daoud is a well-known Palestinian peace activist in the West Bank who has hosted countless delegations of activists at his Tent of Nations farm, an educational compound located in the Bethlehem hills dedicated to bringing people together to work and learn about the land.[57] Ilana had worked closely with Daoud for many years; she had brought numerous delegations of Jews to the Tent of Nations through her work with Encounter, an "educational organization committed to informed, courageous, and resilient Jewish [American] leadership" through trips to Palestine/Israel.[58]

After the tree uprooting, Encounter's new director asked Ilana to facilitate a phone call between Daoud and Encounter alumni who had previously visited the Tent of Nations. During the call, Ilana asked Daoud how Jews in particular could support him. Daoud responded, "You could come replant the trees with us in a show of solidarity, to demonstrate that the Israeli Army's bulldozers don't represent your Jewish values."[59] Ilana, a veteran activist and organizer par excellence, sprang into action. She founded CJNV based on the premise that the solidarity of Jews from around the world willing to engage with co-resistance is necessary and radical, both in working toward justice for Palestinians and in presenting a Jewish politics that refuses to condone acts of Israeli state violence.

In February 2015, less than a year after Daoud made this suggestion, CJNV brought its first delegation of twenty-five Jews from North America and Europe to the West Bank to engage in co-resistance and tree planting. During the weeklong experience, the multigenerational group of activists, including Millennials from the United States, actively subverted the central Zionist tenet of nation building by planting olive trees. The Zionist movement, and the Jewish National Fund (JNF) in particular, has a long tradition of tree planting as a political strategy to displace Palestinians and erase their presence on the land.[60] By heeding Daoud's call to replant the trees uprooted by the Israeli army, CJNV activists repurposed one of Israel's most widely used strategies of control to oppose occupation and act in solidarity with Palestinians.[61] By uprooting a dominant Zionist narrative, the activists participating in the first CJNV delegation showed the symbolic and material possibilities of Jews engaging in co-resistance work on the ground in Palestine/Israel. This action affirmed their Jewish identities and signaled to their Jewish communities that there is an alternative to the discriminatory policies of the state and its supporting institutions, most notably the JNF.[62]

The success of the first CJNV delegation set the stage for the organization's growth in size and prominence, leading to subsequent delegations that have brought hundreds of diaspora Jews to Palestine/Israel since 2015. In addition to learning about the contemporary political situation on the ground in the West Bank, CJNV delegations include serious nonviolent direct action trainings, ensuring that activists are prepared for the main co-resistance element of the delegation, which involves a direct and confrontational action. Since each CJNV delegation centers around one major direct action coordinated with multiple Palestinian partners, following the principles of co-resistance, CJNV participates only when they are invited to do so by Palestinian partners. The Jewish activists know that their presence enables Palestinian activists to potentially elicit a different response from the military and/or settlers.

Another example of a direct action took place in May 2016, when Issa Amro and the Hebron-based Youth Against Settlements invited CJNV to join them in reclaiming stolen Palestinian property. The action aimed to transform an old metal shop into the city's first cinema, thus creating a much-needed safe entertainment space in a neighborhood where Palestinians face daily harassment from Israeli settlers and soldiers. When the Israeli military showed up to the work site and declared the area a closed military zone—thereby making it illegal for nonmilitary personnel to be there—the activists sat down in an act of civil disobedience and began singing songs in Hebrew about justice. "Olam hesed yibaneh" (we will build a world of love/righteousness), they sang, emphasizing their Jewish values and identities in participating in a co-resistance action. Not amused at the activists' defiance and befuddled by their singing, the military promptly moved in and arrested six activists for refusing to leave the area.

Later that evening, in the nearby village of Susya, CJNV activists participated in a Kabbalat Shabbat service, a traditional ritual that welcomes in the Jewish Sabbath. The activists sang and prayed in Hebrew inside of a Palestinian village under constant threat of demolition and settler attacks; their action embodied what it means to show up *as Jews* in solidarity with Palestinians. According to one of the young activists who organized the action, celebrating Shabbat in Susya after a nonviolent direct action enabled him to integrate his Jewish identity with his activism: "I feel Jewish here because I'm standing in solidarity with people facing oppression."[63]

According to Jewish American journalist Peter Beinart, who left a family vacation in Israel to participate in the direct action, celebrating Shabbat in the village after participating in the action helped him connect with his Jewishness in new and reinvigorated ways. In a widely circulated opinion article in *Haaretz*, Beinart later wrote,

> Why were we performing Kabbalat Shabbat? I can't speak for everyone, but for me, it was partly to remind myself of who I am. I had spent the day working alongside Palestinians and being protected by them. I had spent the day fearing Jewish soldiers and police. It was a jarring experience. The normal order of things, as I had learned them since childhood, had been turned upside down. Welcoming Shabbat was a way of centering myself. It was a reminder that no matter how many people tell me I hate Judaism, the Jewish people and the Jewish state—no matter how many people tell me I hate myself—I know who I am. I know when I'm living in truth. And nothing feels more Jewish than that.[64]

For many Jews, young and old, who join CJNV delegations, the co-resistance activism reinforces their connection to their Jewish identities while fortifying the importance of engaging in Palestine solidarity activism *as Jews*. The delegations are transformative for participants, partially because they model the possibilities of a different future in Palestine/ Israel, one rooted in partnerships between Jews and Palestinians. The value of CJNV's co-resistance work and the success of their delegations are based on the sustained presence of Jewish activists in solidarity with Palestinians.

Furthermore, since the delegations bring Jews from the diaspora to engage in co-resistance work, they also provide an opportunity to include a broad-based coalition of activists. Recent delegations have included activists from JStreet, JVP, IfNotNow, and multiple smaller locally based anti-occupation activist groups. As such, one of CJNV's primary modes of engagement has been to bring people who are already involved with diverse groups in the United States and integrate them into their on-the-ground co-resistance work. The delegations thereby act as a catalyst for the activists to bring the work on the ground back to their organizations thereafter.

Just as ATL is a hub for people going to Palestine/Israel to connect to co-resistance work, CJNV makes it possible for young American Jews to participate in activist work on the ground in easier and more accessible ways. According to one CJNV leader, "We hope what folks get out of the delegation experience is the possible points of strategic collaboration back home. We believe that the delegation can be an opportunity for people to take [things back home with them] so that the delegation can be part of their strategic organizing cycle for the activist groups they are working with."[65] It is also important to note that CJNV and ATL work closely with one another, both in planning the delegations and in creating more points of connection for activists after a delegation action has ended, especially for those who want to continue engaging in co-resistance on the ground.

Since CJNV is a self-identified Jewish group, it is a safe and comfortable way for young Jewish activists to participate in co-resistance. On a fairly simple level, as one activist told me, "Someone traveling on their own who is Jewish might not go to the West Bank. Certainly, they would not be welcomed into these communities in the same way without the institutional infrastructure of CJNV that enables that [engagement]."[66] The Jewish nature of CJNV's organizing is sometimes more appealing and easier, for young Jews especially when trying to convince their parents that it is okay to participate in a delegation with a Jewish group organizing within a Jewish framework. The mere name of the organization—the Center for *Jewish* Nonviolence—provides an ease of acceptance and Jewish framing. But it also makes it more comfortable for activists to engage in solidarity and co-resistance activism when there are other Jews around them.

As a Jewish space, it articulates its activism in the language of Jewish values and ethics. Take, for example, the creation of CJNV's newest program, Hineinu: A Sustained Solidarity Project. Hineinu—Hebrew for "here we are"—is based on the Hebrew word *hineini*, which appears in the Torah multiple times. Whenever God calls out a biblical leader, whether Abraham, Moses, or a prophet, they most commonly respond by saying *hineini*, or "here I am." This name is also a response with a purpose; in saying *hineinu* ("here we are"), CJNV activists are engaging in the Jewish biblical tradition of responding to a need that requires action to resolve.

The COVID-19 global pandemic forced the organization to temporarily halt its delegations. But they quickly pivoted to a more sustained and long-term form of co-resistance activism in the South Hebron Hills, a site of previously enduring partnerships. Launched in 2020 through the Hineinu project, CJNV activists spend four months living in a Palestinian village in the South Hebron Hills engaging in daily co-resistance work alongside Palestinians. The sustained presence of Jewish activists in these villages has been integral to the protection of villagers from both settler and military forms of violence; the mere presence of Jewish activists alters the common hostile response of settlers and soldiers through the leveraging of their Jewish privilege. While this sustained activism in the South Hebron Hills has material impacts in villages like Susya, Umm al-Khair, and others, it also impacts the Jewishness of the activists who are using their bodies to express solidarity with Palestinians in radical defiance to the Jewish settlers and soldiers who attempt to destroy and erase Palestinian life in the West Bank.

Leveraging Privilege and Power

One of the reasons that co-resistance is a valuable and powerful method of anti-occupation activism, both materially and symbolically, is that the presence of Jewish activists on the ground can protect Palestinians from both settler and military violence. Essential to this process is the ability of Jewish activists to leverage their privilege, which makes it difficult for those in power to maintain the status quo. According to scholar Kurt Schock, leverage is "the ability . . . to mobilize the withdrawal of support from opponents or invoke pressure against them through the networks upon which opponents defend for power."[67] By leveraging their privilege as Jews, the activists discourage military and settler violence; simply put, the military is less interested in hurting or attacking Jews than Palestinians. Since the Israeli state depends on the support and good will of diaspora communities, and the United States in particular, attacking Jewish Americans not only is a bad look but also can lead to disastrous consequences that could challenge Israel's impunity.

One common critique of Jewish Israeli and diaspora Jewish co-resistance activism raises the ethics of solidarity, questioning the ethical entanglements of the activists with Israeli state violence and power.[68] For example, sociologist Teodora Todorova argues that when Jewish activists leverage their privilege they both enshrine that privilege and seek to dismantle it, which can present a serious obstacle for the possibilities of meaningful co-resistance activism.[69] Scholar Fiona Wright claims that while on the one hand Jewish activists engaging in solidarity with Palestinians on the ground provide "a hopeful subversion of dominant relationalities in Israel/Palestine, this activism is also intimately bound to the very ethical and political paradigms it aims to challenge."[70] Wright contends that this is the case because the subjectivity of these activists is deeply tied to the Israeli state, which connects them to the forms of power they are seeking to challenge.

While Wright concludes that the privilege of these activists complicates their ability to engage in a form of successful radical politics, I observed that activists engage in a robust process of recognizing, grappling with, and leveraging that privilege in order to intervene in and disrupt Israeli state violence. Of particular relevance and importance is that Jewish privilege in this context exists under the direction of Palestinian activists, which enables the Jewish activists to distance themselves—in some central ways—from the Israeli state. In this way, there is an attempt to transfer some of the privilege that the Jewish activists possess to Palestinian communities, thereby giving them the power to direct the forms of activist engagement. This political act of intervention enables a particular form of affective solidarity that is necessary for and acts in service to a radical politics of social and political transformation.[71] In fact, as Wright explains elsewhere, by engaging in co-resistance and solidarity activism on the ground, Jewish Israeli and diaspora Jewish activists negotiate their citizenship and privilege in ways that challenge the Israeli state violence perpetrated in their names.[72]

The activists I interviewed engage in a deeply reflexive process that reveals ways to successfully leverage their privilege in the service of material gains that improve the conditions of everyday life for Palestinians. For example, in reflecting on the attempted arrest of Palestinian activists during a CJNV delegation, one Jewish activist said,

> When soldiers moved in and targeted the Palestinians very aggressively and violently, there were Jewish bodies around Palestinian activists. We enveloped them in a mixture of tactical readiness, nonviolent discipline, and pure solidarity. This was about love, safety, and hope. We modeled what's possible in leveraging our Jewish bodies and our privilege in solidarity with Palestinians. After the action in talking to the Palestinian activists they told me, "I've never had so many bodies trying to prevent my arrest and trying to get between a soldier and me. I've never had so much focus and clarity from an activist on my position vis-à-vis this soldier who is hell-bent on arresting me."[73]

This act of leveraging privilege led to the successful de-arresting of a Palestinian activist, which enabled him to return home safely after the action. Most importantly, in co-resistance activities, Jewish activists show up only when asked to by Palestinian partners and engage in activism only in ways that Palestinians request. This is one of many ways that these activists avoid reproducing some of the pitfalls of Palestine solidarity activism. At the same time, since the activism occurs in the context of the occupied Palestinian Territories, which does not exist in a vacuum, it is also impossible to not perpetuate the hierarchical status of Jews in Palestine/Israel when working in this area, thus reproducing the very power dynamics they seek to disrupt.[74]

Recognizing and leveraging privilege is one of the things that enables Jewish participation in co-resistance to be so profoundly powerful, not just as an act of symbolic solidarity but also in ways that lead to material impacts. Young Jewish American activists not only have the privilege of being Jews but also have the privilege of not experiencing the routine violence of everyday life in Palestine/Israel and the privilege of not needing to be in Palestine/Israel to begin with. Although they can leave whenever they want to, these activists choose to be there to engage in co-resistance. The Jewish privilege they have is therefore also about access. Diaspora Jews can go to Palestine/Israel, and many of the young Jewish American activists who do co-resistance activism do so because they feel as though they have the responsibility to use their privilege in this particular way. It is ultimately through the ability to leverage this privilege that the act of solidarity becomes meaningful and radical.

According to Nina, a veteran activist with copious experience doing co-resistance work, "As Jews, often with a connection to mainstream Jewish communities, we have a very particular role to play. We can put our bodies on the line in ways that our bodies, our privilege, and our presence will help dramatize the violence that is inherent in the system [of Israeli occupation]. That's the basic idea of civil disobedience in general, and there's a very conscious awareness in knowing it's about privileged people using their privilege to be in solidarity with Palestinians."[75] This idea was further argued by CJNV's founder, Ilana Sumka. In an article published in *Tikkun* to mark fifty years of Israel's occupation, she argues that Jews engaging in solidarity work is important "because our presence deters Israeli security forces from coming down overly harshly on the Palestinians who are otherwise prevented from building . . . [and] because our presence deters the neighboring Israeli settlers from harassing the Palestinians and intimidating them from planting their fields."[76]

Nina and Ilana are referencing slightly different goals of diaspora Jewish participation in co-resistance activism. While Nina suggests that the goal is to show the violence of the system to diaspora communities by putting their bodies in the line of fire, Ilana implies that the objective is to prevent the violence in the first place. In actual fact, both of these things often happen simultaneously. The military is undoubtedly less violent with American Jews than with Palestinians, so there is indeed some built-in protection from having Jewish bodies involved in direct actions. Nonetheless, sometimes the military is harsher and more aggressive than expected in its response to protests, which is one way to raise the consciousness of diasporic Jewish communities about Israeli state violence.

This articulation of using Jewish privilege as a radical act of solidarity with Palestinians and as a symbolic act toward ending the occupation elucidates that co-resistance is about leveraging Jewish privilege in a way that centers Palestinian narratives and experiences. Some critics of Jewish participation in anti-occupation activism argue that it revolves around Jewish experiences and thus omits and invisibilizes Palestinians. But according to Jewish Israeli activist Omri Evron, co-resistance is "distinguished from the philanthropic politics of progressive Jews that like to express one-sided solidarity with the Palestinians, which unintentionally reproduces the trope that paints people as either white saviors or black/brown victims."[77]

The challenge for activists, therefore, is to reconcile the necessity of engaging in challenging internal Jewish conversations while also following the lead of Palestinians in order to be in solidarity in the struggle for justice. To that end, in following the lead of Palestinians in co-resistance work the Jewish activists must be willing to use their privilege not for their benefit but for material gains in the Palestinian struggle for justice. "Jews can talk about themselves endlessly without coming up for air," Jacob told me in an interview in a crowded Jerusalem café. "But we must remember that our conversations and actions exist in a context with non-Jewish adjacent experiences. If we forget that our work is about aiding the Palestinian cause, then we are doing a disservice to ourselves and to the Palestinians."[78]

Simply put, Jewish co-resistance activists are able to leverage their privilege for material gains while simultaneously making a symbolic statement as to the power of Jewish-Palestinian alliance building, all while centering the Palestinian story and struggle. Though Jewish American media outlets sometimes cover co-resistance activities to highlight Jewish participation in the Palestine solidarity movement, the activists giving quotes to reporters are careful to ensure that a fundamental element of the story is the injustice that Palestinians experience at the hands of Jewish occupiers, refusing to obfuscate the quotidian violence Palestinians are subject to every day. Jewish American activists are not, like Palestinians, living under occupation. Yet they are willing and able to put their bodies on the line in solidarity with them in order to push for the end of occupation.[79] This is precisely what it means to embody and practice a radical form of solidarity. This insistence on centering Palestinians in the struggle is a profound form of affective solidarity, one based on love, care, and a deep commitment to the Other.

Although a central purpose of co-resistance is to focus on Palestinians, sometimes Jewish activists engaged in this work are arrested, which inevitably shines a spotlight on them, thus centering the Jewish experiences of Palestine solidarity activism. One highly prominent and publicized incident took place during the annual Jerusalem Day Flag March in May 2017. Jerusalem Day is an Israeli national holiday that commemorates and celebrates the "reunification" of Jerusalem during the 1967 War. In 1968, the Israeli government made the 28th of Iyar, the Hebrew date of the "reunification," a holiday, "a day that symbolizes the continued historical connection of the Jewish People to Jerusalem."[80] Thirty years later, in 1998, the government officially passed a law cementing Jerusalem Day as a national holiday in Israel.[81]

The Jerusalem Day Flag March is one of the most racist and violent annual expressions of Israeli nationalism, a day when the systematic exclusion and erasure of Palestinians from the city is on full display. Jerusalem Day is marked by Israeli celebrations throughout the city, capped off by a massive rally of Jewish nationalist youth groups, most of whom are ultra-nationalist religious settlers who do not even live in Jerusalem but rather reside in West Bank settlements, marching with Israeli flags toward the Old City.[82] Since the Flag March is a prominent expression of Israel's ultranationalism, it is also a frequent site of counterprotests waged by Palestinian and Jewish activists. These counterprotests are always met with severe repression and crowd-dispersal tactics carried out by the Israeli police.

In 2017, a small group of Palestinian, Israeli, and young Jewish activists, most of whom were from the diaspora, affiliated with ATL, IfNotNow, and Free Jerusalem, organized a small counterprotest. They stood in front of Damascus Gate with a sign that read "End the Occupation" in Hebrew, Arabic, and English. Since the Israeli settlers and the Flag March were approaching Damascus Gate, the Israeli police asked the group of protestors to leave. In a defiant act of civil disobedience, the activists refused. The protestors instead sat down in place, linking arms. Almost immediately the police grabbed the protestors, shoved and dragged them away, and, in one incredibly violent moment, even broke the arm of Sarah Brammer-Shlay, one of the activists who is now a rabbi; she needed surgery to repair the break.[83]

When asked about the incident, Brammer-Shlay was quick to proclaim, "I am proud to be Jewish, but occupation is not my Judaism," intentionally and clearly linking her anti-occupation activism with her Jewish identity.[84] As someone who has participated in these counterprotests and experienced the violence firsthand, I was both dismayed and not at all surprised when I heard that a police officer had broken Sarah's arm; I had witnessed similarly vile acts of violence toward protestors during Jerusalem Day previously.[85] This violent police action made the news in Israel and in Jewish American communities.[86]

It is also precisely this type of image that, when it circulates in Jewish communities in the United States, polarizes debates about Jews and Palestinians, thus moving the needle ever so slightly in publicizing Jewish anti-occupation politics. In the words of one activist, "Sometimes we see American Jews putting their bodies on the line in solidarity with Palestinians. The image that comes through is really messy. When you see soldiers trying to arrest or beat the shit out of American Jews who are sitting with locked elbows, it evokes the image of what happened in other explicit nonviolent activism campaigns. And those images of nonviolent protestors getting assaulted ultimately helped move the broader community towards justice in other struggles, so maybe that can happen in Israel/Palestine as well."[87] Even though the Jerusalem Day counterprotest was intended to center the Palestinian struggle, it ultimately illuminated Jewish participation in Palestine solidarity activism in a way that made the story about Jewish activism rather than the necessity of ending Israel's occupation. And although this incident is somewhat rare, and Jewish activists are seldom treated with the same malicious intent as are Palestinians, the power and privilege of Jewish activists emerge through the process of arrest and assault.

Co-resistance and Jewish Values

Co-resistance has a larger agenda than Jewish activists supporting and participating as allies in the Palestinian struggle for justice. It is also about Jewish liberation, changing the politics of Jewish identity, and showing other Jews that joint struggle with Palestinians and direct action against the Israeli occupation is possible for Jews. Lucy, an activist involved with CJNV, articulates this quite clearly: "I think there's something very powerful about doing co-resistance because for me it is about living out my Jewish values. I think a lot of people go to Israel and Palestine thinking 'I'm either anti-occupation or Jewish, but I can't be both.' Young Jews participating in co-resistance is powerful because we're trying to challenge these narratives and we do this work from a Jewish space. We are showing people that Palestine solidarity activism is not contrary to our Jewish values. It's modeled and based on our Jewish values."[88] Lucy engages in co-resistance in a way that enacts her Jewish values; these actions show her that it is possible to be both proudly Jewish and steadfastly anti-occupation. She purposefully engages in deep conversations with her family and friends about her activism to ensure that they understand that she spends so much time in places like the South Hebron Hills and other Palestinian areas in the West Bank and East Jerusalem to show solidarity with Palestinians as an expression of her Jewishness.

Another activist, Jess, who has participated in numerous CJNV delegations, said, "To me what CJNV does is impactful on a personal level. We know that we're not going to stop the occupation through the delegations. Instead, we understand that I can be here and see this place (Palestine/Israel) in a different way, and feel my Judaism in a different way through this activism."[89] Jess was socialized into a Zionist ideology through her family and community from a young age. For many years, her Jewish identity was inextricably linked with Zionism. When she became an active participant in Palestine solidarity activism, she decided to engage through specifically Jewish spaces because they felt more comfortable for her. Though she participated in numerous methods of Palestine solidarity activism, including targeting mainstream Jewish institutions in the United States, it wasn't until she engaged in co-resistance activism that she was truly able to disentangle Zionism from her Jewishness. She now understands co-resistance to be an absolute necessity for diaspora Jews and Israeli Jews in that it is a method of improving material conditions on the ground for Palestinians while simultaneously enabling Jews to free themselves from the shackles of being an occupier. Co-resistance is thus not only an instrument of liberation for Palestinians, who often see the material conditions of their lives improve, but also a necessary liberatory practice for Jews.

In fact, one Jewish Israeli activist claimed, "The first time I felt proud to be an Israeli Jew was when I marched alongside Palestinians protesting the apartheid wall in the West Bank village of Bil'in."[90] This sentiment of pride is echoed by young American Jews who feel similarly when they engage in co-resistance activism on the ground. As was clearly evidenced by the queer liberation movement, the feeling of pride can, in and of itself, be understood as a liberatory practice.[91] Many of the Jewish activists I spoke with expressed that at one point they felt tremendous shame in Israeli government actions being perpetrated in their names.

Co-resistance activism is one prominent way that activists reclaim their pride in their Jewishness. According to Elie, "One of the great things about co-resistance is that it's based on shared values. Only by showing up time and again can you prove that you have these shared political commitments and these shared values. When I started doing co-resistance, I was so proud to be showing up as a Jew to show that it is possible for Palestinians and Jews to have shared values and political commitments in this land."[92]

In addition to the pride felt by activists, the presence of Jews exhibiting their Jewish values through co-resistance also disrupts a problematic understanding of Jewishness among Palestinian activists. For Palestinians who grew up knowing Jews only as soldiers or settlers who attack them, the constant presence of Jewish activists provides a new context from which to understand and approach Jewish identity and values. This was reinforced by Gabe, who staunchly supports and participates in co-resistance activism from his current home base in Jerusalem: "Co-resistance helps destabilize for Palestinians the connections between the State of Israel and Jewish values. It interrupts that notion because our presence in co-resistance activism physically places Jewishness in between an armed soldier purporting to represent Jewishness and Jewish activist bodies preventing their physical harm. Our Palestinian partners are conscious of that."[93] If co-resistance can have impacts on both Jewish and Palestinian perceptions of each other and their connections to Israeli state violence, perhaps it can represent a path forward to a more just and equitable society in Palestine/Israel.

Co-resistance shows how the symbolic power of Palestinians, Jewish Israelis, and international Jews coming together as a model for what a future of liberation and equality for all people who live in Palestine/Israel could look like. When Jewish activists join together in co-resistance and engage in projects to make life more livable for Palestinian communities, Jewish activists are refusing to enable those upholding the occupation in their names. Co-resistance is therefore a rejection of the continued annexation of Palestinian land and the erasure of Palestinian life and culture. By engaging in co-resistance, Jewish activists uplift Palestinian resilience and leadership and show through their physical presence that occupation is not their Judaism.

This type of activism is a way of asserting a liberatory Jewish identity based in justice for all people while reclaiming Judaism from Israeli state violence. The participation of Palestinians, Jewish Israelis, and diaspora Jews in anti-occupation and anti-apartheid activities is vital to the struggle for justice because in all settler-colonial situations, both the colonizer and the colonized are impacted by the violence of colonialism.[94] Both Palestinians and Jewish Israelis inhabit the land between the Jordan River and the Mediterranean Sea, and neither group is going anywhere anytime soon, despite the desires of some extremists in both communities to the contrary. In order to survive, the people living in Palestine/Israel must share resources and learn to live together in every facet of a shared society.

Co-resistance provides a window of insight into what a shared society could look like. The co-resistance model rejects normalization as a way to transform the current conditions of occupation and colonization in Palestine/Israel by focusing instead on creating a meaningful, collaborative, and liberatory shared existence between Palestinians and Jews.[95] By resisting together in the struggle for justice as a committed lifestyle, co-resistance activists refuse the violent conditions of the present in order to model a different path forward. Put simply, one of the ultimate end goals of co-resistance work is coexistence predicated on equity and justice for Palestinians and Jewish Israelis.

The solidarity activism and the collective actions of the Jewish and Palestinian activists engaged in co-resistance are slowly forming the building blocks to liberate Palestinians from occupation and Jews from complicity in Israeli state violence. Since this type of activism is based on the possibility of mutual liberation, those who engage in co-resistance do so not as a matter of choice but rather as a necessity. As Nina said, "I think that co-resistance is essential because the fact of the matter is that the future of [Palestine/Israel] is going to require Palestinians and Jewish Israelis living together. I think there is value in young diaspora Jews challenging the paradigms and norms of our community that we can't live together. I think it takes a lot of work to undo that and I feel like young Jews participating in co-resistance has been so essential in really cracking open a space in the community to reimagine how we relate to Israel and to our Jewishness."[96]

This method of activism shows that Palestinians and Jews can live together, that diaspora Jews have a role to play on the ground, and that co-resistance partnerships are beginning to build a society based on equality that is integral to the future. In other words, co-resistance is necessary for decolonization and for creating different conditions on the ground for a just, sustainable, and peaceful future in Palestine/Israel.[97] Co-resistance can therefore be seen as a ray of light that inspires hope for the possibility of a more just tomorrow.

5

Under Pressure

Boycott, Divestment, Sanctions

In a student-wide referendum that took place in December 2020, one with the highest voter turnout in school history, the student body at Tufts University voted to end their campus police's partnership with Israeli law enforcement.[1] The student effort was part of a national campaign led by Jewish Voice for Peace (JVP) called End the Deadly Exchange, which seeks to end programs that send U.S. law enforcement personnel on trips to Israel to train with Israeli police and military. The referendum was the culmination of more than two years of campus organizing and coalition building led by the campus chapter of Students for Justice in Palestine (SJP), a student organization that advocates for Palestinian rights.

The Tufts chapter of SJP was the first U.S. student group to implement the End the Deadly Exchange campaign on a college campus. They were bolstered by a diverse coalition of student on-campus organizations, such as JVP and Alt-J (Alternative Jews), two Jewish-identified groups that operate independently of the university's Hillel chapter.[2] The success of the campaign hinged on the broad-based coalition of supporters, which enabled them to convince people of its importance and validity. The Jewish campus organizations, in addition to the Jewish student members of SJP, were integral to this coalition, as, among other things, they defused accusations of antisemitism from Zionist-affiliated organizations.

The Tufts campaign was part of the global movement to boycott, divest from, and sanction Israel, more commonly referred to as BDS. This movement has grown into one of the most widespread global strategies used to combat Israeli state power and end its policies of occupation and apartheid.[3] As evidenced by the Tufts End the Deadly Exchange campaign, the national BDS movement had played a central role in raising the consciousness of left-wing progressive students across the country around justice struggles in Palestine/Israel. For this movement, U.S. college campuses are among the most important sites of BDS organizing. As I discuss in greater detail below, student involvement in BDS campaigns helped break the hegemonic pro-Israel consensus in Jewish communities and visibilized the Palestinian struggle both within Jewish campus organizations and in students' home communities.

This chapter examines the central role that BDS activism plays among young Jewish American Palestine solidarity activists. After identifying and responding to some of the shifts among BDS activists, I look at how support from young American Jews bolsters the broader movement to boycott, divest from, and sanction Israel. Among the various methods that Jewish Palestine solidarity activists use to combat Israel's system of occupation and apartheid, BDS is uniquely criticized and targeted by Jewish communities because Zionist groups arguably fear the BDS movement more than any other that is currently present on U.S. campuses. This fear is most clearly evidenced by the way that pro-Israel Zionist groups and the American Jewish Establishment have successfully codified BDS activism as the proverbial "red line" for acceptable Jewish behavior and membership into the Jewish community.

Overall, the tactic of BDS is uniquely appealing to organizers and activists due to its perceived effectiveness. It utilizes local strategies and campaigns to impact a global justice issue, thereby harnessing the power of the people to make change on a local level in a way that may also have material impact on the situation in Palestine/Israel. Both BDS activists and their opponents seem to agree that BDS is uniquely effective as a strategy, which is one reason why it receives so much attention. While pro-Israel groups claim that BDS holds Israel to a double standard, Jews active in the BDS movement feel that to not utilize these nonviolent tactics would actually be a double standard because of the Jewish community's historic participation in and valorization of BDS in other contexts such as the farm workers movement, the civil rights movement, and the South African anti-apartheid movement. In recognizing these contradictions, Jews engaged in BDS typically also identify as anti-Zionist, which also renders it distinct from other tactics within the movement space.

The battle over BDS is particularly strong on college campuses because, though most American Jews oppose BDS, a growing number of young Jews support it. Therefore, this chapter also argues that there is a shift in Jewish Palestine solidarity activism with regard to BDS that is mostly occurring among and being galvanized by college students. Like other social movement organizing, successful college BDS campaigns have depended on diverse coalitions that have included anti-occupation and anti-apartheid Jewish youth. Jewish participation in BDS activism is particularly important because accusations of antisemitism can easily shut down these campaigns if they are accepted as accurate. Jewish anti-occupation organizations, especially on campus, provide a needed space for Jewish students to engage in solidarity without forgoing their Jewish identities, which combats the tactics of exclusion drawn by the red lines of the American Jewish Establishment and enables activists to reclaim their Jewishness through BDS organizing. Overall, the participation in and support of BDS campaigns by young Jewish American activists is the most controversial of the strategies used by Palestine solidarity activists described in this book but is also the one that garners the most attention.

Although the referendum at Tufts was the first successful campaign on a U.S. college campus of this kind, it followed End the Deadly Exchange victories in a few other places, including in the cities of Durham, North Carolina (April 2018), and Northampton, Massachusetts (October 2018), as well as with the Vermont State Police (November 2018), all of which ended their participation in police training programs due to pressure by activists organizing local End the Deadly Exchange campaigns.[4] The fact that these campaigns take place both on college campuses as well as in cities and municipalities evidences the ways in which BDS campaigns can provide material wins that connect local issues to a movement and political cause that is relevant both locally and in a different geographical location. With this organizing strategy in mind, JVP launched the End the Deadly Exchange program in 2017. They did so in order to contextualize the relationship between policing in Israel and the United States and contribute to the larger struggle against state violence in both countries. Highlighting the dangers of the U.S.-Israel police partnerships for community safety, JVP's Deadly Exchange program created a template for ending such programs in any city, state, or organization that sends its police officers to train in Israel.

According to JVP's extensive research, thousands of law enforcement officers from the United States have trained in surveillance, crowd control, and counterterrorism strategies with Israeli military, police, and security officials since 2002.[5] The Deadly Exchange report, which influenced the Tufts activists and was published jointly by JVP and Researching the American-Israeli Alliance, "comprehensively documents how these trainings solidify partnerships between the U.S. and Israeli governments to exchange methods of state violence and control, including mass surveillance, racial profiling, and suppression of protest and dissent," all under the official guise of safety and counterterrorism.[6] Ben Lorber, JVP's former campus coordinator, declares, "According to their logic, they're protecting citizens from terror. But our view, and the view of most people, is that real safety does not come through increased surveillance and militarized policing, but real safety for communities comes from the relationships we build and the alliances we form to protect each other."[7]

These training partnerships were notably sponsored by Jewish organizations, including the Anti-Defamation League, the Jewish Institute of National Security in America, the American Jewish Committee, and the American Israel Education Foundation, a group that is associated with the American Israel Public Affairs Committee (AIPAC).[8] By making a link between the dangers of policing in Israel and the United States, and by showing how these partnerships are supported and funded by the American Jewish Establishment, JVP created a manageable and winnable BDS campaign.

But they also created a framework to be successful by tapping into the social and political zeitgeist of the moment of increased anti-police activism after the cataclysmic events of the summer of 2020, such as the murder of George Floyd. Boycotts, divestment campaigns, and sanctions are, more than anything else, tactics that can be used to organize for social and political transformation.[9] In his seminal work on nonviolent resistance, Gene Sharp expanded on each of these tactics as ways to work toward justice.[10] In creating the Deadly Exchange campaign, JVP utilized two of these tactics—boycotts and divestments—in order to end the police partnerships and ensured that U.S. activists could target something local, familiar, and achievable rather than something far away that seemed impossible to win.

Significantly, many left-wing Jewish activists perceive BDS "as a viable and powerful nonviolent tool for resisting and combating the Israeli occupation from the diaspora."[11] Unlike other co-resistance activities that require them to travel halfway across the world to the Middle East, BDS actions enable activists to work toward change from their homes or their campuses in spaces where they have more power to influence their institutions. Local activists in the United States may feel powerless to influence the Israeli Supreme Court or the Israeli military, but they can certainly have a direct influence on what company their school contracts with or with whom their local police force trains.

According to one BDS activist, "Most BDS resolutions and campaigns on college campuses are not actually focused on Israeli corporations at all. They're mostly focused on American corporations that profit off of Israel's apartheid policies. So whether that's multinational corporations that do arms deals in Israel or build surveillance systems for walls, or the police exchanges, the BDS campaigns focus on things that are based in the US."[12] This ensures that the campaigns have a recognizable target that can be adjusted based on a specific context, which makes the tactics malleable and achievable. But it also counters the objection of many right-wing Jews and BDS opponents who claim that the movement targets Jewish and Israeli businesses in a manner that is inherently antisemitic.

Enter the diverse coalition of student activists at Tufts. A Freedom of Information Act request made by JVP revealed that Tufts' director of Public and Environmental Safety, Kevin Maguire, went on the ADL-sponsored trip to Israel in December 2017.[13] In the spring immediately thereafter, 216 members of the Tufts community, including students, faculty, staff, and alumni, wrote and signed a letter expressing concern over the participation of a Tufts official in this trip.[14] A few months later, the Tufts chapter of SJP organized the Deadly Exchange campaign, which centered on putting a vote to the entire student body that would, among other things, prevent Tufts University Police Department (TUPD) personnel from attending similar training programs.

The language of the referendum that students voted on read,

Do you support Tufts University administration 1) apologizing for sending the former Tufts police chief to an intensive week-long course led by senior commanders in the Israel National Police, experts from Israel's intelligence and security services, and the Israeli Defense Force, 2) prohibiting TUPD officers from attending programs based on military strategies and/or similar international trips in the future, and 3) refining the vetting process to prevent prior program attendees from being hired, not including veterans who may have been stationed or trained abroad during their service?[15]

The referendum was the culmination of a two-year organizing campaign that saw students exert tremendous energy into ensuring that the referendum passed by capitalizing on the timing of Maguire's trip to Israel.[16] Despite the tiresome work, students were largely energized by the diverse coalition of student groups that endorsed the campaign. According to one student activist, "With this campaign and coalition we are bringing together a community of Black, Brown, queer, trans, Palestinian, Jewish, and other students who are invested in fighting for each other's safety and know that it will never come from increasing the power of the U.S. and Israeli police and military."[17] This diverse coalition was integral to their success because they harnessed the collective power of the student body, using a clear lesson from social movement organizing. Furthermore, the student activists clearly articulated why this issue of policing and community safety matters to most constituents on campus and not only to Palestinians, in part by drawing on language and strategies of the Black Lives Matter movement and the galvanizing moment of the George Floyd protests across the country earlier that year.

Most of the student activists working on the campaign, regardless of their identities, endured a widespread and vicious smear campaign by mostly off-campus pro-Israel lobby groups that wanted to impact the results of the voting. The smears referred to the referendum as a "modern-day antisemitic blood libel" and demonized the activists as anti-Israel, antisemitic, and misguided.[18] These dangerous smears and charges of antisemitism are predictable backlash to Palestine solidarity organizing on campus and have emerged as a strategy used by the pro-Israel establishment to quell any BDS campaigns on campuses and beyond.[19] Yet despite this constant demonization and vilification, student activists at Tufts and elsewhere continue to fight for justice through End the Deadly Exchange and other BDS campaigns.

The successful campaign at Tufts brings many elements of the BDS movement into sharp relief, including showing how young American

Jews fit into its broader scope. First, the SJP chapter worked closely with JVP, an established national Jewish organization with ties to and direct experience with BDS, in order to launch and implement the campaign. Second, the Tufts campaign shows the possibilities of using the tactics of BDS in strategic ways by targeting something tangibly related to a community that could lead to material (and symbolic) gains. In this case, that was seeking to end the partnership between campus police and the Israeli military, thus forcing Tufts to cease its indirect complicity in Israel's occupation and human rights abuses of Palestinians. Third, it elucidates the ways that the charge of antisemitism is constantly levied against those who support and engage in BDS. Finally, the success of the Tufts campaign shows how BDS relies on building solidarity through coalitions and that Jewish support of BDS campaigns is sometimes integral to their success in part due to their ability to diffuse accusations of antisemitism.

BDS as a Strategic Method of Nonviolent Resistance

The Palestinian call for boycotts, divestment, and sanctions against Israel is the largest global movement advocating for justice for Palestinians. If one were to only consume the mainstream media, it might appear as though Palestinian resistance is singularly about armed struggle. All too often people ask, "Where is the Palestinian Gandhi?" or "Why don't Palestinians use nonviolence more frequently?" These questions, while seemingly legitimate, are rooted in ignorance and orientalism.[20] As the largest movement of Palestinian resistance, the BDS movement is full of Palestinian activists committed to nonviolence as a strategy who turned to the BDS methods to further propel their case for justice. Above all else, the BDS movement must be understood as the largest nonviolent campaign for Palestinian rights in history. As such, its origin story is best understood in its proper historical context.

In 2005, Palestinians were reeling from the catastrophic ramifications of the incredibly violent and bloody Second Intifada. Coming in the wake of the failed peace process during the hopeful Oslo period, the Second Intifada led to a more deeply entrenched occupation with more repression from the Israeli military regime alongside increased settlement activity throughout the West Bank and East Jerusalem. According to scholar Stephen Zunes, "By this point, most Palestinians recognized that in addition to being flagrantly illegal and morally reprehensible, terrorism was politically counterproductive. There was also an awareness that armed struggle against Israeli Occupation forces, while more legitimate, would be utterly futile and lead to additional suffering on a massive scale."[21]

As a result, Palestinian activists from across a broad and diverse spectrum of civil society called for a widespread and coordinated effort of nonviolent strategic resistance to the Israeli regime, its mechanisms of unfettered state violence, and its utter disregard for international law. Much like the co-resistance model discussed in the previous chapter, BDS emerged out of the confluence of the failure of the Oslo Accords with the nonviolent joint activism that materialized during the Second Intifada. According to journalist Nathan Thrall, much to the chagrin of the Israeli government and its supporters, "the nonviolent activism of the second intifada was a prelude to what would become a worldwide boycott campaign."[22]

Palestinian activists decided to make a widespread call for solidarity with Palestinians by "people of conscience" around the world to support their struggle for justice by participating in a campaign to boycott, divest from, and apply international sanctions to Israel. To that end, on July 9, 2005, Palestinian civil society groups launched the call for a global BDS movement, thereby launching "what is now widely recognized as a different phase in the global struggle for Palestinian freedom, justice, and self-determination."[23] This date was strategically planned as it represented the one-year anniversary of the International Court of Justice's advisory opinion on the illegality of Israel's separation wall.[24]

A coalition of 173 Palestinian civil society groups made the BDS call, representing a broad range across the political and geographic spectrums including trade unions, activists, academics, and cultural organizations. These organizations, representing Palestinian civil society, called upon the international community to implement this call "until Israel meets its obligation to recognize the Palestinian people's inalienable right to self-determination and fully complies with the precepts of international law by: (1) Ending its occupation and colonization of all Arab lands and dismantling the Wall; (2) Recognizing the fundamental rights of the Arab-Palestinian citizens of Israel to full equality; and (3) Respecting, protecting and promoting the rights of Palestinian refugees to return to their homes and properties as stipulated in UN resolution 194."[25]

These three demands are all in and of themselves significant toward ensuring Palestinian justice, but they all revolve around the necessity of Israel complying with international law. This emphasis on international law is vital to the movement's successful framing since critics of the BDS movement often claim that the movement advocates for a one-state solution and therefore an end to Israel's existence as a Jewish (and democratic) state. But this is an erroneous understanding of the BDS movement, which has openly published their platform, for all to see, on the internet: "The BDS movement does not advocate for a particular solution to the conflict and does not call for either a 'one state solution' or a 'two state solution.' Instead, BDS focuses on the realization of basic rights and the implementation of international law."[26]

Palestinian civil society ensured that each of these demands would include a particular segment of the fragmented Palestinian population. The first demand undergirds justice for the stateless Palestinians living in the West Bank, Gaza, and East Jerusalem and ensures that the wall, the most visible mechanism of Israel's architecture of occupation, is dismantled. This demand is most fundamentally about ending Israel's occupation and settlement expansion. The second demand focuses on Palestinian citizens of Israel, who compose 22 percent of the state's citizens. Finally, the third and most controversial demand, which includes Palestinian refugees living in the diaspora, mandates the return of refugees to the homes and properties taken from them as a result of the 1948 and 1967 wars. Currently numbering more than seven million people, Palestinian refugees compose the largest and longest unresolved refugee case in the world.[27]

This threefold framing of the demands is all quite significant. As journalist Nathan Thrall explains,

> The chief innovation of the BDS call was not in the tactics that it advocated: boycott and divestment campaigns were already pervasive in 2005, and even sanctions and arms embargoes had been proposed previously, including by the UN general assembly. What was new about BDS was that it took disparate campaigns to pressure Israel and united them around three clear demands, with one for each major component of the Palestin-

ian people. First, freedom for the residents of the occupied territories; second, equality for the Palestinian citizens of Israel; and third, justice for Palestinian refugees in the diaspora—the largest group—including the right to return to their homes.[28]

Though these demands clearly stipulate justice for each of the three different geographical sectors of Palestinian society, it is this final one, about the right of return for Palestinian refugees, that most frequently leads to the criticism that the BDS movement is both antisemitic and committed to Israel's destruction. According to BDS critics, demanding the right of return for seven million Palestinian refugees would alter Israel's demographic balance such that Jews would no longer maintain their demographic majority. This would end the Jewish character of the state. Such a goal, say these critics, is a veiled call for Israel's destruction, which is also antisemitic.[29]

At the same time, there are some people in the BDS movement who advocate for an end to Israel, which leads to tremendous fear among some Jews and pro-Israel groups. It is quite difficult to delineate those critical of Israel from those who are antisemitic. As Aaron Hahn Tapper notes, "Many antisemitism watchdog groups, such as the Anti-Defamation League (ADL), label anti-Israelism (also referred to as anti-Zionism), or criticism of Israeli governmental policies, as 'the new antisemitism.' Even though some people who are critical of the State of Israel and its policies are motivated by antisemitism, certainly not all are."[30] It is important to note, therefore, that there are non-Jewish participants in the BDS movement who are antisemitic and who are motivated by a hatred of Jews. This must be taken seriously and is one potential place where Jewish BDS supporters can have an impact.

However, in the eyes of most BDS activists, and Palestine solidarity activists more broadly, the call for the return of Palestinian refugees and support for the demands of the BDS movement is solely about justice for Palestinians and is not a call for the destruction of Israel. As they have made clear, and as Jewish activists involved in the movement have repeatedly emphasized, Jewish safety and Palestinian justice are not mutually exclusive; they must go hand in hand. Interpreting the Palestinian demand for the right of return as an antisemitic move toward Israel's destruction fundamentally misunderstands the fact that Jewish safety, and Israel's future, must be predicated on Palestinian justice as well as the radical realignment of Jewish values toward the realization that Jewish and Palestinian liberation are inextricably linked to one another.

Jewish activists supporting the BDS movement argue that the current Zionist and pro-Israel model of Jewish safety, which is based on Jewish supremacy in Israel, is not sustainable because it involves human rights abuses toward Palestinians. In turn, this makes Israel and its Jewish population less safe; increased human rights abuses lead to increased violent resistance from Palestinian militants. If Israel continues its current policies toward Palestinians, conflict will persist and Israel may not always be victorious. The social and political cost is quite high and has led to the increasingly radical right-wing tendencies of the current Israeli political system, resulting in the increased international isolation of Israel alongside the strengthening of the global pro-Palestine movement for justice. Jewish safety must therefore be decoupled from Jewish political supremacy in Israel if the safety of Jews is to be sustainable.

Em Hilton, an Australian Jewish activist based in London who is deeply involved with the Center for Jewish Nonviolence, makes this point quite clearly. As she wrote in an op-ed during the May 2021 Israel-Hamas War, "A feeling of safety cannot be predicated on the oppression and subjugation of another people, on ethnic cleansing and state sanctioned violence."[31] Furthermore, she contends, when charges of antisemitism or the destruction of Israel are levied at Palestinian solidarity activists, it "restricts our ability to build greater solidarity and joint struggle based in equality and shared humanity. When Palestinians tell us that this is a call for liberation, not genocide, we should believe them."[32] This articulation of the fact that justice and freedom for Palestinians should not be seen as a threat to Jews extends to the demands of the BDS movement, which seeks justice for Palestinians and *not* the destruction of Israel. Rather, BDS is about using a particular set of nonviolent strategies to force Israel to comply with international law and to end its institutionalized and systemic abuses of Palestinian human rights.

The BDS call is therefore based on using a set of tried and trusted tactics of nonviolent resistance that have already been successfully implemented in other historical and cultural contexts, including against the oppressive Jim Crow laws in the U.S. South and most famously against the policies of apartheid in South Africa.[33] Learning from these past successes, BDS utilizes a framework that is simultaneously top-down, as evidenced through international sanctions, and grassroots organizing, seen in the use of boycotts and divestment campaigns in both local and global contexts. The ultimate goal of the BDS movement is to apply international pressure to force Israel to comply with international law and change its treatment of Palestinians by making it into a pariah state in the same way that South Africa was ostracized by the world during its apartheid era.[34]

Drawing on the South African anti-apartheid movement, Palestinian activists initially sought to replicate some of the strategies that helped end apartheid in their own fight for justice. They were particularly inspired by South Africa's successful academic and cultural boycott. By adopting the academic and cultural boycott from South Africa, Palestinian activists distinguished between the earlier BDS campaigns that focused on corporate profiteering and cultural boycotts intended to isolate Israel until it complies with international law. South African activists first called on the international community to boycott South African academic, sports, and cultural institutions in the 1950s, but it wasn't until the 1980s that this boycott reached a fever pitch.[35] The sports boycott was particularly powerful as the white community in South Africa was impacted by the international community's boycott of their beloved Springboks rugby team, which was barred from competing in international competition.[36]

Inspired by these successes, in 2004 Palestinian activists preceded the broader BDS call by creating the Palestinian Academic and Cultural Boycott of Israel (PACBI), which has advocated for a boycott of Israeli academic and cultural institutions due to their complicity in Israel's human rights violations.[37] Applying strategic boycotts to these institutions, as well as pressuring international artists to boycott Israel by refusing to perform there, much like the cultural boycott in South Africa, the PACBI catapulted BDS into the international conversation on Palestinian rights. In pressuring international artists to boycott Israel and organizing to prevent Israel from participating in international FIFA competitions, the PACBI laid the groundwork for a robust BDS movement and started the process of turning Israel into a pariah state in the eyes of left-wing progressives around the world. PACBI, along with the wider BDS movement, seeks to bring Israel's human rights violations into sharp relief on a global scale, raising awareness and combatting Israel's "sportwashing" attempts to enhance its image.[38]

In drawing on this history, BDS uses a set of tried-and-true tactics of social movement organizing to end Israeli state violence toward Palestinians.[39] The call for BDS against Israel makes it clear that anyone who supports these tactics and believes in Palestinian rights is welcome to participate in BDS efforts, including Israeli Jews and diaspora Jews.[40] Jews did, in fact, take the Palestinian civil society call for BDS seriously and have been part of the movement since its inception in Israel, the United States, and globally. According to Omar Barghouti, one of the Palestinian founders of the BDS movement, "Anti-colonial Jewish Israeli BDS supporters play a significant role in exposing Israel's regime of oppression and advocating for its isolation."[41] In Israel, for example, a group called Boycott from Within was founded by a group of Israeli citizens (both Jewish and Palestinian) to support the BDS movement from within Israel. Since it emerged as an internal support to the BDS movement, it has been essential to the growth of boycott and divestment campaigns in Israel and around the world, acting as a moral compass of Israelis who support the boycott of their own country. More relevant to this book, however, is the presence and impact Jews in the United States have had in and on the BDS movement.

Jewish Voice for Peace and the Role of Jews in BDS

Though most Jews in the United States either don't support or have never heard of BDS, there is growing backing for the movement among Jewish American youth. As discussed elsewhere in this book, Jews in the United States have the potential to impact Israeli policies and can influence U.S. governmental support for Israel in many ways. As Stephen Zunes argues, "Using BDS to challenge Israeli policies is one way of attempting to redress the ways in which Israel is already being singled out by the U.S. government for support."[42] Though statistical survey data show that the BDS movement does not have widespread support from U.S. Jews, the fact that surveys are beginning to ask about the BDS movement indicates its growing influence.

According to the 2020 Pew Survey on Jewish Americans, 43 percent of American Jews oppose BDS and 44 percent of American Jews haven't even heard of it, leaving a mere 10 percent of American Jews who support BDS.[43] Interestingly, though most American Jews don't support BDS, the fact that the survey asked questions about BDS indicates that the movement has successfully inserted itself into the American Jewish conversations about Israel, which is significant since the previous Pew Survey on Jewish Americans, conducted in 2013, did not include questions about BDS. These statistics complement the findings of the University of Maryland Critical Issues Poll, published in January 2020, which showed that 27 percent of Americans (Jewish and not Jewish) who have heard of BDS either somewhat or strongly support the BDS movement.[44]

Perhaps more significantly, even if they don't support the movement itself, 42 percent of Americans support the tactics that BDS uses and believe that it is a peaceful way of opposing Israeli occupation.[45] Although opposition to boycotts against Israel remains widespread among American Jews, research shows that a growing number of young Jews in the United States support the tactics and strategies of BDS. This fact is most prominently evidenced through a survey conducted by JStreet in November 2020 revealing that 13 percent of Jews in the United States and 22 percent of those under age forty support a full boycott of Israel.[46]

Though these statistics reveal that generating support for BDS within the American Jewish community is an uphill battle, many young American Jews are participating in the movement because they believe it provides the opportunity to highlight a strategy of nonviolent resistance to Israeli policies of state violence. According to Rae Abileah, a veteran activist who was instrumental in pushing young Jewish American resistance to occupation into the mainstream, "Here in the United States, while lobbying Congress is important, it's up to the grassroots to lead, seeing as our elected representatives are still in thrall to the far-right Israel lobby—AIPAC specifically. Boycott, divestment, and sanctions (BDS) campaigns offer a way for people to help take the profit out of the Occupation and to focus attention on Israel's flagrant violations of international law. . . . BDS offers activists a way to support human rights without waiting around for the U.S. government to broker a peace deal."[47]

Numerous BDS activists reiterated a similar sentiment in my interviews with them, noting the significance of "hitting Israel in the pocketbook" and ensuring constant external pressure on Israel and the United

States to end the occupation. In the words of one BDS activist, "I think BDS is especially important in the American and American Jewish context because the U.S. is bankrolling Israel, and the fact that we give them all this money, which then bounces back to our weapons manufacturers . . . is awful. Once you hone in on that and bring people's attention to the ways that their lifestyles and their institutions are actively complicit, that's when the game starts to change."[48]

Offered as a tangible, nonviolent method of resistance to Israeli violations of human rights and noncompliance with international law, BDS is now a firmly entrenched internationally known element of the Palestinian struggle against Israeli state violence and oppression. In fact, it is the most significant and effective contemporary form of international solidarity with the Palestinian struggle for justice.[49] Omar Barghouti suggests that support for BDS is now "a litmus test for meaningful international solidarity with the Palestinian liberation struggle."[50] So it should not be surprising that many Jewish activists in the Palestine solidarity movement see BDS as a key element to their solidarity and activism.

Invigorated by a broad coalition of organizational support, both in and beyond the Jewish community, BDS became much more widespread and popular in the United States despite the efforts of the Israeli government and the American Jewish Establishment to quash and delegitimize it. A few Jewish groups, including JVP, Independent Jewish Voices, the International Jewish Anti-Zionist Network, and American Jews for a Just Peace, among others, have publicly endorsed BDS since it grew into a full-fledged movement and are active participants in the movement. These groups bravely go against the current in the Jewish community and actively present a dissenting voice to the Jewish Establishment seeking to silence BDS and its activists.

Interestingly, one commonality that the Jewish groups who endorse BDS have is their adamantly anti-Zionist political stance. In fact, "the crucial difference between the Jewish groups endorsing or supporting BDS and those that opposed it was the separation of Jewishness from Zionism, and the willingness to combat, or at least consider an alternative to, the fundamentally racist notion of a Zionist state, while still upholding Jewish identity."[51] This is a key point for understanding the participation of young American Jews in the broader social movement for Palestinian justice and liberation. Jews who support other tactics criticizing Israel and its occupation may still identify as Zionist. But most of the Jews who embrace BDS identify as anti-Zionist or non-Zionist. Integral to this identification and the willingness to accept BDS and its demands is the ability to let go of the idea of a Jewish-majority state (examined more thoroughly in chapter 2). Whereas anti-occupation tactics such as targeting the American Jewish Establishment and participating in co-resistance activities on the ground in Palestine/Israel are more palatable to those who identify as liberal Zionists, BDS activists are almost exclusively anti-Zionist. This is one reason why the Jewish Establishment works tirelessly to discredit BDS and to exclude BDS activists from the Jewish community.

JVP is the primary American Jewish organization active in the BDS movement. Arguably, it has cemented itself as the premier Jewish space for anti-Zionist and BDS organizing. Founded in 1996 in Berkeley, California, by three young left-wing Jewish women, JVP has grown into one of the most important and the most maligned (by Jews) Jewish organizations in the American Jewish peace camp. At its core, JVP works at the grassroots level, both in the Jewish milieu and in the broader community, to lend a Jewish voice to the movement for justice in Palestine, including ending Israeli occupation. Since its inception, JVP has been deemed too radical by the Jewish Establishment. They continue to be ostracized by the American Jewish Establishment and labeled antisemitic despite their commitment to maintaining a vibrant Jewish identity.[52]

The group has never been accepted by the mainstream Jewish community, and the organization has been written out of or glossed over in media articles reporting on Jewish anti-occupation activism in the United States, which represents one meaningful way that American Jews learn about things in American Jewish life. For example, in a 2021 article published in *Jewish Currents* about IfNotNow, Aaron Freedman dismissively writes about JVP's status during the cataclysmic summer of 2014, referring to them as a "small but active group."[53] Though this type of reductive analysis of JVP's role in the Jewish American movement working for justice in Palestine/Israel is commonplace, Rebecca Vilkomerson, the former executive director of JVP, took her displeasure to Twitter, where she has a meaningful following. Noting the article's dismissive tone, she offered data showing the significance and growth of the organization and its solidified place as a major player in the movement.

By 2014, JVP had already played a considerable role in two major BDS-related victories: the Presbyterian Church's divestment campaign and the successful efforts to get TIAA-CREF to divest from companies that profit from the occupation.[54] Vilkomerson also offered statistical data to support JVP's importance and their evolution as a major participant in the Palestine solidarity movement. "After dozens of actions, incl. civil disobedience in summer of 2014," she tweeted, "JVP tripled in size in every measure. 'Small but active' is a pretty serious erasure of the largest & most dynamic org in this sphere."[55] What started as a small group of activists meeting in a Berkeley living room has since grown into an organization with more than sixty chapters across the country, a staff of more than twenty-five, over twenty thousand dues-paying members, and over two hundred thousand recipients of the organization's mailing list.[56]

JVP is a relatively large and long-lasting organization with international renown in the Palestine solidarity movement. It has grown in part because the organization intentionally stakes out some of the most radical positions within the Jewish ecosystem of Palestine solidarity activism, including declaring itself anti-Zionist and fully supporting BDS. While JVP is a multigenerational organization, IfNotNow has been youth centered since its inception. Interestingly, the Jewish Currents article that dismisses the importance of JVP as a national organization was actually able to assist in the growth and prominence of IfNotNow. Furthermore, JVP's strength and radicalism is one of the things that enabled IfNotNow to grow so quickly. When contrasted with JVP, IfNot-Now, which did not take a position on either BDS or Zionism, seemed like a more palatable option for young Jewish activists seeking a place to participate in Palestine solidarity activism.

One of the many valuable contributions of JVP to Jewish Palestine solidarity activism is that it has dramatically shifted the goalposts of what is understood as acceptable for Jewish activism vis-à-vis Israel. Over the course of more than a quarter century of activism, JVP has participated in countless anti-occupation campaigns and diverse interfaith and multiracial coalitions, started a wing of political advocacy to pressure members of Congress to put conditions on U.S. aid to Israel, and created innovative curricula to teach about topics such as the Israeli occupation and the Palestinian Nakba. JVP also formed a Rabbinic Advisory Council and an Academic Advisory Council in order to develop a network of rabbis and academics committed to justice in Palestine. Perhaps most significantly, in 2015 JVP as an organization officially endorsed BDS through a vote of the entire JVP membership.[57]

After the vote, JVP released a statement confirming their commitment to justice: "We join with communities of conscience around the world in supporting Palestinians, who call for BDS until the Israeli government [complies with the three BDS demands]. . . . JVP is committed to supporting and organizing all kinds of powerful and strategic campaigns to secure a common future where Palestinians, Israeli Jews, and all the people of Israel/Palestine may live with dignity, security, and peace."[58] Though the American Jewish Establishment viewed JVP's endorsement as too radical, that paled in comparison to the earthquake JVP caused in the Jewish organizational world a few years later when, in 2019, they adopted anti-Zionism as its official political position.[59] By declaring themselves unequivocally opposed to Zionism, JVP both opened themselves up to a maelstrom of hate (primarily from Jews) and created a much-needed Jewish home and organizing space for Jewish anti-Zionist activists in need of a validating and welcoming environment to engage in Palestine solidarity activism.[60]

In addition to being a Jewish home for anti-Zionist Jewish activists, JVP also solidified the role of Jewish activists in the much larger BDS movement. As is the case with any social movement that wants to succeed, BDS activists know that building a broad-based coalition is integral to its chances of success, which means that there is an important role for Jews to play in BDS alongside Palestinian and other activists. Though Jewish activists who engage in BDS understand that it is a unique form of Palestinian-led co-resistance, there are four key ways that American Jews participate meaningfully in this arena. First, Jews show up as allies in the struggle for Palestinian liberation. As the new wave of co-resistance activism teaches, the presence of Jews as allies is symbolically meaningful as it represents a counternarrative to the hegemonic viewpoint that Jews and Palestinians are enemies. The presence of Jewish allies in the BDS movement is particularly important because those who engage in BDS are slandered and demonized more than activists who engage with many other methods or strategies of Palestine solidarity activism.

The most common way that the pro-Israel establishment discredits and smears BDS activists is by calling them antisemitic. Accusations of antisemitism constitute a widespread and effective tool in silencing Palestinian solidarity activism. Therefore, the second core way that Jews can make an important contribution to the BDS movement is by deflecting such smears. Jewish BDS activists can make it clear that boycotts, divestment, and sanctions levied at Israel are not inherently based on antisemitism but rather are rooted in the principles of justice, equality, and human rights for Palestinians, which do not need to come at the direct expense of Jews. One activist who was deeply involved in BDS organizing when she was a student pointedly told me that "we need a Jewish wing of the BDS movement because we need somebody to deflect accusations of antisemitism."[61] This same sentiment was repeatedly mentioned by BDS activists I spoke with.

All of these activists also agreed that antisemitism exists in the BDS movement but that it is not widespread. As Jews they can deflect the smears while also educating others and resisting the claim that Palestine solidarity is coterminous with antisemitism. When Jews are present in BDS campaigns, they can be the ones to respond to antisemitism and use the opportunity to teach about histories of Jewish oppression and persecution. According to one activist, there is tremendous value in Jews taking on these actions. "Having Jewish people do that," she said, "is monumentally important because it is one of the most effective ways to materially impact the opinions of the activists, meaning that it could actually change people's views and prevent future instances of antisemitism."[62]

Furthermore, some BDS campaigns are best led by Jews because they require confronting Jewish organizations. The Deadly Exchange program, for example, has close ties to the American Jewish Establishment, including powerful Jewish groups like the ADL and AIPAC. It would be more difficult for non-Jewish activists to challenge U.S.-Israel police exchanges because, as the Tufts campaign brought into focus, the charges of antisemitism fly fast at the activists. Since JVP, as a Jewish organization, led the Deadly Exchange campaign, it meant that groups like the Tufts SJP chapter could build a coalition of activists to take on this BDS target in a meaningful way.

Finally, as previously mentioned, many Jewish BDS activists, especially young American Jews on campus, need a safe space to organize as Jews. According to a veteran BDS activist, the significance of BDS organizing in a Jewish context cannot be understated:

> In college organizing, especially, there are a lot of people who are working through their feelings and thoughts in real time as they're doing the activism. Typically, college students are forming political opinions and trying things on and making decisions on what is right for them. Therefore, having other Jews to work through your feelings about Zionism, or your feelings about Israel, or BDS, is really important for a lot of the young people because they didn't always feel comfortable going to SJP. That was not the right place to have those feelings. You can't go to SJP and say you're having all these feelings about Israel. But if you have a place that's with other Jews, that's a more open space for folks to have those conversations, then it makes a big difference.[63]

Recent studies show that there is not an abundance of antisemitism on campus despite claims by mainstream Jewish organizations about a rise in antisemitism on campus due to BDS activism.[64] Despite the inaccuracy of this contention, the discourse still circulates that BDS campaigns on campus make them less safe for Jews.[65] In fact, it is tensions between pro-Israel Jewish students and Palestinian solidarity activists that most often make Jewish students uncomfortable, especially when discussing Israel.[66] Simply witnessing this political conflict manifest on college campuses makes some Jewish students feel unsafe, even if incidents of antisemitism have not occurred. Since Zionist rhetoric equates Jewish identity and Jewish safety with support for the State of Israel, Jewish students who have been immersed in mainstream pro-Israel rhetoric may perceive legitimate political disagreements as an attack on their identities.

Further, such Jewish students have a welcoming and safe Jewish environment where they can go: Hillel, which has explicitly rejected BDS supporters. In 2010, as a result of a rising wave of BDS resolutions on campuses, Hillel International developed an official policy prohibiting Hillel chapters from hosting or cosponsoring an event with individuals or organizations that Hillel believed to be anti-Israel or that supported the BDS movement. In what they refer to as the Standards of Partnership, Hillel states that they "will not partner with, house, or host organizations, groups, or speakers that as a matter of policy or practice: Deny the right of Israel to exist as a Jewish and democratic state with secure and recognized borders; Delegitimize, demonize, or apply a double standard to Israel; Support boycott of, divestment from, or sanctions against the State of Israel; Exhibit a pattern of disruptive behavior towards campus events or guest speakers or foster an atmosphere of incivility."[67]

The Standards of Partnership policy, which was based on "the three Ds of antisemitism" (Demonization, Double Standards, and Delegitimization) originally articulated by Natan Sharansky, who at the time served in the Israeli government as the minister in charge of Jewish diaspora affairs, effectively shut the doors of the largest Jewish on-campus space to countless Jewish student activists across the country.[68] Anyone deemed to delegitimize, demonize, or subject Israel to double standards—as they believe BDS does—is considered antisemitic and is thus not allowed to partner with Hillel. Furthermore, the Standards of Partnership policy led to Jewish BDS activists on campus experiencing vitriolic treatment from pro-Israel students with the backing of Hillel and other right-wing groups such as Stand With Us and Campus Watch. Though the Standards of Partnership did not begin the demonization of BDS activists, even Jewish ones, it most certainly played a major role in cementing BDS as the absolute red line in Jewish communal spaces, especially on college campuses.

Despite this codification of BDS as a political boundary in the Jewish community, Jewish activists refused to acquiesce to Hillel's attempt to silence Palestine solidarity activism on campuses. The most profound student response to this silencing occurred at Swarthmore College, where Jewish students declared their campus had the country's first Open Hillel, a new student-led group that would brazenly defy the Hillel International guidelines.[69] Since its founding in 2012, Open Hillel (mentioned in chapter 1) has become a significant space on college campuses to challenge the acceptability of Jewish participation in Palestine solidarity activism, which has continued since their 2020 rebranding as Jews on Our Own Terms. As Atalia Omer notes, Open Hillel's "challenge to the Jewish establishment's policing of the boundaries of debate indeed attracts a diversity of Jewish supporters, located across the spectrum regarding relations to Zionism and Israel, on the one hand, and BDS campaigns, on the other."[70] Alongside other Jewish organizations that counter Hillel's exclusion of Jewish activists, Open Hillel functions to disrupt the status quo surrounding the question of Palestinian rights. It challenges Jewish communal red lines that ostracize BDS supporters from inclusion in mainstream Jewish spaces.[71]

Open Hillel is significant to this movement as it combatted the red lines and opened room for dissent within Jewish communities on campus, but they do not actively organize BDS campaigns. JVP stepped in, somewhat reluctantly, to help Jewish students with various BDS initiatives. Despite their initial reticence, JVP's national organization eventually capitulated due to student interest. Students on campuses across the country demanded that JVP start chapters on campus because they wanted a "specifically Jewish space, and specifically a JVP space, for Palestine Solidarity work to happen."[72] JVP is successful on college campuses because there has been such high demand for what they can do because Jewish student support for BDS is growing and JVP is the Jewish organization best equipped to assist.

For many Jewish student activists on campuses, starting JVP chapters was a saving grace that enabled them to continue the activist work to which they were committed. Though they were shut out of Hillel and were often excluded from their synagogues upon returning home, JVP empowered them to organize around Palestine/Israel issues, such as BDS, all while feeling proud of their Jewishness. Marla, an activist who experienced both the ostracization from community and the resurgent feeling of acceptance through JVP and BDS activism, articulates the struggle well:

Some of my organizing experience is in the context of starting a Jewish Voice for Peace chapter. Being one of the few Jews [in my community] that is publicly in support of things like BDS or criticizing Zionism meant that I was not very welcome. Many of the rabbis in [my community] have blocked me from being part of their synagogue and some have spat on me or otherwise let me know I'm not welcome. Although I continued to feel Jewish because it had been so formative for my entire life, I felt very disconnected from Jewish community. That changed when I joined Jewish Voice for Peace. I started doing some work with them . . . and then I cofounded a JVP chapter. Since then I have been able to find more meaningful Jewish communities, primarily among other young Jews, other

Millennials and Gen Z Jews who are also engaged in anti-occupation work on some level.[73]

Marla's experience speaks to how she was able to both find Jewish community through JVP and also find support for her political activism. These red lines that transform BDS into scarlet letters have had dramatic impacts on the lives of individual activists as well as on the Jewish conversation around Palestine/Israel more broadly.

BDS and the Impacts of the Communal Red Lines

As explained, the American Jewish Establishment is preoccupied with ensuring widespread American support for Israel. Therefore they are willing to go to great lengths to ensure the continued strong ties between the two countries. Of particular importance is maintaining Jewish connections to and support of Israel. To that end, the Jewish Establishment created a set of guidelines that would include or exclude certain people or groups based on their politics and beliefs vis-à-vis Israel. BDS activists became the eventual target of these guidelines and the policies that accompanied them because the Jewish Establishment believed then and believes now that BDS demonizes and delegitimizes Israel in ways that are dangerous and harmful for Jews. As Atalia Omer noted, "In the same way that the supporters of BDS aim at crumbling not only the economic but also (and primarily) the symbolic and cultural capital authorizing Israeli policies, opponents of the BDS movement are concerned with bolstering their narrative. The critique articulated by BDS activists challenges Israel's moral standing and is accordingly interpreted by the political echelon as a symbolic threat to its identity."[74]

This interpretation of BDS—as a threat to Israel's Jewish character—led the Reut Institute, one of Israel's most notable think tanks, to argue that BDS and Palestinian armed resistance are the two most significant existential threats facing Israel.[75] In a Reut Institute policy paper from 2010 that condemns BDS, they recommended a new strategy for the Israeli government: to direct significant human and financial resources to stop the spread of the many international hubs of BDS activism. While this strategy has been applied globally, the American Jewish Establishment implemented it in attempts to eradicate BDS activism in the Jewish community in the United States. In other words, the Reut Institute's articulation of BDS as a threat was instrumental in creating the very red lines that excluded BDS activists from mainstream Jewish communal spaces, as seen with the case of Hillel International's Standards of Partnership. These communal red lines make clear the inclusion/exclusion of the Jewish Establishment regarding "loyalty to the collective and differentiation between insiders and outsiders" and shunning BDS supporters as outsiders.[76]

In order to enforce these red lines, pro-Israel advocates developed an intense machine to halt and silence BDS activism thanks to financial and political support from the Israeli government. According to most activists I interviewed, pro-Israel advocates developed these tactics because (1) they felt they were losing the ideological battle and (2) pro-BDS efforts were detracting pro-Israel advocates from their mission to defend Jews and Israel at all costs. BDS threatens the status quo, which they are willing to go to great lengths to maintain. They are also scared of the "delegitimization" of Israel, an idea the Reut Institute used to sound the alarm bells to Israel's defenders.[77]

The Reut Institute's role in developing the anti-BDS campaign cannot be understated. Their published reports serve as the foundation of the pro-Israel establishment's response to the BDS movement and its activists. For example, the Zionist Organization of America (ZOA), a far right-wing organization, AIPAC, and the Anti-Defamation League all worked tirelessly to target individual BDS activists and the larger movement as antisemitic and dangerous for the global Jewish community. Among pro-Israel organizations, only JStreet upheld the right to free speech by BDS activists, even as they condemned the movement for its "punitive approach to Israel."[78] T'ruah: The Rabbinic Call for Human Rights similarly disagrees with the BDS movement itself but vociferously defends the right to boycott as a free speech issue and a Jewish value.[79]

Just five years after Palestinian civil society issued the BDS call, the Jewish Establishment in the United States started targeting the BDS movement with coordinated and well-funded efforts aimed at delegitimizing the movement, and its tactics, altogether. In 2010, the Jewish Federations of North America and the Jewish Council for Public Affairs (JCPA) launched the Israel Action Network (IAN). Established with millions of dollars in seed funding, IAN was tasked with opposing BDS campaigns.[80] According to activist Sriram Ananth,

> The millions of dollars in funding was for hiring people in universities, NGOs, civic institutions, etc., to primarily combat BDS. One could see the effects of these heavily funded efforts almost immediately. The Reut Institute contacted many BDS groups around North America with strange requests for meetings. Zionist groups on campuses across the nation targeted BDS efforts and the Palestine-solidarity groups via large national bodies like the Israel on Campus Coalition (ICC), which includes Hillel, the Jewish Community Relations Council (JCRC), and almost all other Zionist groups as members. Various Students for Justice in Palestine (SJP) chapters involved in Palestine-solidarity work across North America were attacked in different ways, including having their posters torn down and members slandered.[81]

In addition to targeting student activists, the anti-BDS machine attacked university faculty. In one extremely high-profile case, Palestinian professor Steven Salaita had his appointment to a tenured professorship in American Indian studies revoked by the University of Illinois Urbana-Champaign just days before he was to begin. The university's president and board of directors had buckled to pressure from pro-Israel lobby groups who cited his support for BDS as evidence of his being unfit to serve on the university's faculty.[82] "Witch hunts" intended to eradicate BDS and pro-Palestine activism on campuses like the one that prevented Salaita from teaching at the University of Illinois effectively suppress academic freedom with the goal of eliminating BDS from campus politics. As part of these targeted campaigns, websites like the Canary Mission (see chapter 1) created "blacklists" of campus activists who participate in BDS in the attempt of quelling BDS campaigns.

As a direct result of the Jewish Establishment's successful campaign to delegitimize BDS, supporting BDS in the Jewish community became as controversial as being a Jesus-believing Jew, more commonly referred to as Messianic Judaism.[83] When it comes to the quintessential red line in Jewish communities regarding "who is a Jew," the only thing Jewish denominations can agree upon is that this subgroup should be rejected by the Jewish community. Similarly, support for BDS became a way to exclude Jews from participation and belonging in Jewish spaces. According to one activist I interviewed, "The right has pretty successfully demonized BDS so that it becomes this scary monster. But they also successfully defined antisemitism in such a way that if you're criticizing Israel, you are criticizing all Jews."[84] As such, in their attempts to control the narrative about BDS, mainstream Jewish organizations successfully convinced the majority of American Jews that pro-BDS folks, Jewish or otherwise, have no place in American Jewish life. This myopic view has had catastrophic consequences for BDS activists, especially for Palestinian and Muslim activists who are repeatedly targeted with vicious smear attacks, but also for Jews who support BDS.

The impact of these targeted campaigns is the silencing of critics of Israel; they prevent dissenting Jewish voices from speaking out on BDS, publishing about it, or participating in BDS efforts. When I interviewed Nina, an activist and prominent member of the anti-occupation movement, she made it abundantly clear that although she has played a major role in confronting mainstream American Jewish institutions and has engaged in co-resistance activism in Palestine/Israel, including with the Center for Jewish Nonviolence, she has purposefully stayed away from engaging in BDS in any meaningful way.

When I asked her if that was as a direct result of the communal red lines that demonize BDS activists, she was unwavering in her response:

Yeah, of course it's because of the red lines. Absolutely. I think it's amazing that this whole conversation around cancel culture that is happening right now because you know who is terrified to speak their minds about Israel? Jews and Palestinians because their activism and even their thoughts have been policed for decades, but in particular this decade. I was on campus right as the BDS strategy really started and saw how it's made people terrified to speak out. Even with you, [in this anonymous interview], I still do not even feel comfortable saying to you that I support BDS. I can say that I think it is a legitimate nonviolent protest movement and I support everyone's right to engage in nonviolent resistance. Of course, personally, I support the individual Bs and Ds and Ss, and yet that three letter word, BDS, has been so effectively demonized in our culture to the point that it's just so threatening to people, and to me personally. The ability to get jobs, to get speaking opportunities, to be welcomed in communities, to be welcomed in their family's homes if you say you support the BDS movement. It has been so deeply demonized and so I don't say that I support it.[85]

Nina's support for the nonviolent tactics of BDS but refusal to publicly state her support for the movement illustrates how successful the anti-BDS machine has been in suppressing activists even as it has failed to stop its momentum. Though Nina's experience is merely one of many, it exemplifies the fear many activists feel about participating in BDS activism because of the possibility of reprisal or being ostracized from family or community.

I can personally relate to Nina's decision to remain on the sidelines of BDS activism. Though I have been an active part of movements for peace and justice in Palestine/Israel for many years, until now I have never spoken publicly or published anything about BDS. As a graduate student, I watched BDS activists on campuses across the country lose funding for their research, be passed over for job opportunities within and outside of academia, and discover their names published on "blacklist" websites such as the Canary Mission and other iterations like the SHIT (Self-Hating, Israel Threatening) List. Seeing friends, colleagues, and activists whom I admired experience such a damaging backlash for their activism scared me.[86] Even though I knew that this fear was a tactic used by the pro-Israel establishment as a political tool to silence, it was nevertheless effective.[87] For some activists, perhaps those with far more confidence and conviction than I, it is a rite of passage and great accomplishment to be listed on a pro-Israel "blacklist."[88] But for me and my hopes to have a career in the academy generally and within Jewish communities specifically, I wanted to avoid these lists at all costs. Therefore, I policed myself to avoid all BDS activities.

I was advised by friends to remain silent and not publish on or speak about BDS. I internalized the absolute necessity, for my career and for my ability to remain in communities that mattered to me, of remaining silent on BDS. This internalization was so powerful that when I was first starting research for this book, I refused to engage with BDS as a meaningful part of the anti-occupation and Palestine solidarity movement even though it is among the most, if not the most, significant and widespread methods of activism today.

I'll never forget the conversation I had with a colleague during a break from the annual Association for Jewish Studies conference where I explained my ideas and outline for this book. When she asked me why I was not planning to write a chapter on BDS, I shuddered with fear. "You want me to write about BDS?" I asked her. "I'm not protected by tenure. If I write about BDS I could lose my job. I could lose funding that I rely on for my livelihood," I quipped. "I know all of that," she calmly responded. "And yet I think you should write about BDS." She argued that without a careful examination of BDS this book would be incomplete; it would be missing a crucial element to the participation of young Jews in Palestine solidarity activism. I knew in the moment that she was right. I could not justifiably exclude BDS from the conversation about Palestine solidarity activism, especially since young American Jews are such active participants in the BDS movement. But I was so afraid, based on my internalized fear of reprisal, that for months I could not even consider writing about BDS.

Much like Nina, I fully believed in nonviolent resistance. When speaking about BDS I always made the point that BDS is the most widespread *nonviolent* global movement for justice in Palestine. I support boycotts, divestments, and sanctions as viable, legitimate, and justified strategies that social movements can and in certain cases should use. I learned the significance of boycotts in particular from a young age. As a child growing up in California in the 1980s, we never had grapes in my home. Although the Delano Grape Boycott ended before I was born, my parents supported it and never went back to buying grapes.[89] In learning about the grape boycott and hearing why my parents were such avid supporters, I came to understand the value of boycotts as a strategy of social movements to force change. Coupled with learning about this strategy of activism during the civil rights movement in the U.S. South throughout my formal education, I knew that boycotts were significantly important, and I became a big supporter of them as a strategy of change.

This naturally caused confusion for me when I encountered the BDS silencing campaign. I wondered why Jewish communities in the United States who had been so supportive of other boycotts would be so forceful in their opposition to BDS. Why wouldn't people apply their beliefs in and support of this nonviolent strategy evenly? What made Israel different? Why would those who said that BDS activists are targeting Israel be the ones singling out Israel? They support boycotts in other places and circumstances, so why wouldn't they also support them in Israel? Though this confusion about the uneven application of values and political commitments to Israel initially became evident to me through the BDS movement, I soon began to see it in every element of the Jewish Establishment's relentless defense of Israel, which inevitably led me to examine how young American Jews are forcing a reckoning about these values in the Jewish community.

Having followed the BDS movement closely since its inception, learning about its tactics and principled stance on issues of justice, I realized that it plays a significant part in building a global intersectional movement for justice. I was impressed to see how quick the BDS movement was to respond to other struggles of justice. Notably, in the aftermath of the murder of Michael Brown by police in Ferguson, Missouri, and the subsequent Black-led uprisings on the streets of U.S. cities (2014), the BDS National Committee endorsed the Movement for Black Lives, lending support to the struggle for racial justice in the United States.[90] Also, the Palestinian BDS National Committee lent its support to and stood in solidarity with the Standing Rock Sioux Tribe in its campaign against the Dakota Access Pipeline (2016).[91]

In those moments, witnessing how quickly and easily the leading Palestinian BDS committee spoke out in support of these contemporary justice struggles in the United States, I was reminded how important international and intersectional solidarity is in the never-ending struggle for justice both globally and specifically in Palestine. This witnessing reminded me how troubling it is that the Jewish Establishment perceives outspoken support of the largest nonviolent movement for Palestinian justice (BDS) as dangerous. Just as Palestinians can so easily make the connection between Palestine and Standing Rock, it should be easy for Jews to understand the necessity of supporting (or at least not brazenly organizing to stop) the most widespread, successful, and *nonviolent* movement for justice for Palestinians.

BDS advocates are on the front lines of Palestinian solidarity activism in the United States today. With each campus resolution or divestment campaign, the activists raise the stakes of their activism by attempting to shift the status quo and breaking from the business-as-usual routines of pro-Israel activism. By engaging in BDS campaigns, they make themselves vulnerable to attacks and risk losing friendships due to commitments to their resistance to Israeli policies. In another example of the "witch hunt" against BDS activists, Yael Horowitz, a Jewish student who attended Wesleyan University, felt ostracized by the Jewish community on campus after she was involved with passing a BDS resolution with SJP. In reflecting on her experience, Yael said the following:

> After publicly endorsing BDS, I began feeling less automatically welcome in the Jewish community. At Shabbat services and dinners, I would feel as though I was not truly communing with the people sitting around me. I sensed that my politics served to alienate me from others, not just because the community didn't share my political views but also because I now felt I had to prove my Judaism—as if my Judaism had been called into question because I was not a Zionist or because I supported BDS. Conversely, I sometimes felt that I could not be fully Jewish in activist settings, or that talking about Judaism to people who did not know me well would lead them to assumptions about my politics. Whenever I was among my fellow Jews, I would feel myself getting "prickly." In an attempt to resolve the situation, a friend and I decided to lead a Jewish Voice for Peace Shabbat.[92]

While Yael's experience makes clear the significant role that JVP plays for young Jews seeking a safe place to engage in Palestine/Israel political activism, it also shows how BDS activism is grounds for exclusion from Jewish communal spaces. Once she spoke publicly about BDS on campus, the Jewish community where she once felt welcomed and safe shunned her.

In dividing the Jewish community over BDS activism, pro-Israel advocates have attempted to claim ownership over Jewish identity by demonizing BDS activists as bad or disloyal Jews, which has inevitably caused significant rifts and divisions in Jewish communities. To illustrate the ways in which Jewish identity itself is contested vis-à-vis BDS activism, we can look to the experience of Shoshana, a Jewish student who helped pass a BDS resolution at an elite university in the Northeast. Shoshana recalled her experience after a hotly contested vote in the Student Senate that resulted in the passage of a BDS bill:

After the BDS resolution passed, all the pro-Israel students walked out and they were singing *Oseh Shalom*. I got on the microphone and started singing with them. When they confronted me, I said, "This is my song as well. You don't get to claim this song as only yours. I can sing it, as well." It was a very emotional moment for me. But to me that symbolizes the reclamation of Jewishness through BDS activism. That came from a place of deprivation, feeling deprived of acceptance in the Jewish community. Even though I grew up in a big Jewish community, I always went to Jewish summer camp, and all of my best friends from childhood are Jewish. Once I started doing BDS activism I was no longer accepted in the Jewish community on campus.[93]

Singing a Jewish song about peace at the same time as other Jewish students, even those who disagreed with her politics, enabled Shoshana to proudly illustrate that BDS activism does not separate her from Judaism. Rather, participating in BDS activism is a reflection of her Jewish values.

While some, like Shoshana, have been shunned from Jewish community on campus, other Jewish BDS activists have been barred from entry into Israel on account of their activism. As a direct response to the growth of the global BDS movement, in 2017 the Israeli government passed a law that barred entry into the country of any foreigner who "makes a public call for boycotting Israel . . . or any area under its control."[94] Passed as an amendment to the state's Law of Entry, this bill had a clear anti-BDS intention and was meant to intimidate BDS activists and deter them from coming to Israel.[95] In reality, the law revealed the increasingly fascist nature of Israel's right-wing government under then–prime minister Benjamin Netanyahu. One of the consequences was the fact that this new law bumped up against one of Israel's most hallowed and fundamental laws, the 1950 Law of Return, which allows all Jews to become Israeli citizens.

On multiple occasions since 2017 this law has been used to prevent the entry of Jewish activists who support BDS. In one high-profile case, Ariel Gold, the national co-director of the activist group CODEPINK, was barred entry to Israel despite the fact that she had obtained a student visa to study Judaism at the Hebrew University in Jerusalem.[96] Another highly publicized instance occurred when Israel refused to allow five members of an interfaith delegation, including three Jews, to board their Israel-bound plane in the United States. One of the people prevented from traveling to Israel was Rabbi Alissa Wise, who at the time served as the deputy director of JVP.[97] This was likely the first time in Israeli history that the country refused to allow an ordained rabbi to enter.

Another person from the interfaith delegation who was also banned from entering Israel was Noah Habeeb, an Arab Jewish Tufts University graduate student. In reflecting on this experience, Habeeb said, "Our denial of entry was meant to weaken us and convince us our efforts were meaningless. It was meant to deny us access to the land in which we call for justice. It was meant to deny us the ability to continue to call for justice. Yet it had the opposite effect. . . . I am now even more intimately invested in the Palestinian struggle for dignity and freedom, and more convinced of the power of human solidarity."[98] Habeeb's clear articulation of solidarity is evidence of why the BDS movement will continue to be successful. Abigail B. Bakan and Yasmeen Abu-Laban argue that BDS, as a method of solidarity with Palestinians and resistance to Israeli occupation, is deeply tied to challenging the hegemony of Zionism in Israel and the West.[99] When Jewish activists such as Habeeb are barred entry to Israel due to their support for BDS, it highlights the disconnect between the values that most American Jews hold regarding democracy, human rights, and free speech and Zionism and the actions of the Israeli government.

This clear act of suppressing BDS activism, and all other efforts aimed at stopping and delegitimizing the movement, does not appear to have a great chance to succeed in fully stopping the BDS movement. The State of Israel has a dedicated branch of the government, the Ministry of Strategic Affairs, with a massive budget of over $70 million annually, that is tasked with combatting the BDS movement.[100] As is evidenced by an Israeli report published in 2020 that admitted Israel's failure to "disrupt the BDS momentum," the incredible investment of human and financial resources to combat BDS is not an effective strategy to stop a global nonviolent movement of international solidarity with Palestinians.[101] BDS campaigns won't stop just because they encounter resistance. Instead, they continue to grow and manifest in various places and in different ways despite the coordinated opposition to the movement. Furthermore, as Omar Barghouti claims, "Israel's full enlistment of Washington in its war on the Boycott, Divestment, Sanctions (BDS) movement for Palestinian rights is the strongest indicator of the movement's impact on its regime of military occupation, settler colonialism, and apartheid, and of its failure to crush the movement."[102] BDS is yet another example of how any attempts by Israel and its allies to quell support for the Palestinian cause will only invigorate and strengthen the movement.

Though they know it may be difficult to convince their Jewish family or friends to support BDS, the young American Jews I interviewed frequently expressed their desire for consistency from the Jewish community regarding its response to BDS. They watch with confusion as Jewish community federations divest from the fossil fuel industry just as they demonize BDS activists for seeking to divest from companies that profit from Israel's occupation.[103] Activists are shocked to see Jewish communities celebrate the Montgomery Bus Boycott during the Civil Rights era or, as was the case with my family, the outward support of the grape boycott, while condemning others for promoting the boycott of Israeli institutions for their complicity with Israeli human rights abuses. They simply want a consistent application of their values, which should lead them not to defend Israel at all costs but rather to seriously engage with Israeli human rights violations and recognize BDS as an entirely legitimate strategy meant to pressure Israel to comply with international law and end its occupation of the Palestinian Territories. Instead, activists are confronted with demonization, delegitimization, smear tactics, and a coordinated network set on toppling the entire BDS movement and ostracizing Jews who dare participate in this form of activism.

The American Jewish Establishment's strategy to delegitimize BDS will ultimately fail. In the articulation of BDS activists, they are not the ones who are delegitimizing Israel. Rather, through their political tactics, BDS activists are merely bringing certain tensions surrounding Israel to the surface. They argue that Israel delegitimizes itself through the state's constant and persistent refusal to comply with international law, which is, above all else, the BDS movement's chief demand. Israel's refusal to do so renders the state vulnerable to challenges by movements working for justice. Furthermore, the blatant attempts to delegitimize BDS activists by labeling them as antisemitic dilute accurate charges of antisemitism, which, in turn, makes it harder to challenge antisemitism when it actually exists. Given the rampant white supremacist activism in the United States, this is a cause of concern.[104]

Ultimately, many young Jewish American activists are attracted to BDS as a strategy both because it is nonviolent and because it has historical precedent as one of the effective tools that helped end the apartheid system in South Africa, thereby indicating that it just may prove successful in ending Israel's occupation of the Palestinian Territories and have material impacts on Palestinian liberation. The participation of young American Jews in BDS activism is yet another powerful way that they are building inclusive and thriving new Jewish communities that reflect their own liberatory politics.

Conclusion

Occupation Is Not Our Judaism

As violence erupted in Palestine/Israel in May 2021, the American Jewish community experienced yet another reckoning regarding its engagement with the State of Israel. As with previous moments of cleavage among American Jews, young Jews committed to ending American Jewish support for Israel's apartheid policies led the charge. Their activism led numerous domestic Jewish American justice organizations to rethink their approaches to Palestine/Israel. Perhaps the most prominent Jewish justice organization that was forced to reconcile its social justice values with its relationship to Israel was Avodah: The Jewish Service Corps. Formed in 1998, Avodah brings together young Jewish activists between the ages of twenty-one and twenty-six to engage in a yearlong process of social justice activism. While living together in a communal house in a few cities across the United States, Jewish Service Corps members work at antipoverty nonprofit organizations and learn about Jewish social justice ethics, values, and organizing strategies.[1] Since its formation, Avodah has trained over thirteen hundred Jewish social justice activists and created a vast alumni network of people who are working for justice in various capacities and in multiple geographical locations.[2]

The diverse nature of Avodah's alumni network relates also to their vast politics and approaches to Palestine/Israel. So when the violence started between Israel and Hamas in May 2021, it was not surprising that a select group of program alumni organized to push Avodah to make a public statement about the violence and take a direct stance on Palestine/Israel.[3] The following month, 274 alumni wrote a letter to Avodah organizational leadership demanding that they take a more forceful and clearer stance on Palestine/Israel. These alumni, nearly all of whom are in the demographic of activists documented in this book, argued that as a Jewish justice organization it had a moral and ethical imperative to make a statement about Israeli state violence and the injustices Palestinians face on a daily basis.

The letter strategically used the language of Jewish values and ethics, directly linking the training they received from Avodah in explaining their political position: "Our Jewish values call us to solidarity with oppressed people. . . . You trained us to act collectively and seek systemic responses to systemic injustice." Both pointing to Avodah's history of speaking out and aligning with movements for change, the letter made four requests of the organization: (1) publicly endorse the BDS movement; (2) commit to annual educational programming about the Nakba and the occupation with Palestinian trainers and resources; (3) release a public statement supporting the Palestinian Children and Families Act and the Joint Resolution of Disapproval to block the proposed U.S. arms sale to the Israeli government; and (4) end official gag rules that prevent program participants and staff from speaking freely about their support for BDS and Palestinian liberation.[4] Though these were clear demands, they were also very bold, especially in asking Avodah to publicly endorse the BDS movement, which includes serious risks, as I discussed in chapter 5. But the letter also argued that the risks of not taking action are far greater, such as the possibility of losing credibility, trust, and support with BIPOC organizers and community leaders, its alumni base, and future Avodah participants.

This letter embodied the shifting narrative of how young Jewish American social justice activists orient toward Palestine/Israel. It brought into sharp relief some of the ways that they participate in the broad global social movement for justice in Palestine/Israel and beyond. For example, they made the intersectional argument that all successful social movements must make, pointing to the interconnected nature of justice struggles. They argued that Avodah could lose its credibility and damage its integrity as a domestic Jewish social justice organization by not speaking out forcefully and clearly against Israeli state violence and for Palestinian liberation and justice. Furthermore, the letter pointed to both the risks and the significance of supporting the BDS movement. The alumni who wrote and signed this letter indicated the ways that BDS aligns with Avodah's values, noting that it is nonviolent, has clear and achievable demands, is led by those most impacted by violence, and encourages people to make change based on their money, all of which are organizing strategies and principles that Avodah teaches its participants. Additionally, the letter noted the ways that Jewish ethics, values, and morals are the driving factors behind the call to engage meaningfully with Palestine/Israel as a Jewish justice organization. Finally, this letter highlighted an escalation of tactics that young Jews use to force a reckoning among Jewish American organizations around Israel and to challenge the communal red lines. Whereas in early instances students targeted Hillel, a student organization with a clear Zionist agenda, here we see how young American Jews targeted a Jewish organization that has tried to avoid the conversation about Israel and Zionism altogether.

Above anything else, this letter was about imagining a different future for the American Jewish Establishment more than the practical implications of the demands of activists. Quite simply, the alumni who signed the letter asked Avodah to apply the same values and teachings evenly across all justice issues, even and especially when it comes to justice for Palestinians. The reckoning with Avodah over Palestine/Israel is evidence of the fact that anti-occupation and anti-apartheid activists simply want consistency with values from the Jewish community and its institutions. If a Jewish justice organization is going to "talk the talk," they want them to similarly "walk the walk." But activists want the application of justice and equality as a Jewish value to be applied evenly, in every context, thereby highlighting the intersectional nature of justice struggles.

What made this internal organizational discord so unique was that Avodah is one of many Jewish justice organizations that intentionally declined to take any public stance on Palestine/Israel, claiming that it is beyond the scope of their work. In a letter to the Avodah alumni network, leaders of the organization said that their approach has always been "to not engage with Israel/Palestine on an organizational level . . . seeing it as outside the bounds of our mission and focus on U.S. social and economic justice."[5] In some ways it makes sense for a U.S.-based Jewish social justice organization that focuses intentionally on domestic justice struggles to "not engage with Israel/Palestine" on any meaningful level. Why would they engage on something outside their stated mission? Does every Jewish organization need to engage with Palestine/Israel? Does demanding that every Jewish organization speak about or engage with Zionism and Israel traffic in antisemitic tropes that conflate all Jews with Israel and the political ideology of Zionism?

I don't think that every Jewish American organization needs to engage with Palestine/Israel for this very reason. It is important to reinforce the separation between Jews and Zionism and to cement the idea that not all Jews in the United States have an interest in or connection to Palestine/Israel on any meaningful level. Many young Jews choose to participate in the Avodah program because they are committed to domestic struggles for justice and want to learn to engage with justice in a distinctly Jewish framework. Ultimately, however, the skills that many activists learn from Avodah and other justice-based organizations are being applied not only to the domestic context but also to Palestine/Israel organizing. Therefore, the alumni community's demands were legitimate and could ultimately help this very important Jewish justice organization remain relevant into the future.

While a multigenerational cohort of American Jews oppose Israeli occupation and apartheid, young Jewish activists are the primary driving force behind the communal reckoning about how Jewish institutions engage with Israel. Activists are very clearly stating that occupation is not their Judaism, and if Jewish institutions are not willing to say the same thing, then many young Jews will steer clear of those organizations. This is not representative of a fringe minority within the Jewish community. Rather, it brings into sharp relief the demands that young Jews have on their community if they want to remain relevant and continue to have young Jewish participation.

Avodah is one of the most established and well-known Jewish justice organizations in the United States working with young people. The communal reckonings highlighted by this example represent a harbinger of things to come. While the events of May 2021 were cataclysmic in shifting the terrain of the conflict in Palestine/Israel as well as its proxy battles in U.S. Jewish communities, there will no doubt be future instances as earth-shattering as those that took place that summer. With each catalyzing moment, there will be more demands by young Jewish American activists for communal change in regard to institutional attitudes toward Israel. And if these institutions don't take meaningful action, they will risk becoming irrelevant to the future of the Jewish community.

Shabbat in Bethlehem

Throughout this book, I have provided autoethnographic accounts in order to highlight the ways in which my participation in the Palestine solidarity movement influenced the research. By sharing and analyzing my experiences, I have elucidated the ways that my connections to the social and political networks in this book formed a "relational ethics" that implicate myself and others within Jewish participation in the Palestine solidarity movement.[6] Throughout the process of researching and writing this book, I learned a lot from the activists about how and why young American Jews participate in Palestine solidarity activism. In this project, I intentionally researched a demographic to which I am proximate but not party to, knowing that my experiences with Palestine solidarity activism would be different from those of the activists I interviewed. In part, this was a strategy to analyze what was familiar to me, a way of investigating certain things that I took for granted as a means to better understand their underlying unrecognized power and cultural significance.[7] In starting with what was simultaneously familiar and strange, I sought to understand both my own activism and my Jewish identity on a deeper level. I did not expect to be so personally transformed by the experience of learning from the activists, but I was profoundly impacted by the care and passion for justice that I witnessed.

One moment in particular stands out as being both personally significant and epiphanous for the overall research for this book. It involved the soundtrack to my experience during the winter 2019–2020 Center for Jewish Nonviolence (CJNV) delegation (see chapter 4). During that delegation, music was a constant presence. I have a deep and passionate love for music, so I immediately connected with the songs we sang, some of which were familiar but most of which were new to me. Each of the songs contained a connection to the delegation, because they had either justice-themed lyrics or explicitly Jewish content. The song that I enjoyed the most was a version of "Mi'mayaneh Hayeshua," which translates from Hebrew as "from the wellspring of liberation" and is a central prayer of the Havdallah service that marks the conclusion of Shabbat. The lyrics come from the biblical book of Isaiah, which states, "with joy you shall draw water from the wellsprings of liberation."[8] Multiple times throughout the delegation we sang these words to a melody I had just learned and thought was beautiful.

Then, on the final Friday of the delegation, we engaged in a direct action to enable Palestinians from the South Hebron Hills to access and draw water from the Ein Albeida spring. This action helped me understand co-resistance as a tactic and the significance of Jewish participation in Palestine solidarity activism more broadly. It was most clear to me when I realized that we had been singing a song all week about joyously drawing water from a spring of liberation and that the main direct action of the delegation was centered around a well. We were working to realize exactly what the lyrics of the song are about.

Later that evening, the CJNV group sang Friday evening Shabbat prayers together in our hotel in Bethlehem. I had mixed feelings about engaging in these Jewish rituals in this ancient city. On the one hand, it was meaningful to celebrate Shabbat with other activists on the evening of the direct action. But on the other hand, I felt incredibly uncomfortable engaging in a vocal Jewish ritual in the Occupied West Bank, where most people who observe Shabbat are Jewish settlers, people with whom I vehemently disagree and have no personal connection. (I later discovered that I was not alone in my feelings when the *Unsettled* podcast published a miniseries on the delegation that featured a story about a delegate named Lilly who expressed a similar sentiment.)[9] Although I had a lot of experience with anti-occupation and Palestine solidarity activism, the tensions I felt were new to me because I had never engaged in Jewish rituals in the context of my activism. At first, I struggled to make sense of it.

During the Shabbat prayers I closed my eyes while the group sang "Shalom Aleichem," which means "may peace be upon you," a central prayer marking the beginning of Shabbat. I noticed a surprising and overwhelming internal shift. I started crying. This was the first time in years that I felt comfortable engaging in a Jewish ritual practice. For far too long I had had an incredibly hard time performing Jewish rituals because I was unable to dissociate Jewishness from the Israeli state project. But in this moment, because I was in a community of fellow anti-occupation and anti-apartheid Jewish activists with similar political commitments as me, I experienced a spiritual alignment. I realized that far too often I suffer from the shackles of internalized antisemitism; I

Figure c.1. The author with members of the Adara family at Ein Albeida in the South Hebron Hills, January 2020. Photo by Emily Glick.

understood that I had been resisting Jewish ritual practice partly due to my thought that, for me, Judaism has been co-opted by Israel and Zionism. As a result, Jewish ritual had lost a lot of its significance for me as religious and cultural practice. Our Shabbat singing on CJNV felt like an opportunity to reclaim Judaism from Zionism and to reassert a liberatory Jewish identity based in justice for all people. While I knew this to be true on an intellectual level, and though I had spoken with many activists who related similar experiences, that Shabbat in Bethlehem helped me understand it in a profoundly personal and emotional way.

This was further reinforced for me the following evening when we marked the end of Shabbat with the Havdallah service. We gathered in a building in the heart of Bethlehem, a five-minute walk away from Manger Square, and it was very cold and rainy. Just as we had started the Havdallah service, the power went out in the building, making the room pitch black. A few people turned on flashlights; one of our prayer leaders lit two candles, placing the wicks together. Then one of the group leaders started singing the first part of the Havdallah service, the very words from the song we had been singing all week. I didn't know this particular melody, but as soon as we got to the section that says "U'shavtem mayim besasson mimay'nei ha'Yeshua," I was again overcome by emotions. For the second time in as many days, tears filled my eyes.

This time I cried for two new reasons. First, in that moment I thought about my children, who often sing a different version of this song and love it dearly. I felt sad thinking about them and other children growing up in a world with so much violence, where the Jewish state commits egregious human rights violations toward Palestinians in their name. I wondered what kind of Jewish community they would grow up in and what I could do to help them live in a more just and peaceful world. Second, I cried because we had just the day before helped Kifah Adara return to Ein Albeida for the first time in fifteen years. We had been singing these words about drawing water from a wellspring of liberation, and I thought about the connections between the song, the action, and the future possibilities of justice, peace, liberation, and equality in Palestine/Israel. The action itself was truly a celebration of the possibilities of a more just future. We had literally witnessed Kifah Adara successfully draw water from the wellspring of liberation.

Performing the Havdallah service and singing those words were powerful and transformative. My emotional response was a mixture of sadness and hope—I was saddened by the reality of what is happening in Palestine/Israel, but singing provided a spark and insight into the possibility of reclaiming Jewishness and not acquiescing to Israel's co-optation of Jewish identity. Being surrounded by young American Jewish activists provided a semblance of hope for a better and more just future, and it cemented my understanding of the fact that these activists are sowing the seeds of a powerful American Jewish resistance movement against Israel's occupation and policies of apartheid.

The leaders of the CJNV delegation—all of whom were young American Jews—taught me how to infuse Palestine solidarity activism into my Jewishness. Though I knew on an intellectual level that it was possible to do so, I did not experience it for myself until that CJNV delegation. The Havdallah experience was the first time I understood, on a deep and visceral level, the slogan "occupation is not our Judaism." For the first time, I actually understood this as more than just a saying printed on T-shirts and written on signs for demonstrations. "Occupation is not our Judaism" is a lifestyle. It is not a fleeting moment in time but rather a way of being, a symbolic and material expression of a commitment to Palestinian liberation that simultaneously reinforces a connection to Jewish life devoid of Israeli state violence.

Occupation Is Not Our Judaism

This book argues that young American Jews are at the forefront of a broad social movement of Palestine solidarity activists working to end unequivocal American Jewish support for Israeli occupation and apartheid. The individuals documented in this book are mostly engaged in this activism as an expression of their Jewish identity, a demonstration of their commitment to justice and other Jewish values. While critics might see these young American Jewish activists' opposition to Israeli occupation as resistance to Jewish communities, it in fact reflects their deep commitment to their Jewish identities. Instead of walking away from their community in protest, they have drawn on history in an effort to shift contemporary politics into alignment with these deep-seated values. They see Israeli actions toward Palestinians, and unequivocal American Jewish support for Israel, as both morally and ethically inconsistent with the Jewish values of justice, freedom, and equality that they were taught by their parents, teachers, rabbis, and other Jewish elders. In this way, Jewish anti-occupation and anti-apartheid activism is a direct result of their desire to see Jewish life thrive all around the world and to ensure the disentanglement of Judaism and Zionism.

Young Jews in the United States increasingly understand Israel's treatment of Palestinians as a moral and ethical disaster and are waking up to the role that their communities play in upholding Israel's occupation and its policies of apartheid. As a result, they are rising up in dissent, working toward ending American Jewish support for the occupation while also actively participating in and influencing the global Palestinian solidarity movement. Through their activism, young American Jews working toward Palestinian liberation are forcing an internal reckoning within the Jewish community, seeking to disrupt the status quo and challenge American Jewish institutional relationships to Israel and Zionism.

This book also contends that young Jewish American participation in the broader social movement for Palestinian liberation is important both materially and symbolically. Through the process of writing this book I have come to understand that while the material impact is meaningful, it is not as significant as the symbolic impact on the activists, their families, their communities, and the American Jewish conversation about Palestine/Israel more broadly. While the three main strategies of activism documented in this book had small material impacts, most notably through BDS and co-resistance activism, these strategies are not doing enough to erode the deeply entrenched status quo of occupation, apartheid, and Israeli state violence perpetrated against Palestinians. From a symbolic standpoint, however, young American Jewish activists are having a profound impact on how people understand and approach Palestine in the American Jewish community. This signals hope for a different future in American Jewish life, including changes in the Jewish Establishment's unequivocal support for Israel.

All the while Israel continues to be emboldened by unchecked and unconditional support from the U.S. government in its enterprise of occupation and apartheid. This has led to a more deeply entrenched status quo and a seeming impossibility of freedom, equality, and liberation for Palestinians. Therefore, the material impact of this activism, while important, pales in comparison to the symbolically meaningful factors of young American Jewish Palestine solidarity activism, which has pushed the American Jewish community to a tipping point.

Throughout this book I have provided qualitative data to elucidate the myriad levels of anti-occupation and Palestine solidarity activism with which young American Jews engage. I have also provided quantitative data, where available, to show that young Jews are at the forefront of the changing relationship between American Jews and the State of Israel. The Jewish activists featured in this book are working tirelessly to push American Jews to understand that they must no longer uphold the status quo of unequivocal support for Israel and instead must, at the very least, accept into their communities those who don't toe the party line. If mainstream Jewish communal institutions don't want to be irrelevant to a new generation of Jews, they need to be ready, willing, and able to adapt to the changing nature of young Jews' relationships to Israel, Zionism, and their Jewish identities. The institutions need to openly teach critical histories of Israel and Zionism but must also be open to teaching and engaging with Palestine and Palestinian histories and narratives. Furthermore, they must be open to and accepting of differing viewpoints rather than ostracizing people based on their Israel politics, which will go a long way toward building a more inclusive and justice-oriented Jewish community.

The activists highlighted in this book developed their Jewish identities within the same institutional framework where they target their activism. Their Jewish cultural and religious acculturation taught and encouraged them to celebrate justice and participate in movements for social change. As the activists grew older and more aware of the complex realities of Israel and Zionism, tensions within their Jewishness bubbled to the surface. Forced to make a stark choice, they refused to accept Israeli state violence perpetrated in their name. Many young American Jews today view their Jewishness as rooted in the idea of justice for all, even for Palestinians, which encourages them to participate in Palestine solidarity activism as a way of living in and creating the world they want to inhabit.

All of the tactics described in this book where young American Jews participate in Palestine solidarity activism are ways of reclaiming and asserting Jewishness through activism. These acts and the politics associated with them are all too often unwelcome by the American Jewish Establishment, which sees them as a threat to Jewishness and as attempts to stop them. Jewish institutions are placing borders around the community, seeking to define acceptable parameters of Jewish identity in regard to politics around and attitudes toward Israel and Zionism. But this redlining has strengthened the Jewish identities of the activists forced to defend their Jewishness. It has created a context to establish alternative Jewish spaces in the face of political exclusion.

Perhaps most importantly, the activists' commitment to a Jewishness rooted in justice for all is helping the American Jewish community adapt to the changing social, cultural, and political conditions of our time. Jewish survival has always been, and will continue to be, predicated on the ability to adapt. The activists described in this book are forcing a change in the American Jewish community that could eventually lead to its ability to survive and thrive in the twenty-first century. Ultimately, this book answers particular questions about potential future directions of Jewish life in the United States. How will American Judaism and its institutions continue to be relevant to young people? Will the Jewish community adapt as more young people are defecting from mainstream

Jewish life in favor of creating new spaces that are more in line with their political worldviews? With American Judaism at a crossroads over its engagement with and connections to Israel, young American Jews are demanding the necessary adaptations to the changing nature of the contemporary social, cultural, and political milieu.

Jewish activists often like to quote Dr. Martin Luther King Jr., who reminds us that although the moral arc of the universe is long, it bends toward justice. The activists in this book and the broad ecosystem of Jews and Jewish organizations engaged in Palestine solidarity activism are bending the arc by performing acts of justice. They are reshaping American Jewish life to more accurately represent a politics that distances themselves from Israeli state violence. These young Jews are building inclusive and thriving new Jewish communities that reflect their own liberatory politics. They have demanded a communal reckoning, and if mainstream Jewish institutions fail to properly adapt to the demands of the social movement to cease their support for Israel's policies of occupation, they will become irrelevant to an entire generation of Jews.

In order to remain relevant, they must be willing to critically engage with Israeli state violence and work to end the occupation. Once Jewish institutions take the demands of this generation of activists seriously, perhaps then a new Jewish future rooted in equity, justice, and liberation for all will arrive. As IfNotNow's slogan emphasizes, Millennial and Gen Z Jews "will be the generation" that plays a pivotal role in ending the occupation and Jewish American support for it, thereby ushering in a new era of Jewish life and liberation.

U'shavtem mayim besasson mimay'nei ha'Yeshua. With joy, may we draw water from the fountains of freedom.

ACKNOWLEDGMENTS

Although writing is often a very solitary act, life is with people. And many different people helped me throughout the process of researching and writing this book. Above all I would like to thank the activists who agreed to be interviewed for this book. Although none of them are named here, I am extraordinarily grateful to all of them for taking the time to speak with me and for allowing me a window into their lives as activists and Jews. Many thanks to the myriad activists from the organizations and groups featured in this book who spoke with me, introduced me to others, or told me various elements of the inner workings of their organizations. Thank you to everyone who spoke to me as a representative of or affiliate with Jewish Voice for Peace, IfNotNow, the Center for Jewish Nonviolence, and All That's Left. I would like to thank Simone Zimmerman in particular for introducing me to others and making important connections that were integral to the research for this book. I am also very grateful for the guidance, friendship, and inspiration of Erez Bleicher, Sarah Brammer-Shlay, Oriel Eisner, Elisheva Goldberg, Em Hilton, Karen Isaacs, Edo Konrad, Isaac Kates Rose, Maya Rosen, Daniel Roth, Moriel Rothman Zecher, Ilana Sumka, Sam Sussman, and Aviva Zimmerman, who were always available to answer questions, introduce me to people, and challenge my thinking on Palestine solidarity activism and Palestine/Israel more broadly.

I am grateful for the support of the University of San Francisco for helping make this book possible. The support of the Faculty Development Fund Research Grants and Travel Grants enabled both my research travel and the ability to work with some remarkable research assistants. Many thanks to the three student research assistants, Dana Baskett, Ali Billow, and Sophie Spievak, who helped me in both early and late stages of research for this book. To my colleagues in the Swig Program in Jewish Studies and Social Justice, I am eternally grateful to you for creating a stimulating intellectual and engaging social environment. Thanks to Noa Bar Gabai, Shaina Hammerman, and Alexis Herr for numerous conversations that helped me craft and shape the research. Camille Shira Angel was a constant sounding board who helped me think about the topic from different angles and encouraged me to keep writing even when it seemed impossible. Without the friendship, mentorship, vision, and incredible editing of Aaron Hahn Tapper, in addition to a fateful conversation some fifteen years ago that set me on a whole new personal and professional journey, this book would not be what it is. I would also like to thank my colleagues in the Middle East Studies program—Nora Fisher Onar, Lindsay Gifford, Ilaria Giglioli, Aysha Hidayatullah, Sadia Saeed, and Stephen Zunes—for their support. Many thanks to Josh Gamson for his help and early championing of this project, as well as to Jeff Paris for his guidance and encouragement.

Other scholars and friends helped shape this book through conversations that were both inspiring and challenging. Tallie Ben Daniel, Matt Berkman, Marjorie Feld, Emmaia Gelman, Brooke Hotez, Emily Schneider, Mira Sucharov, Orian Zakai, and Sivan Zakai provided feedback on ideas and chapter drafts and inspired this research through their own work and conversations at conferences and other venues. Special thanks to Ariella Werden-Greenfield, my thought partner and friend who helped me hone my writing and editing skills through our Phish collaboration. I am particularly grateful to Sarah Anne Minkin for being the ultimate comrade, constantly pushing and challenging me to think deeper about this work and for always being willing to think with me. My friends and colleagues in my writing group—Eleanor Paynter, Gabriella Soto, and Abby Wheatley—provided me with the keen editing skills, analytic minds, and constant encouragement necessary to get this book to the finish line. I am also enormously thankful to Moriah Ella Mason for providing remarkable editing, feedback, and analysis to the entire manuscript as an insider to the movement and editor extraordinaire.

Special thanks go to Emily Glick for providing me with the remarkable photos in this book and offering me a much deeper understanding of what it means to be committed to Jewish life, ritual, and identity through activism. Anne Germanacos also deserves special gratitude for her friendship, guidance, and belief in me, but also for putting together the Thursday Morning group. Thursday mornings became a much-needed sanctuary, a place of creativity, connection, and humor for which I am eternally grateful.

To the incredible staff at NYU Press, thank you for your support in steering this book through to publication. I really appreciate the professionalism and encouragement of Yasemin Torfilli. And I am particularly indebted to my editor, Ilene Kalish, who believed in this project from the outset and helped me understand that this book was worthy of publication.

To all of my friends who asked questions about the research and writing, encouraged me to get to the finish line, and hung out with me even when I was most stressed, thank you! Special thanks to The Thread for your humor, distractions, and constant cheering, without whom this book maybe would have been published a year or two earlier.

Most importantly, none of this would be possible without my family, who really are the bedrock of my life. Thanks to my parents, Leah Kroll and Michael Zeldin, who gave me the gift of Jewish education and inspire me to be the best version of myself. To Noga, Stav, and Ido—I am so grateful for everything that you do and for all that you are. Thank you for enduring my time away for research and writing and for maintaining my happiness while we are together. I love you more than you could ever imagine.

NOTES

INTRODUCTION

1 Matar, "Israel Chooses Violence."
2 United Nations Office for the Coordination of Humanitarian Affairs Occupied Palestinian Territories, "Response to the Escalation."
3 Sokol, "Israel Demolished Tower Blocks in Gaza."
4 Kingsley, "Evictions in Jerusalem."
5 Rosenfeld, "Conflict in Gaza Rages Again."
6 Cramer, "Dozens of US Rabbinical Students."
7 The letter can be read in its entirety through this online article: Cramer, "Dozens of US Rabbinical Students."
8 Personal interview, May 30, 2021.
9 See Tracy, "Inside the Unraveling of American Zionism."
10 Hasson, "Jerusalem Police Raided Pro-Palestinian Activists' Apartment."
11 Eisner, "I Was Arrested for a Crime I Didn't Commit."
12 Throughout this book I use the term "Palestine/Israel" (rather than "Israel/Palestine," "Palestine," or "Israel") to intentionally posit a shift in the dynamics of power between Israel and Palestine. It is important to highlight Palestine as a distinct place due to the attempts by Israeli and Zionist discourse to erase Palestine from the map and convince people that Palestine does not exist. In this book "Palestine/Israel" refers to the contested territory between the Jordan River and the Mediterranean Sea. The term "Israel," when used on its own, refers to the American Jewish communal relationship to the Jewish state.
13 Eisner, "I Was Arrested for a Crime I Didn't Commit."
14 For information on the Save Masafer Yatta campaign, see https://savemasaferyatta.com.
15 Association of Civil Rights in Israel, "Info-Sheet." Although this document identifies approximately 1,300 people living in the area, more updated information from the Save Masafer Yatta campaign website lists the total of 2,800 noted here, which is based on a census carried out by the residents and members of the Masafer Yatta Regional Council.
16 See B'Tselem, "Firing Zone 918."
17 Abraham, "Classified Document." The classified document can be viewed here: www.archives.gov.il/archives/Archive/0b0717068649ce86/File/0b0717068751e066/Item/090717068754901e.

18 United Nations Office for the Coordination of Humanitarian Affairs Occupied Palestinian Territories, "Humanitarian Impact."

19 Glick and Rosen, "Portraits of Resistance."

20 Abraham and Adra, "Armed with High Court Expulsion Order."

21 For a discussion on the use of the term "apartheid," see the section "A Note on Terminology—'Occupation' and 'Apartheid,'" found later in this chapter.

22 Eisner, "I Was Arrested for a Crime I Didn't Commit."

23 Eisner, "I Was Arrested for a Crime I Didn't Commit."

24 Tarrow, *New Transnational Activism.*

25 Lough and Thomas, "Building a Community of Young Leaders."

26 Lough and Thomas, "Building a Community of Young Leaders."

27 I place the terms "support for Israel" and "pro-Israel" in quotation marks to il-lustrate that in this context I am using them as spoken phrases used by those with right-wing politics to actually mean uncritical and unwavering support for Israel.

28 See Omer, *Days of Awe*; Landy, *Jewish Identity and Palestinian Rights*; Schneider, "Pathways to Global Justice"; Hill, Ben Hagai, and Zurbriggen, "Intersecting Alli-ances."

29 Auerbach, *Are We One?*

30 Omer, *Days of Awe*; Landy, *Jewish Identity and Palestinian Rights.*

31 Personal interview, August 3, 2021. The name of every activist in this book is a pseudonym used to protect their identity, unless first and last names are given. In such cases full names are used because they already appear in the public record.

32 Minkin, "Fear, Fantasy, and Family."

33 Cavari and Freedman, *American Public Opinion.*

34 Cavari and Freedman, *American Public Opinion.*

35 All data in this paragraph come from the Pew Research Center, "Jewish Ameri-cans in 2020."

36 Beinart, *Crisis of Zionism*; Sucharov, "Values, Identity, and Israel Advocacy"; Wax-man, "Young American Jews and Israel."

37 Alterman, *We Are Not One*; Wertheimer, "American Jews and Israel."

38 Kolsky, *Jews Against Zionism*; Rabkin, *Threat from Within.*

39 Ross, *Rabbi Outcast*; Raider, Sarna, and Zweig, *Abba Hillel Silver.* See also Brown and Silberstein, "Contested Diaspora."

40 Ganin, *Uneasy Relationship*; Katz, *Bringing Zion Home.*

41 See Raider, *Emergence of American Zionism*; Cohen, *Americanization of Zionism.*

42 Kaplan, *Our American Israel*, 12.

43 Kaplan, *Our American Israel*, 39.

44 Mitelpunkt, *Israel in the American Mind.*

45 Brodkin, *How Jews Became White Folks*; Goldstein, *Price of Whiteness*; Kranson, *Ambivalent Embrace.*

46 Raider, *Emergence of American Zionism.*

47 Silver, *Our Exodus.*

48 Waxman, *Trouble in the Tribe.*

49 Sasson, *New American Zionism.*

50 Cohen and Liebman, "Israel and American Jewry."

51 Sasson, "Mass Mobilization to Direct Engagement," 173.

52 Sasson, *New American Zionism.*

53 Waxman, *Trouble in the Tribe.*

54 Graizbord, *New Zionists*; Rosner and Hakman, *Challenge of Peoplehood*; Waxman, "Young American Jews and Israel."

55 Cohen and Kelman, *Beyond Distancing*; Cohen and Kelman, "Thinking about Distancing from Israel."

56 Sasson et al., *Still Connected.*

57 Dias and Graham, "Gaza Conflict Stokes 'Identity Crisis'"; Kabas, "Young American Jews"; Riesman, "Jewish Revolt."

58 Sunshine, "Get Ready for the New Wave"; Rose, "Generational Shift"; Essa, "New Faces of Jewish-American Resistance."

59 Angel, "Jewish Americans."

60 Wertheimer, *Generation of Change.*

61 Beinart, *Crisis of Zionism.*

62 Beinart, "Failure of the American Jewish Establishment."

63 Karcher, *Reclaiming Judaism from Zionism.*

64 Groesberg, *Jewish Renewal*; Magid, *American Post-Judaism.*

65 Omer, *Days of Awe.*

66 Waxman, *Trouble in the Tribe.*

67 For Jewish social justice values, see Jacobs, *Where Justice Dwells.*

68 Zakai, "Values in Tension."

69 Waxman, "Young American Jews and Israel."

70 Waxman, "Young American Jews and Israel."

71 For a discussion on the ways in which the Holocaust is an element of the foundational narrative of the State of Israel, see Wermenbol, *Tale of Two Narratives.* Furthermore, this connection between the Holocaust and the State of Israel was concretized in Israel's Declaration of Independence, which says, "The recent holocaust, which engulfed millions of Jews in Europe, proved anew the need to solve the problem of the homelessness and lack of independence of the Jewish people by means of the re-establishment of the Jewish State, which would open the gates to all Jews and endow the Jewish people with equality of status among the family of nations."

72 My grandfather, Rabbi Isaiah Zeldin, founded Stephen S. Wise Temple in Los Angeles, California, which eventually grew to be one of the largest Reform synagogues in the United States.

73 Gross, *Beyond the Synagogue.*

74 Seliktar, *Divided We Stand.*

75 Waxman, "Young American Jews and Israel," 189.

76 Gerbaudo, *Tweets and the Streets.*

77 Omer, *Days of Awe,* 21.

78 Penslar, "What's Love Got to Do with It?"

79 In some ways, the political activism of young American Jews discussed in this book is a form of political activism and a contemporary expression of the Jewish idea of *avodah*. According to a famous passage in Pirkei Avot (Ethics of the Fathers), a tractate of the Mishnah that deals with ethical and moral teachings, "The world rests on three pillars: Torah, *avodah*, and acts of loving kindness." Normative takes on this Talmudic passage interpret "Torah" to refer to the study of the Five Books of Moses and *avodah* to mean worship or prayer. However, in Hebrew the word *avodah* has many meanings, including work, worship, and service. In contemporary iterations, *avodah* is sometimes interpreted to mean work in service to God. *Avodah* is a way that American Jews today participate in community engagement and activism, specifically as a method of working toward social and political transformation; helping shape the world from what it is to what it could be, one rooted in justice, liberation, and equality. Young American Jews engaging in Palestine solidarity activism are reimagining *avodah*, one of the three pillars on which the world stands, as a powerful form of activism that is rooted in Jewish teachings and values. Of particular importance to this conception of *avodah* are the ways in which young Jewish American activists are reimagining and reinscribing the classical Zionist understanding of the concept. In labor Zionist ideology, which developed prior to the establishment of the State of Israel, *avodah* referred to getting one's hands dirty, doing the actual physical work and labor of settling and colonizing the Land of Israel. In this regard, young American Jewish anti-occupation and anti-apartheid activists' conceptions of *avodah* as community activism in solidarity with Palestinians subvert the traditional meaning of the terms as well as the Zionist interpretation of working the land.

80 Kaplan, *Our American Israel*; Mitelpunkt, *Israel in the American Mind*.

81 Auerbach, *Are We One?*

82 Dollinger, *Black Power, Jewish Politics*.

83 Alterman, *We Are Not One*, 10.

84 Fischbach, *Black Power and Palestine*; Kaplan, *Our American Israel*.

85 Feld, *Nations Divided*.

86 Ticktin, *Casualties of Care*, 136.

87 Ticktin, *Casualties of Care*, 137.

88 Dimock, "Defining Generations."

89 Kaplan, "Millennial/Gen Z Leftists."

90 Fischbach, *Movement and the Middle East*, 7.

91 Kolsky, *Jews Against Zionism*; Berkman, "Antisemitism, Anti-Zionism, and the American Racial Order."

92 Staub, *Torn at the Roots*.

93 Kushner and Solomon, *Wrestling with Zion*; Becker, *American Jewish Peace Movement*; Farber, *Radicals, Rabbis, and Peacemakers*; Butler, *Parting Ways*; Rabkin, *Threat from Within*; Karpf et al., *Time to Speak Out*; Shatz, *Prophets Outcast*.

94 Azoulay, "'We,' Palestinians and Jewish Israelis," 85.

95 For example, see Schultz, *Going South.*

96 Omer, *Days of Awe.*

97 Chenoweth and Stephan, *Why Civil Resistance Works*, 39.

98 See Erakat, *Justice for Some*; Sfard, *Wall and the Gate*; Shulman, *Freedom and Despair*; Hallward, *Struggling for a Just Peace*; Weiss, *Conscientious Objectors in Israel*; Higgins-Desbiolles, "Justifying Tourism"; Schneider, "Touring for Peace"; Kelly, *Invited to Witness.*

99 Hafsa, "Role of Arab American Advocacy Groups"; Siapera, "Tweeting #Palestine"; Nabulsi, "'Hungry for Freedom.'"

100 Minkin, "Invitation to Belong."

101 For example, see Kroll-Zeldin, "Institutionalized Separation and Sumud"; Kroll-Zeldin, "Separate, Excluded, Unequal."

102 Fleischmann, *Israeli Peace Movement*, 5; Hallward, *Transnational Activism*; Ziv, "Performative Politics"; Pallister-Wilkins, "Radical Ground."

103 Bakan and Abu-Laban, "Israel/Palestine, South Africa, and the 'One-State Solution'"; Zreik, "Palestine, Apartheid, and the Rights Discourse"; Shahak, "Israeli Apartheid and the *Intifada*"; Davis, *Apartheid Israel.*

104 Human Rights Watch, "Threshold Crossed"; Amnesty International, "Israel's Apartheid Against Palestinians"; B'Tselem, "Regime of Jewish Supremacy."

105 Kroll-Zeldin, "Does Israel Function as an Apartheid State?"

106 Juris and Khasnabish, *Insurgent Encounters.*

107 Bochner and Ellis, *Evocative Autoethnography.*

1. THE PALESTINE SOLIDARITY MOVEMENT

1 As noted in the introduction, the name of every activist in this book is a pseudonym used to protect their identity unless first and last names are given. In such cases full names are used because they already appear in the public record.

2 The Presidents' Conference is one of the most powerful Jewish nonprofit organizations in the United States. It is composed of fifty-one Jewish organizations and is tasked with addressing some of the most pressing concerns of the American Jewish community. Though it is a conglomeration of Jewish organizations that focus on diverse issues regarding the Jewish community, the Presidents' Conference is an unequivocal supporter of Israel and is widely considered to have a right-wing and hawkish view on Israeli politics and U.S.–Israel relations.

3 Blumberg, "Jewish Group Delivers Mourner's Kaddish."

4 IfNotNow's origin story was reported in various media publications. For example, see Freedman, "What Happened to IfNotNow?"; Riesman, "Jewish Revolt."

5 Personal interview, February 11, 2019.

6 Zborowski and Herzog, *Life Is with People.*

7 I do not mention this to imply that all Jews in the movement are Ashkenazi. In fact, there are significant numbers of Sephardi and Mizrahi Jews intimately involved in organizing spaces, and there are even specific caucus groups of Sephardi and Mizrahi Jews working to ensure their inclusion in Jewish anti-occupation organizing.

8 Sutherland, Land, and Böhm, "Anti-leaders(hip) in Social Movement Organizations."

9 Klein, *On Fire*, 133.

10 In contrast to this central principle of social movement organizing, Jewish tradition emphasizes that one person indeed can make a difference. An ideal example of this is the biblical figure Nachshon ben Aminadav, who during the Israelite exodus from Egypt jumped into the Sea of Reeds when everyone else was afraid. The Talmud explains that his bravery led the seas to part and enabled the Israelites to escape bondage. In this story, it truly was one person who was able to make a profound difference and change for the community.

11 Omer, *Days of Awe*.

12 McAdam, McCarth, and Zald, *Comparative Perspectives on Social Movements*; McAdam, Tarrow, and Tilley, *Dynamics of Contention*; Staggenborg, *Social Movements*; Tarrow, *Power in Movement*.

13 Zibechi, *Dispersing Power*.

14 Polletta, "Culture and Movements."

15 Johnston, Laraña, and Gusfield, "Identities, Grievances, and New Social Movements."

16 See chapter 3 for a more in-depth investigation of the American Jewish Establishment and its role in upholding the occupation.

17 Meyer and Tarrow, *Social Movement Society*; Tilly and Tarrow, *Contentious Politics*.

18 Meyer, *Politics of Protest*, 23.

19 Passy and Giugni, "Social Networks and Individual Perceptions."

20 McCarthy and Zald, "Resource Mobilization and Social Movements."

21 See Eric Blanc's interview with prominent labor activist and organizer Jane McAlevey in *Jacobin* magazine. Blanc, "It's Not Enough to Fight."

22 Personal interview, August 29, 2019.

23 Chenoweth and Stephan, *Why Civil Resistance Works*; Engler and Engler, *This Is an Uprising*.

24 Engler and Engler, *This Is an Uprising*.

25 Engler and Engler, *This Is an Uprising*.

26 Stewart, "We Are (Still) the 99 Percent."

27 See Black Lives Matter, "Black Lives Matter 2020 Impact Report."

28 Nardini et al., "Together We Rise."

29 Momentum, "About Momentum" (2023), www.momentumcommunity.org.

30 Kingkade, "These Activists Are Training."

31 Engler and Lasoff, *Resistance Guide*, 30.

32 Lawson, "Freedom Then, Freedom Now"; Ball, *After Marriage Equality*.

33 Dinas et al., "From Dawn to Dusk"; Fisher and Tamarkin, "Right-Wing Organizers Do This Too."

34 Engler and Engler, *This Is an Uprising*.

35 Personal interview, June 12, 2019.

36 King, *Letter from a Birmingham Jail*.

37 IfNotNow, "IfNotNow DNA Guide." Though this document was never published, one of the activists I interviewed for this book gave me a copy of the DNA guide to use in my research.

38 Personal interview, February 22, 2019.

39 Riesman, "Jewish Revolt."

40 Freedman, "What Happened to IfNotNow?"

41 Personal interview, February 11, 2019.

42 Personal interview, August 4, 2019.

43 Chenoweth and Stephan, *Why Civil Resistance Works*.

44 Tighe et al., *American Jewish Population Project*.

45 This 3.5 percent statistic is relevant only to the Jewish American population and for Jewish American support for the occupation. The 3.5 percent threshold becomes much more complex when thinking about support for Israel and the occupation in the United States more broadly because Evangelical Christians and hawkish Republicans also support the occupation and are a very significant portion of the American public. This is further complicated by the fact that many American Jewish institutions are building strong coalitions and relationships with non-Jewish American Zionists, thereby decreasing the odds of ending American, and not only Jewish American, support for the occupation.

46 Cortellessa, "How IfNotNow Is Getting 2020 Democrats to Talk Occupation"; Mackey, "Pete Buttigieg and Joe Biden Condemn Israeli Occupation."

47 Plitnick, "More Than 100 Progressive Groups Push Biden."

48 Wilner, "Ocasio-Cortez, Tlaib and Other Star Freshmen Crash into Congress."

49 Einhorn, "Democratic Presidential Candidates."

50 Freedman, "What Happened to IfNotNow?"

51 Meyer, "Protest and Political Opportunities."

52 Tarrow, *Power in Movement*.

53 Suh, "How Do Political Opportunities Matter for Social Movements?"

54 Lowery, *They Can't Kill Us All*.

55 Jasper, *Art of Moral Protest*.

56 Chenoweth and Stephan, *Why Civil Resistance Works*.

57 Chen and Gorski, "Burnout in Social Justice."

58 Biekart and Fowler, "Transforming Activisms 2010+."

59 While it is a far more recent event and therefore difficult to understand how much of a catalyst it was, Israel's announcement to annex the Jordan Valley and part of the West Bank will be another critical moment in bringing more young Jews into the anti-occupation movement. The same is true for Israel's attempted judicial overhaul and subsequent protests as well as the 2023 Israel-Hamas War. See Farb, "Israel Will Lose My Entire Generation"; Rosenfeld, "What Does Annexation Mean for American Jews?"

60 Tatour, "'Unity Intifada' and '48 Palestinians."

61 Pfeffer, *Bibi*.

62 Pappe, "What Is Left of the Israeli Left? (1948–2015)."

63 Waxman, "Young American Jews and Israel."

64 United Nations Human Rights Council, "Report of the Independent Commission."

65 According to David Lloyd, "Disproportionate response is by now the IDF's official military doctrine." See Lloyd, "Settler Colonialism and the State of Exception," 70.

66 Beaumont, "Israel Kills Scores in Gaza City Suburb."

67 Borschel-Dan, "In Wake of War."

68 Borschel-Dan, "In Wake of War."

69 Personal interview, October 3, 2019.

70 Chenoweth and Pressman, "This Is What We Learned."

71 Moynihan, "About 20 Rabbis Arrested."

72 Kampeas, "With History in Mind."

73 Perea, *Immigrants Out!*

74 Personal interview, October 3, 2019.

75 Crenshaw, "Mapping the Margins"; Hancock, *Intersectionality*.

76 Tatum, "Complexity of Identity."

77 Fischbach, *Black Power and Palestine*; Davis, *Freedom Is a Constant Struggle*.

78 Kroll-Zeldin, "U.S. Jews Are Standing Up for Black Lives."

79 Ayoub, "Black-Palestinian Solidarity"; Bailey, "Black-Palestinian Solidarity"; Erakat, "Geographies of Intimacy."

80 See, for example, Schultz, *Going South*; Klapper, *Ballots, Babies, and Banners of Peace*; Landy, *Jewish Identity and Palestinian Rights*; Svirsky, *Arab-Jewish Activism*.

81 JStreet, "About Us," www.jstreet.org.

82 JStreet defined itself as "anti-occupation" in a 2017 statement. See JStreet, "Anti-BDS, Anti-occupation."

83 Interestingly, after I mentioned this to numerous activists during interviews and conversations, some people said that IfNotNow also acts as a gateway drug to more potent and radical forms of activism. This is evidenced by the fact that after getting involved with the Palestine solidarity movement through IfNotNow, many people go on from there to engage in co-resistance work on the ground in Palestine with All That's Left and the Center for Jewish Nonviolence. Many other activists move from IfNotNow to get involved with BDS campaigns through Jewish Voice for Peace.

84 Personal interview, July 23, 2020.

85 Landy, *Jewish Identity and Palestinian Rights*.

86 Independent Jewish Voices Canada, "About IJV," www.ijvcanada.org.

87 Na'amod, "Home," www.naamod.org.uk.

88 Personal interview, June 24, 2019.

89 Personal interview, June 25, 2019.

90 Personal interview, June 25, 2019.

91 Dolsten, "Jewish Currents."

92 Omer, *Days of Awe*, 47–49.

93 See chapter 5 for a more robust discussion on these guidelines.

94 Pink, "New Independent Jewish Student Network."

95 Kehilla Community Synagogue in Oakland, California, and Tzedek Chicago are two prominent examples. There is also Synagogues Rising, which is "a network of seven synagogues across the U.S. that integrate justice and spiritual practice at the heart of their missions." They are working to expand the Jewish presence and solidarity in justice and liberation movements across the country. See Rise Up, "Rise Up Grantees."

96 Personal interview, June 25, 2019.

97 Minkin, "Fear, Fantasy, and Family," 19.

98 Meyer, *Politics of Protest*, 51.

99 Personal interview, February 11, 2019.

100 Omer, *Days of Awe*.

2. UNLEARNING ZIONISM

1 Urofsky, *Voice That Spoke for Justice*; Urofsky, *Louis D. Brandeis*.

2 Isaiah Zeldin founded Stephen S. Wise Temple in 1964. See Greenberg, "Jewish Pass"; Dash Moore, *To the Golden Cities*.

3 Benson, *Harry S. Truman*.

4 See Schorr and Graf, *Sacred Calling*.

5 An excellent examination of the role that Jewish overnight summer camps play in the Zionist socialization of young Jews is Rudow, "'Camp Is Life, the Rest Is Just Details.'" More recently, a doctoral dissertation also examined this very topic. See Mitchell, "Building Home/Land."

6 See Ofer, *Escaping the Holocaust*.

7 NFTY is the National Federation of Temple Youth, the youth movement affiliated with Reform Judaism. NFTY-EIE, which is now called the Isaac and Helaine Heller EIE High School in Israel, is a semester program for high school students in Israel. My personal experience is in line with empirical research on the transformative nature of immersive Israel experiences. For example, see Kelner, "Impact of Israel Experience Programs."

8 See Shtern and Yacobi, "Urban Geopolitics of Neighboring."

9 See Zink, "Quiet Transfer"; Habash, "Unmaking of Palestinian Neighborhoods."

10 Rose, *Myths of Zionism*; Laor, *Myths of Liberal Zionism*; Piterberg, *Returns of Zionism*.

11 Pappe, *Ten Myths about Israel*, preface.

12 I'm grateful for the work of other scholars who use this language as well, all of whom helped me understand the significance of this framework for thinking about how Jewish activists break away from their conditioning as Jews regarding unequivocal support for Israel. See Omer, *Days of Awe*; Knopf-Newman, *Politics of Teaching Palestine to Americans*; Abdo and Lentin, *Women and the Politics of Military Confrontation*. Additionally, the International Jewish Anti-Zionist Network officially adopted an unlearning Zionism framework as part of their educational training, even creating a workshop with the same name.

13 Karcher, *Reclaiming Judaism from Zionism*.

14 See chapter 3 for a more detailed discussion of Birthright.

15 Kober, "Israel Defense Forces."

16 Bomb shelters are ubiquitous in Israel. Most buildings have them, in addition to the public bomb shelters dispersed throughout Israeli cities and towns.

17 See the conclusion.

18 Pappe, *Ethnic Cleansing of Palestine*.

19 Veracini, "Other Shift"; Ghanem and Khateeb, "Israel in One Century," 80.

20 This of course pales in comparison to Palestinian experiences of exile and dispossession, which I would later learn about.

21 Neumann, *Land and Desire in Early Zionism*; Abufarha, "Land of Symbols."

22 Due to rigid restrictions imposed by the Israeli military, travel to Gaza is extremely difficult.

23 Finkelstein, "May Your Classroom Be a Sea Change."

24 I teach in the Swig Program in Jewish Studies and Social Justice. It is the first academic program that formally links these two fields of study. The "Social Justice and the Israeli-Palestinian Conflict" course is actually cross-listed with the department of politics and is not, per se, a Jewish studies class but is a class taught by a professor affiliated with our Jewish Studies and Social Justice program.

25 See Pappe, *Ethnic Cleansing of Palestine*; Saʿdi and Abu-Lughod, *Nakba*.

26 See Madmoni-Gerber, *Israeli Media and the Framing of Internal Conflict*; Bernstein, "Conflict and Protest in Israeli Society"; Elia-Shalev, *Israel's Black Panthers*. See also a special issue of *Women in Judaism: A Multidisciplinary e-Journal* 17, no. 2 (2020), with a focus on the Yemenite Babies Affair.

27 Ben Hagai and Zurbriggen, "Between Tikkun Olam and Self-Defense."

28 See Zimmerman and Lieberman, "Which Side Are You On, My People?"; Cooper, "What They Didn't Teach Me."

29 See Roberts, *Party and Policy in Israel*.

30 Beinart, *Crisis of Zionism*.

31 Fishman, "Why Young Jews Don't Trust."

32 Schiff, "Towards a Mission Statement"; Horowitz, *Defining Israel Education*; Grant and Kopelowitz, *Israel Education Matters*.

33 Hahn Tapper, *Judaisms*, 14.

34 Althusser, "Ideology and Ideological State Apparatuses."

35 For example, see Karcher, *Reclaiming Judaism from Zionism*; Levit, *Wrestling with Zion*; Kushner and Solomon, *Wrestling with Zion*; Beinart, *Crisis of Zionism*; Jewish Voice for Peace, NYC, *Confronting Zionism*; Chabon and Waldman, *Kingdom of Olives and Ash*.

36 Although this chapter centers the experiences of young American Jews in their processes of personal transformation, I am in no way suggesting that their voices are more important than others in the conversation (i.e., Palestinians). Instead, I am proposing that the process of unlearning Zionism is integral to young

American Jews' becoming powerful allies and solidarity activists in the struggle for Palestinian liberation. By omitting the experiences of Palestinians from this chapter (except for the one individual mentioned) and largely from this book, I am not seeking to reproduce the American Jewish educational experience that erases Palestinians and omits them from the conversation. On the contrary, I hope that readers will understand the process of unlearning Zionism as central to one's liberation from the constraints of an exclusive Jewish ethnonationalism, one that is integral to practicing solidarity with Palestinians.

37 Tatum, "Teaching White Students about Racism."

38 In 1975, the United Nations General Assembly adopted Resolution 3379, which stated that Zionism is a form of racism. This determination was revoked by the General Assembly in 1991, but it remains a highly contested notion. See also Massad, "Ends of Zionism"; Fishman, "'Disaster of Another Kind.'"

39 See Ben-Eliezer, "Multicultural Society and Everyday Cultural Racism"; Abu, Yuval, and Ben-Porat, "Race, Racism, and Policing"; Daniele, "Mizrahi Jews and the Zionist Settler Colonial Context"; Massad, "Zionism's Internal Others."

40 Newstrom, "Management of Unlearning," 36.

41 Becker, "Individual and Organizational Unlearning."

42 Karcher, "Afterword," 366.

43 Yiftachel, *Ethnocracy.*

44 Shuman, *Other People's Stories.*

45 Adichie, "Danger of a Single Story."

46 Lentin, "Palestinian Lives Matter."

47 Said, "Zionism from the Standpoint of Its Victims"; Shohat, "Sephardim in Israel."

48 Applebaum and Zakai, "Pretend Trips to Israel"; Pomson, Wertheimer, and Wolf, *Hearts and Minds*; Sales and Saxe, *"How Goodly Are Thy Tents"*; Gerber and Mazor, *Mapping Israel Education.*

49 Krasner, "Place of Tikkun Olam"; Cherian, "'Tikkun Olam.'"

50 Schleifer, "Jewish and Contemporary Origins"; Sucharov, "Values, Identity, and Israel Advocacy."

51 Waxman, "Young American Jews and Israel."

52 Mitchell, "Beyond Resolution"; Lederach, *Preparing for Peace.*

53 This is most clearly evidenced by the personal stories of activists involved with numerous joint Palestinian-Israeli organizations and groups such as Combatants for Peace, Parents Circle–Bereaved Families Forum, and Ta'ayush, among others.

54 Most of the information I provide here on Robi Damelin is based on two documentary films in which she is featured, *Encounter Point* (2006) and *One Day After Peace* (2012).

55 Horowitz and Kimmerling, "Some Implications of Military Service."

56 See www.parentscirclefriends.org.

57 See www.theparentscircle.org.

58 Hill and Plitnick, *Except for Palestine.*

59 Sulaiman is featured in the documentary film *Disturbing the Peace* (2016). The information about him in this section comes from that film as well as from Eilberg-Schwartz and Khatib, *In This Place Together*.

60 See www.cfpeace.org.

61 See Hassenfeld, "Negotiating Critical Analysis and Collective Belonging"; Zakai, "Values in Tension"; Zakai, *My Second Favorite Country*.

62 Reingold, "Not the Israel of My Elementary School"; Knopf-Newman, *Politics of Teaching Palestine to Americans*.

63 This is a nod to the legendary R&B singer Ms. Lauryn Hill (Hill, *Miseducation of Lauryn Hill*).

64 Solomon, "IfNotNow Launches #YouNeverToldMe."

65 See www.younevertoldme.org.

66 See, for example, Fishman, "Why Young Jews Don't Trust"; Simpson, "Why Didn't They Teach Me about the Occupation?"

67 hooks, *Teaching to Transgress*, 4.

68 Personal interview, June 25, 2019.

69 Personal interview, May 12, 2020.

70 Personal interview, May 12, 2020.

71 Personal interview, July 14, 2020.

72 Personal interview, July 14, 2020.

73 Cook, *Disappearing Palestine*.

74 Makdisi, "Architecture of Erasure."

75 Black, *Maps and History*; Hodgson, *Rethinking World History*, 3–5.

76 This incident is one of many factors that prompted Elon to walk off his Birthright trip. I explore the 2018 Birthright walk-off in greater depth in chapter 3.

77 Collins-Kreiner, Mansfield, and Kliot, "Reflection of a Political Conflict in Mapping."

78 Now This News, "Birthright Participant Questions Israel Map."

79 Kroll-Zeldin, "Does Israel Function as an Apartheid State?"

80 Personal interview, December 17, 2018.

81 Personal interview, June 25, 2019.

82 Omer, *Days of Awe*.

83 Personal interview, February 12, 2020.

84 Karni and Broadwater, "Biden Signs Law."

85 Weiner and Weiner, "When My Daughter Called Israel an Apartheid State, I Objected."

86 Personal interview, June 24, 2019.

87 Personal interview, February 12, 2020.

88 Omer, *Days of Awe*.

89 Cruger-Zaken, "Questioning Zionism."

90 Habeeb, "Denial," 183.

91 Personal interview, September 24, 2019.

3. #NOTJUSTAFREETRIP

1 Subsequent news coverage of the walk-off similarly received widespread attention online. Most notably, a video posted online by Now This was viewed more than four million times. The video can be viewed at www.facebook.com.

2 IfNotNow, "Beyond Talk."

3 See chapter 2.

4 Hasson, "For Second Time in Two Weeks."

5 Waxman, *Trouble in the Tribe*.

6 Personal interview, September 17, 2019.

7 Minkin, "Fear, Fantasy, and Family," 19.

8 Corwin Berman, *American Jewish Philanthropic Complex*.

9 Beinart, "Failure of the American Jewish Establishment."

10 Goldberg, *Jewish Power*.

11 Kaye/Kantrowitz, *Colors of Jews*; Dash Moore, *American Jewish Identity Politics*.

12 Sasson, *New American Zionism*.

13 Liebman and Cohen, *Two Worlds of Judaism*; Pew Research Center, "Jewish Americans in 2020"; American Jewish Committee, "2021 Survey of American and Israeli Jewish Opinion."

14 Pew Research Center, "Jewish Americans in 2020." This figure is notably lower than in the previous Pew Survey on American Jews, which was conducted in 2013 and found that 87 percent of American Jews believed that caring about Israel is either "essential" or "important" to their identity as Jews. See Pew Research Center, "Portrait of Jewish Americans."

15 For example, see Dash Moore, "Bonding Images"; Corwin Berman, *American Jewish Philanthropic Complex*.

16 Tobin, *Transition of Communal Values*; Shaul Bar Nissim, "'New Diaspora Philanthropy?'"

17 IfNotNow, "Beyond Talk."

18 IfNotNow, "Beyond Talk."

19 Blau, "Does Your Jewish Charity Donate to the Settlements?"

20 Blau, "Jewish Federations Donated Millions to Israeli Settlements."

21 Blau, "Jewish Federations Donated Millions to Israeli Settlements."

22 Corwin Berman, *American Jewish Philanthropic Complex*.

23 Nathan-Kazis, "REVEALED."

24 Kane, "'It's Killing the Student Movement.'"

25 Landau, "Official Documents Prove."

26 Kershner, "U.S. Student."

27 Diller Teen Foundation Alumni, "We Alumni of the Diller Teen Foundation."

28 Nathan-Kazis, "Canary Mission Dumped."

29 IfNotNow, "Beyond Talk," 12.

30 Brown, "I'm Jewish"; Weinthal, "Ilhan Omar."

31 Berlet and Planansky, "Silencing Dissent."

32 Zunes, "Israel Lobby."

33 Beinart, "It's Time to End America's Blank Check."

34 Pew Research Center, "U.S. Public Has Favorable View."

35 See www.jewishvote.org.

36 Kampeas, "Fallout from Eliot Engel's Likely Defeat."

37 IfNotNow, "Beyond Talk."

38 "Sheldon Adelson."

39 Black, "Inside Story."

40 Maltz, "Jewish Group Releases Blacklist."

41 IfNotNow, "Beyond Talk," 28.

42 Beinart, *Crisis of Zionism*.

43 For a similar argument extended to the progressive American community, see Hill and Plitnick, *Except for Palestine*.

44 Saxe et al., *Young Adults and Jewish Engagement*.

45 Saxe et al., *Israel, Politics, and Birthright Israel*, 4.

46 Kelner, *Tours That Bind*, 196.

47 Saxe et al., *Generation Birthright Israel*.

48 Saxe et al., *Generation Birthright Israel*; Saxe, Sasson, and Hecht, *Taglit-Birthright Israel*; Saxe et al., "Intermarriage"; Saxe et al., *Beyond 10 Days*; Sasson et al., "Does Taglit-Birthright Israel Foster Long-Distance Nationalism?"

49 IfNotNow, "Not Just a Free Trip," www.notjustafreetrip.com.

50 Abramson, "Securing the Diasporic 'Self'"; Abramson, "Making a Homeland, Constructing a Diaspora."

51 This quote from Barry Chazan comes from Kelner, *Tours That Bind*, 65.

52 Personal interview, March 13, 2019.

53 *Hasbara* literally means "explaining," but the term colloquially refers to Israeli propaganda. See Schleifer, "Jewish and Contemporary Origins."

54 Personal interview, January 15, 2019.

55 Personal interview, October 3, 2019.

56 Abowd, "Moroccan Quarter."

57 Personal interview, March 1, 2019.

58 "Young U.S. Jews Aim 'Occupy' Movement at Birthright Israel."

59 The entire video can be found on the JVP website at www.jewishvoiceforpeace.org.

60 "Young U.S. Jews Aim 'Occupy' Movement at Birthright Israel."

61 "Young U.S. Jews Aim 'Occupy' Movement at Birthright Israel."

62 To read the manifesto written by the young JVP activists, visit www.jewishvoiceforpeace.org.

63 Sommer, "Jewish Voice for Peace."

64 See Mlyn, "Why I Refuse to Go on Birthright"; Kaplan, "Three Reasons to #ReturnTheBirthright"; Neuman, "Return the Birthright."

65 Breaking the Silence is an Israeli NGO composed of former soldiers in the Israeli military that is dedicated to exposing the realities of everyday life in the occupa-

tion. By collecting testimonials, engaging in public education and advocacy, and leading tours in the occupied territories, the organization refuses to turn a blind eye to the impacts that Israeli occupation and military activities have on Palestinian society. As a result of their work, the group has become the subject of a coordinated media and political smear campaign and violent assaults and threats toward its staff. See Zonszein, "Breaking the Silence."

66 Danielle Raskin, Twitter post, June 28, 2018, www.twitter.com/DanielleRaskin1/status/1012333187085856769.

67 Birthright was originally a program for Jews between the ages of eighteen and twenty-six years old. In 2017, the program raised the eligibility age to thirty-two in order to increase the pool of potential participants.

68 Kelner, *Tours That Bind*, 60.

69 Personal interview, September 17, 2019.

70 Personal interview, October 3, 2019.

71 For examples, see Sommer, "Principled Activists or Entitled Brats?"; Epstein, "#IfNotNow Is Not Jewish Virtue."

72 See Zaiman, "Of Birthright Transgressions"; Wagner, "Why I Walked Off a Birthright Trip"; Curcie, "Why Walking Off My Birthright Trip Was the Jewish Thing to Do"; Nagel, "Why I Walked Off My Birthright Israel Trip"; Raskin, "We Had to Meet Our Peers Where They Were".

73 Zakai, *My Second Favorite Country*.

74 Zakai, "'Bad Things Happened.'"

75 Arnett, *Emerging Adulthood*.

76 Ben Hagai, Whitlatch, and Zurbriggen, "'We Didn't Talk about the Conflict.'"

77 Personal interview, December 17, 2018.

78 Personal interview, January 15, 2019.

79 Habib, *Israel, Diaspora, and the Routes of National Belonging*.

80 Schneider, "It Changed My Sympathy, Not My Opinion."

81 Hahn Tapper, *Judaisms*, 232.

82 For a critical view of the Jewish continuity issue, see Corwin Berman, Rosenblatt, and Stahl, "Continuity Crisis."

83 Personal interview, December 13, 2018.

84 Noy, "Political Ends of Tourism."

85 Landy, "Place of Palestinians."

86 Rothman, "10 Reasons the 'City of David' Is Not the Wholesome Tourist Site."

87 Hasson, "Israeli Court Clears the Way."

88 B'Tselem, "Hebron City Center."

89 Griffiths, "Hope in Hebron."

90 +972 Magazine Staff, "Everything You Need to Know."

91 Personal interview, December 13, 2018.

92 Cannon, "Walking Off a Birthright Trip Isn't 'Stealing.'"

93 Maltz, "Sharp Decline."

94 Tunis and Breza, "Boycott Birthright—Unconditionally."

95 Sales, "15 Jewish Anti-Occupation Activists Arrested."

96 Maltz, "J Street Launches Birthright Alternative."

97 Maltz, "After Summer Walkouts."

98 Magarik, "Birthright Is Chasing Away Engaged Jews."

99 Feldman, "After Getting Kicked Off Birthright, Trio Regroups in West Bank."

100 Raskin, "We Had to Meet Our Peers Where They Were."

101 See www.extendprograms.org.

102 See www.birthrightunplugged.org.

4. CO-RESISTANCE

1 I originally wrote a description of this action in an op-ed published shortly after it took place, from which this is taken. See Kroll-Zeldin, "Activists Reclaimed a Water Source."

2 Ziv, "Palestinian, Israeli, and Diaspora Jewish Activists Reclaim Spring."

3 Ziv, "Palestinian, Israeli, and Diaspora Jewish Activists Reclaim Spring."

4 See Peace Now, "Return of the Outpost Method."

5 Hass, "Israel Pushing to Legalize West Bank Outpost."

6 Gordon, *Israel's Occupation*; Allegra, Handel, and Maggor, *Normalizing Occupation*.

7 Gale, "'Coloniser Who Refuses.'"

8 Freire, *Pedagogy of the Oppressed*, 128.

9 Hill, Ben Hagai, and Zurbriggen, "Intersecting Alliances."

10 Svirsky and Ben-Arie, *From Shared Life to Co-resistance*, 44.

11 Gordon, "Against the Wall"; Pallister-Wilkins, "Radical Ground"; Hallward, "Creative Responses to Separation"; Gawerc, "Building Solidarity across Asymmetrical Risks."

12 Fleischmann, *Israeli Peace Movement*; Daniele, *Women, Reconciliation, and the Israeli-Palestinian Conflict*; Gawerc, "Solidarity Is in the Heart."

13 Landy, *Jewish Identity and Palestinian Rights*; Omer, *Days of Awe*.

14 Gale, "'Coloniser Who Refuses.'"

15 Maoz, "Peace Building in Violent Conflict"; Hammack, "Identity, Conflict, and Coexistence"; Schroeder and Risen, "Befriending the Enemy."

16 Allport, *Nature of Prejudice*; Hahn Tapper, "Pedagogy of Social Justice Education"; Pettigrew, "Intergroup Contact Theory"; Gross and Maor, "Is Contact Theory Still Valid in Acute Asymmetrical Violent Conflict?"

17 Dixon, Durrheim, and Tredoux, "Beyond the Optimal Contact Strategy"; Torstrick, *Limits of Coexistence*; Thiessen and Darweish, "Conflict Resolution and Asymmetric Conflict."

18 Maoz, "Does Contact Work in Protracted Asymmetrical Conflict?," 118.

19 Hammack and Pilecki, "Power in History"; Hantzopoulos, "Encountering Peace"; Hammack, "Exploring the Reproduction of Conflict."

20 It is important to note that Encounter articulates their mission as being rooted in education rather than coexistence. Although coexistence is part of the frame-

work behind the organization's activities, it is not the driving force. According to Encounter, their vision is that "Jewish communities in Israel and the United States will be a positive force in the pursuit of advancing a durable resolution to the Israeli-Palestinian conflict that upholds the dignity, security, and rights of all parties." Such a model explicitly aims to educate Jews alone. After years of working within the education framework laid out by Encounter, Sumka observed that education was a necessary but insufficient strategy in the work of justice and peace, which was one of many things that led her to found CJNV.

21 Mi'Ari, "Attitudes of Palestinians toward Normalization with Israel"; Salem, "Anti-normalization Discourse"; Barakat and Goldenblatt, "Coping with Anti-normalization."

22 Rahman, "Co-existence vs. Co-resistance."

23 Uri and Evron, "Forget about Dialogue Groups."

24 Roy, "Why Peace Failed"; Gelvin, *Israel-Palestine Conflict.*

25 Track II diplomacy refers to the back-channel discussions held by everyday people and grassroots organizations rather than official politicians working on behalf of a state, which is considered to be a Track I diplomatic effort. See Agha et al., *Track-II Diplomacy*; see also Kaufman, Salem, and Verhoeven, *Bridging the Divide.*

26 Gale, "'Coloniser Who Refuses,'" 49.

27 Katz, *Connecting with the Enemy*, 163.

28 Pallister-Wilkins, "Separation Wall"; Hallward, "Creative Responses to Separation"; Todorova, "Vulnerability as a Politics of Decolonial Solidarity."

29 Dolphin, *West Bank Wall*; Sfard, *Wall and the Gate.*

30 Usher, "Unmaking Palestine"; Sfard, *Wall and the Gate.*

31 Tamimi, "Socioeconomic and Environmental Impacts"; Dana, "West Bank Apartheid/Separation Wall."

32 Gordon, "Against the Wall"; Hallward, "Creative Responses to Separation."

33 Barakat and Goldenblatt, "Coping with Anti-normalization"; Simons, "Fields and Facebook"; Gordon and Grietzer, *Anarchists Against the Wall.*

34 Hallward, "Creative Responses to Separation."

35 See Naaman, "Silenced Outcry"; Keshet, *Checkpoint Watch.*

36 Wilmer, *Breaking Cycles of Violence*; Head, "Politics of Empathy."

37 Personal interview, May 22, 2020.

38 Donitsa-Schmidt and Vadish, "American Students in Israel."

39 Personal interview, May 12, 2020.

40 Personal interview, June 25, 2019.

41 Tarlau, "'We Do No Need Outsiders to Study Us.'"

42 Calhoun, "Occupy Wall Street in Perspective"; Gordon, "Israel's 'Tent Protests.'"

43 Personal interview, June 29, 2019.

44 For an analysis on how Occupy influenced political and social movements, see Levitan, *Generation Occupy.*

45 See www.allthatsleftcollective.com.

46 Goldberg, "Why Don't Young Diaspora Jews Like Naftali Bennett?"

47 Goldberg, "Why Don't Young Diaspora Jews Like Naftali Bennett?"

48 A short video documenting the action is available on YouTube: All That's Left, "Redrawing the Green Line," YouTube, June 5, 2013, www.youtube.com/watch?v=2KQkjvyMubA&ab_channel=AllThatsLeftAntiOccupationCollective.

49 Bargeles, "Do Not Forget the Green Line."

50 Zink, "Quiet Transfer."

51 Zonszein, "IDF Maps Village of Susya."

52 Omer-Man, "Diaspora Jews Bring Solidarity."

53 Omer-Man, "Diaspora Jews Bring Solidarity."

54 Personal interview, June 24, 2019.

55 Personal interview, May 12, 2020.

56 Prusher, "Tree Uprooting Heard around the World."

57 Seidel, "'We Refuse to Be Enemies.'"

58 See www.encounterprograms.org.

59 See www.cjnv.org.

60 Cohen, *Politics of Planting*; Masalha, "Remembering the Palestinian Nakba."

61 Bohrer, "Jewish Activists Plant Trees in Palestine."

62 Rosen and Roth, "Progressive Jewish Response."

63 Schindler, "What's Shabbat Like."

64 Beinart, "What I Saw Last Friday in Hebron."

65 Personal interview, February 6, 2019.

66 Personal interview, February 3, 2020.

67 Schock, *Unarmed Insurrections*, 142.

68 Wright, "Palestine, My Love."

69 Todorova, "Vulnerability as a Politics of Decolonial Solidarity."

70 Todorova, "Vulnerability as a Politics of Decolonial Solidarity," 131.

71 Hemmings, "Affective Solidarity."

72 Wright, *Israeli Radical Left*.

73 Personal interview, June 17, 2019.

74 Pollock, "Using and Disputing Privilege."

75 Personal interview, July 17, 2020.

76 Sumka, "It's Time to Put Our Privileged Jewish Bodies on the Line."

77 Uri and Evron, "Forget about Dialogue Groups."

78 Personal interview, June 17, 2019.

79 Prescod-Weinstein, "Black and Palestinian Lives Matter."

80 Knesset, "Jerusalem Day."

81 Lustick, "Reinventing Jerusalem."

82 Most of the youth at the march are bussed in from various locations throughout Israel and the West Bank to inundate Jerusalem with nationalist pride.

83 Roth-Rowland, "U.S. Jewish Activist."

84 Sommer and Silber, "Jewish-American Protestor Hurt."

85 Kroll-Zeldin, "Ethnography of Exclusion."

86 In addition to the previously cited articles, see Brammer-Shlay, "Israeli Police Broke My Arm."
87 Personal interview, July 14, 2020.
88 Personal interview, February 8, 2020.
89 Personal interview, February 12, 2020.
90 Uri and Evron, "Forget about Dialogue Groups."
91 See Britt and Heise, "From Shame to Pride in Identity Politics"; Riemer and Brown, *We Are Everywhere.*
92 Personal interview, May 20, 2020.
93 Personal interview, June 18, 2019.
94 Cesaire, *Discourse on Colonialism.*
95 Svirsky and Ben-Arie, *From Shared Life to Co-resistance*, 150.
96 Personal interview, July 17, 2020.
97 Svirsky and Ben-Arie, *From Shared Life to Co-resistance.*

5. UNDER PRESSURE

1 Tufts University Students for Justice in Palestine, "Tufts Students Pass Referendum."
2 Campus Hillel chapters usually allow Jewish student groups and clubs to operate through the Hillel itself. These groups did not organize through Hillel because their politics vis-à-vis Israel do not align with Hillel International's guidelines for student groups since they support BDS.
3 Barghouti, *BDS: Boycott, Divestment, Sanctions.*
4 Kane, "States Are Cracking Down."
5 Researching the American-Israeli Alliance and Jewish Voice for Peace, "Deadly Exchange."
6 Researching the American-Israeli Alliance and Jewish Voice for Peace, "Deadly Exchange."
7 Knox, "Tufts Police Chief Travels to Israel."
8 Researching the American-Israeli Alliance and Jewish Voice for Peace, "Deadly Exchange."
9 Di Stefano and Henaway, "Boycotting Apartheid."
10 Sharp, *Politics of Nonviolent Action.*
11 Magid, "Jewish American Peace Camp," 159.
12 Personal interview, December 15, 2021.
13 Al-Subaey, Skinner, and Drezner, "Deadly Exchange."
14 Members of the Tufts Community, "Letter Regarding TUPD Training in Israel," March 4, 2018, https://docs.google.com/forms/d/e/1FAIpQLSdwUnMfcSdExGTYk_TUk6q5CB9ogRPTfDAUoUPXahivON-weg/viewform.
15 Tufts University Students for Justice in Palestine, "Tufts Students Pass Referendum."
16 Tufts University Students for Justice in Palestine, "Op-Ed."

17 Tufts University Students for Justice in Palestine, "Tufts Students Pass Referendum."

18 See Kerstein, "Tufts University Group Condemns Passage"; Bandler, "Tufts Student Body Condemns"; Barrows-Friedman, "Boston Students Vilified."

19 Elman, "Antisemitism and BDS on US Campuses."

20 Said, *Orientalism*. For an interesting discussion on orientalism in the context of BDS, see Pegues, "Empire, Race, and Settler Colonialism."

21 Zunes, "Reflections on BDS."

22 Thrall, "BDS."

23 Barghouti, *BDS: Boycott, Divestment, Sanctions*, 4.

24 Barghouti, *BDS: Boycott, Divestment, Sanctions*, 56; For a discussion on the 2004 ICJ opinion, see Sfard, *Wall and the Gate*.

25 BDS National Committee, "Palestinian United Call for Boycott, Divestment and Sanctions."

26 See the FAQs on the official BDS website at www.bdsmovement.net.

27 Ghanayem, Mogannam, and Sharif, "Locating Palestinians at the Intersections."

28 Thrall, "BDS."

29 See Fishman, "BDS Message of Anti-Zionism"; Barnett and Karsh, *Soft Threats to National Security*; Sheskin and Felson, "Is the Boycott, Divestment, and Sanctions Movement Tainted by Anti-Semitism?"

30 Hahn Tapper, *Judaisms*, 117.

31 Hilton, "Palestinian Freedom Isn't a Threat to Jews."

32 Hilton, "Palestinian Freedom Isn't a Threat to Jews."

33 Feldman, *Boycotts Past and Present*.

34 Barghouti, *BDS: Boycott, Divestment, Sanctions*.

35 Hyslop, "South African Boycott Experience"; Booth, *Race Game*.

36 MacLean, "Revisiting (and Revising?) Sports Boycotts."

37 See www.bdsmovement.net.

38 Liew, "Sportswashing Is Associated with Certain Countries"; see also Francesco Belcastro, "Sport, Politics, and the Struggle over 'Normalization.'"

39 Bakan and Abu-Laban, "Palestinian Resistance and International Solidarity."

40 Barghouti, "Opting for Justice."

41 Barghouti, "BDS: Nonviolent, Globalized Palestinian Resistance," 113.

42 Zunes, "Reflections on BDS."

43 Pew Research Center, "Jewish Americans in 2020." The final 3 percent did not respond to the query.

44 Telhami, "What Do Americans Think of the BDS Movement, Aimed at Israel?"

45 Telhami, "What Do Americans Think of the BDS Movement, Aimed at Israel?"

46 JStreet, "National Jewish Survey Results."

47 Abileah, "Fresh Tactics and New Voices," 20.

48 Personal interview, July 6, 2021.

49 Barghouti, "BDS: Nonviolent, Globalized Palestinian Resistance."

50 Barghouti, "BDS: Nonviolent, Globalized Palestinian Resistance," 110.

51 Ananth, "Politics of the Palestinian BDS Movement," 135.

52 Elman, "Antisemitism and BDS on US Campuses."

53 Freedman, "What Happened to IfNotNow?".

54 See Goodstein, "Presbyterians Vote to Divest Holdings"; Cunningham, "BDS Victory at TIAA-CREF."

55 Rebecca Vilkomerson, Twitter post, April 12, 2021, https://twitter.com/rvilkomerson/status/1381703709843918851?s=11.

56 See www.jewishvoiceforpeace.org.

57 See www.jewishvoiceforpeace.org.

58 See www.jewishvoiceforpeace.org.

59 Omer-Man, "JVP Just Declared Itself Anti-Zionist."

60 See Mason, "Epiphany in Slow Motion."

61 Personal Interview, July 6, 2021.

62 Personal Interview, July 6, 2021.

63 Personal interview, December 15, 2021.

64 Kelman et al., "Safe and on the Sidelines"; see also my analysis of this report: Kroll-Zeldin, "Jewish Students Feel Unsafe on Campus?"

65 Elman, "Antisemitism and BDS on US Campuses"; Pessin and Ben-Atar, *Anti-Zionism on Campus*; Saxe et al., *Antisemitism and the College Campus.*

66 Saxe et al., *Hotspots of Antisemitism and Anti-Israel Sentiment*; Stern, *Conflict over the Conflict.*

67 See Hillel International, "Hillel Israel Guidelines."

68 Sharansky, "3D Test of Anti-Semitism."

69 Kirk, "Open Hillel."

70 Omer, *Days of Awe*, 47.

71 Svirsky, "BDS as a Mediator."

72 Personal interview, December 15, 2021.

73 Personal interview, June 24, 2019.

74 Omer, *Days of Awe*, 28.

75 Reut Institute, "Delegitimization Challenge."

76 Minkin, "Fear, Fantasy, and Family," 50.

77 See Olesker, "Delegitimization as a National Security Threat."

78 JStreet, "Boycott, Divestment, and Sanctions Movement."

79 T'ruah, "Freedom of Speech in Jewish Tradition."

80 Berkman, "Federations, JCPA Teaming."

81 Ananth, "Politics of the Palestinian BDS Movement," 133.

82 Salaita, *Uncivil Rights.*

83 Messianic Jews are members of a religious community that combines Jewish practice with a theological belief in the divinity of Jesus. Jews for Jesus is the most well-known and largest Messianic Jewish group. See Cohn-Sherbok, *Messianic Judaism*; Hahn Tapper, *Judaisms*, 226–228.

84 Personal interview, April 29, 2021.

85 Personal interview, July 23, 2020.

86 See Sirri, "BDS in a Time of Precarity."

87 Sarah Anne Minkin includes a section in her dissertation, "Fear, Fantasy, and Family," about the use of fear as a political tool.

88 Kaufman, "Best Day of My Life."

89 Garcia, "Moveable Feast."

90 Palestinian BDS National Committee, "Palestinians Salute the Movement for Black Lives."

91 See the BDS Committee's Open Letter of Support to the Standing Rock Sioux Tribe, available at www.bdsmovement.net.

92 Horowitz, "Moving Away from Zionism."

93 Personal interview, July 6, 2021.

94 See Amendment No. 28 to the Entry into Israel Law; see also Maltz, "Israel's New Travel Ban."

95 Notably, this same law was used to bar the entry into Israel of two members of the U.S. Congress, Rashida Tlaib and Ilhan Omar, both of whom publicly support BDS.

96 Landau and Berger, "Israel Denies Entry."

97 Wise, "I'm the First Jew Banned from Israel for Supporting BDS."

98 Habeeb, "Denial," 184.

99 Bakan and Abu-Laban, "Palestinian Resistance and International Solidarity."

100 "Israeli Government OKs $72 Million Anti-BDS Project."

101 Freedman, *Battle over BDS*, 3.

102 Barghouti, "BDS: Nonviolent, Globalized Palestinian Resistance," 108.

103 Rosenfeld, "Roadblocks Ahead."

104 Onishi, *Preparing for War*.

CONCLUSION

1 Avodah has houses and programs in Chicago, New Orleans, New York, and Washington, D.C.

2 See www.avodah.net.

3 Cohen, "Avodah Considers Stepping Out on Israel/Palestine."

4 The Avodah alumni letter is available here: https://docs.google.com/forms/d/e/1 FAIpQLSf_1pn0imZJxcAEwWE2pBv9BiB3LRBDCd-yH7AYdad9TpTNEg/view-form.

5 An activist in the Avodah alumni network sent me the email correspondence between the alumni and the Avodah leadership, which I am quoting here.

6 Ellis, "Telling Secrets, Revealing Lives."

7 Delamont and Atkinson, *Ethnographic Engagements*.

8 Isaiah 12:3.

9 Freedman, "Birthday Party, Part 3."

BIBLIOGRAPHY

+972 Magazine Staff. "Everything You Need to Know about Khan Al-Ahmar." *+972 Magazine*, October 16, 2019. www.972mag.com.

Abdo, Nahla, and Ronit Lentin. *Women and the Politics of Military Confrontation: Palestinian and Israeli Gendered Narratives of Dislocation*. New York: Berghahn Books, 2004.

Abileah, Rae. "Fresh Tactics and New Voices in the Movement for Justice and Freedom in the Middle East." *Tikkun* 26, no. 4 (2011): 19–44.

Abowd, Thomas. "The Moroccan Quarter: A History of the Present." *Jerusalem Quarterly* 7 (2000): 6–16.

Abraham, Yuval. "Classified Document Reveals IDF 'Firing Zones' Built to Give Land to Settlers." *+972 Magazine*, July 11, 2022. www.972mag.com.

Abraham, Yuval, and Basil Adra. "Armed with High Court Expulsion Order, Israel's Bulldozers Arrive in Masafer Yatta." *+972 Magazine*, May 12, 2022. www.972mag.com.

Abramson, Yehonatan. "Making a Homeland, Constructing a Diaspora: The Case of Taglit-Birthright Israel." *Political Geography* 58, no. 58 (2017): 14–23.

———. "Securing the Diasporic 'Self' by Travelling Abroad: Taglit-Birthright and Ontological Security." *Journal of Ethnic and Migration Studies* 45, no. 4 (2019): 656–673.

Abu, Ofir, Fany Yuval, and Guy Ben-Porat. "Race, Racism, and Policing: Responses to Ethiopian Jews in Israel to Stigmatization by the Police." *Ethnicities* 17, no. 5 (2017): 688–706.

Abufarha, Nasser. "Land of Symbols: Cactus, Poppies, Orange and Olive Trees in Palestine." *Identities: Global Studies in Culture and Power* 15, no. 3 (2008): 343–368.

Adichie, Chimananda N. "The Danger of a Single Story." www.ted.com.

Agha, Hussein, Shai Feldman, Ahmad Khalidi, and Zeev Schiff, eds. *Track-II Diplomacy: Lessons from the Middle East*. Cambridge, MA: MIT Press, 2003.

Allegra, Marco, Ariel Handel, and Erez Maggor. *Normalizing Occupation: The Politics of Everyday Life in the West Bank Settlements*. Bloomington: Indiana University Press, 2017.

Allport, Gordon. *The Nature of Prejudice*. Cambridge: Addison-Wesley, 1954.

Al-Subaey, Amira, Leila Skinner, and Sam Drezner. "A Deadly Exchange: The Implications and Effects of American-Israeli Police Relations." *Tufts Observer*, February 25, 2019. www.tuftsobserver.org.

Alterman, Eric. *We Are Not One: A History of America's Fight over Israel*. New York: Basic Books, 2022.

Althusser, Louis. "Ideology and Ideological State Apparatuses (Notes towards an Investigation)." In *The Anthropology of the State: A Reader*, edited by Aradhana Sharma and Akhil Gupta, 86–111. Malden, MA: Blackwell, 2006.

American Jewish Committee. "2021 Survey of American and Israeli Jewish Opinion." 2021. www.ajc.org/survey2021.

Amnesty International. "Israel's Apartheid Against Palestinians: Cruel System of Domination and Crime Against Humanity." 2022.

Ananth, Sriram. "The Politics of the Palestinian BDS Movement." *Socialism and Democracy* 27, no. 3 (2013): 129–143.

Angel, Arielle. "Jewish Americans Are at a Turning Point with Israel." *Guardian*, May 22, 2021. www.theguardian.com.

Applebaum, Lauren, and Sivan Zakai. "'I'm Going to Israel and All I Need to Pack Is My Imagination': Pretend Trips to Israel in Jewish Early Childhood Education." *Journal of Jewish Education* 86, no. 1 (2020): 94–119.

Arnett, Jeffrey. *Emerging Adulthood: The Winding Road from the Late Teens through the Twenties*. New York: Oxford University Press, 2015.

Association of Civil Rights in Israel. "Info-Sheet: The 12 Villages of Firing Zone 918 in the South Hebron Hills." 2016.

Auerbach, Jerold S. *Are We One? Jewish Identity in the United States and Israel*. New Brunswick, NJ: Rutgers University Press, 2001.

Ayoub, Joey. "Black-Palestinian Solidarity: Towards and Intersectional Alliance." In Hahn Tapper and Sucharov, *Social Justice and Israel/Palestine*, 204–213.

Azoulay, Ariella. "'We,' Palestinians and Jewish Israelis: The Right Not to Be a Perpetrator." In *Assuming Boycott: Resistance, Agency, Cultural Production*, edited by Kareem Estefan, Carin Kuoni, and Laura Raicovich, 81–90. New York: OR Books, 2017.

Bailey, Kristian Davis. "Black-Palestinian Solidarity in the Ferguson-Gaza Era." *American Quarterly* 67, no. 4 (2015): 1017–1026.

Bakan, Abigail B., and Yasmeen Abu-Laban. "Israel/Palestine, South Africa and the 'One-State Solution': The Case for an Apartheid Analysis." *South African Journal of Politics* 37, no. 3 (2010): 331–351.

———. "Palestinian Resistance and International Solidarity: The BDS Campaign." *Race and Class* 51, no. 1 (2009): 29–54.

Ball, Carlos A., ed. *After Marriage Equality: The Future of LGBT Rights*. New York: New York University Press, 2016.

Bandler, Aaron. "Tufts Student Body Condemns Israel Security Program." *Jewish Journal*, December 21, 2020. www.jewishjournal.com.

Barakat, Riman, and Dan Goldenblatt. "Coping with Anti-normalization." *Palestine-Israel Journal of Politics, Economics, and Culture* 18, no. 2/3 (2012): 86–95.

Bargeles, Claire. "Do Not Forget the Green Line." *Palestine-Israel Journal Blog*, n.d. www.pij.org.

Barghouti, Omar. *BDS: Boycott, Divestment, Sanctions: The Global Struggle for Palestinian Rights*. Chicago: Haymarket Books, 2011.

———. "BDS: Nonviolent, Globalized Palestinian Resistance to Israel's Settler Colonialism and Apartheid." *Journal of Palestine Studies* 50, no. 2 (2021): 108–125.

———. "Opting for Justice: The Critical Role of Anti-colonial Israelis in the Boycott, Divestment, and Sanctions Movement." *Settler Colonial Studies* 4, no. 4 (2014): 407–412.

Barnett, Dana, and Efraim Karsh, eds. *Soft Threats to National Security: Antisemitism, BDS and the De-legitimization of Israel*. New York: Routledge, 2011.

Barrows-Friedman, Nora. "Boston Students Vilified for Tackling How Israel Trains US Cops." *Electronic Intifada*, May 1, 2020. www.electronicintifada.net.

BDS National Committee. "Palestinian United Call for Boycott, Divestment and Sanctions Against Israel." July 9, 2005. www.bdsmovement.net.

Beaumont, Peter. "Israel Kills Scores in Gaza City Suburb in Deadliest Assault of Offensive So Far." *Guardian*, July 20, 2014. www.theguardian.com.

Becker, Aliza. *The American Jewish Peace Movement for a Two-State Solution to the Israeli-Palestinian Conflict: An Overview of National Initiatives, 1969-2012*. Washington, DC: Brit Tzedek v'Shalom, 2013.

Becker, Karen. "Individual and Organizational Unlearning: Directions for Future Research." *International Journal of Organizational Behaviour* 9, no. 7 (2005): 659–670.

Beinart, Peter. *The Crisis of Zionism*. New York: Picador, 2012.

———. "The Failure of the American Jewish Establishment." *New York Review of Books* 57, no. 10 (2010): 10–21.

———. "It's Time to End America's Blank Check Military Aid to Israel." *Forward*, May 20, 2019. www.forward.com.

———. "What I Saw Last Friday in Hebron." *Haaretz*, July 19, 2016. www.haaretz.com.

Belcastro, Francesco. "Sport, Politics, and the Struggle over 'Normalization' in Post-Oslo Israel and Palestine." *Mediterranean Politics* 27, no. 5 (2022): 644–664.

Ben-Eliezer, Uri. "Multicultural Society and Everyday Cultural Racism: Second Generation of Ethiopian Jews in Israel's 'Crisis of Modernization.'" *Ethnic and Racial Studies* 31, no. 5 (2008): 935–961.

Ben Hagai, Ella, Adam Whitlatch, and Eileen L. Zurbriggen. "'We Didn't Talk about the Conflict': The Birthright Trip's Influence on Jewish Americans' Understanding of the Israeli-Palestinian Conflict." *Peace and Conflict* 24, no. 2 (2018): 139–149.

Ben Hagai, Ella, and Eileen L. Zurbriggen. "Between Tikkun Olam and Self-Defense: Young Jewish Americans Debate the Israeli-Palestinian Conflict." *Journal of Social and Political Psychology* 5, no. 1 (2017): 173–199.

Benson, Michael T. *Harry S. Truman and the Founding of Israel*. Westport, CT: Praeger, 1997.

Berkman, Jacob. "Federations, JCPA Teaming to Fight Delegitimization of Israel." *Jewish Telegraphic Agency*, October 24, 2010. www.jta.org.

Berkman, Matthew. "Antisemitism, Anti-Zionism, and the American Racial Order: Revisiting the American Council for Judaism in the Twenty-First Century." *American Jewish History* 105, no. 1/2 (2021): 127–155.

Berkson, William. *Pirke Avot: Timeless Wisdom for Modern Life*. Philadelphia: Jewish Publication Society, 2010.

Berlet, Chip, and Maria Planansky. "Silencing Dissent: How Biased Civil Rights Policies Stifle Dialogue on Israel." *Tikkun* 30, no. 1 (2015).

Berman, Lila Corwin, Kate Rosenblatt, and Ronit Y. Stahl. "Continuity Crisis: The History and Sexual Politics of an American Jewish Communal Project." *American Jewish History* 104, no. 2 (2020): 167–194.

Bernstein, Deborah. "Conflict and Protest in Israeli Society: The Case of the Black Panthers of Israel." *Youth and Society* 16, no. 2 (1984): 129–152.

Biekart, Kees, and Alan Fowler. "Transforming Activisms 2010+: Exploring Ways and Waves." *Development and Change* 44, no. 3 (2013): 527–546.

Black, Edwin. "The Inside Story of J Street's Rejection by the Conference of Presidents." *Times of Israel*, May 30, 2014. www.timesofisrael.com.

Black, Jeremy. *Maps and History: Constructing Images of the Past*. New Haven, CT: Yale University Press, 1997.

Black Lives Matter. "Black Lives Matter 2020 Impact Report." 2020.

Blanc, Eric. "It's Not Enough to Fight—Labor and the Left Have to Be Serious about How to Win: An Interview with Jane McAlevey." *Jacobin*, October 19, 2020. www.jacobinmag.com.

Blau, Uri. "Does Your Jewish Charity Donate to the Settlements?" *Haaretz*, August 12, 2015. www.haaretz.com.

———. "Jewish Federations Donated Millions to Israeli Settlements over Four Years." *Haaretz*, October 30, 2017. www.haaretz.com.

Blumberg, Antonia. "Jewish Group Delivers Mourner's Kaddish for Gaza Victims." *HuffPost*, July 26, 2014. www.huffpost.com.

Bochner, Arthur P., and Carolyn Ellis. *Evocative Autoethnography: Writing Lives and Telling Stories*. Vol. 17. New York: Routledge, 2016.

Bohrer, Ashley. "Jewish Activists Plant Trees in Palestine, Uprooting Zionist Narratives." *Truthout*, February 12, 2015. www.truthout.org.

Booth, Douglas. *The Race Game: Sport and Politics in South Africa*. London: Frank Cass, 1998.

Borschel-Dan, Amanda. "In Wake of War, Leftist 'Self-Hating Jews' Find a Voice." *Times of Israel*, August 27, 2014. www.timesofisrael.com.

Both, Douglas. *The Race Game: Sport and Politics in South Africa*. London: Frank Cass, 1998.

Brammer-Shlay, Sarah. "Israeli Police Broke My Arm, but They Can't Stop Me from Resisting—Or Speaking Out." *Forward*, May 30, 2017. www.forward.com.

Britt, Lory, and David Heise. "From Shame to Pride in Identity Politics." In *Self, Identity, and Social Movements*, edited by Sheldon Stryker, Timothy J. Owens, and Robert W. White, 252–268. Minneapolis: University of Minnesota Press, 2000.

Brodkin, Karen. *How Jews Became White Folks and What That Says about Race in America*. New Brunswick, NJ: Rutgers University Press, 1998.

Brown, Maia S., and Sandra Silberstein. "Contested Diaspora: A Century of Zionist and Anti-Zionist Rhetorics in America." *Journal of Language, Identity, and Education* 11, no. 2 (2012): 85–95.

Brown, Scott. "I'm Jewish, and I'm Ashamed of How We're Treating Ilhan Omar." *+972 Magazine*, March 6, 2019. www.972mag.com.

B'Tselem. "Firing Zone 918." 2017.

———. "Hebron City Center." May 26, 2019. www.btselem.org.

———. "A Regime of Jewish Supremacy from the Jordan River to the Mediterranean Sea: This Is Apartheid." 2021.

Butler, Judith. *Parting Ways: Jewishness and the Critique of Zionism*. New York: Columbia University Press, 2012.

Calhoun, Craig. "Occupy Wall Street in Perspective." *British Journal of Sociology* 64, no. 1 (2013): 26–38.

Cannon, Benjy. "Walking Off a Birthright Trip Isn't 'Stealing.'" *Jewish Currents*, July 20, 2018. www.jewishcurrents.org.

Cavari, Amnon, and Guy Freedman. *American Public Opinion toward Israel*. New York: Routledge, 2021.

Cesaire, Aime. *Discourse on Colonialism*. Translated by Robin D. G. Kelley. New York: Monthly Review Press, 2000.

Chabon, Michael, and Ayelet Waldman, eds. *Kingdom of Olive and Ash*. New York: HarperCollins, 2017.

Chen, Cher Weixia, and Paul C. Gorski. "Burnout in Social Justice and Human Rights Activists: Symptoms, Causes and Implications." *Journal of Human Rights Practice* 7, no. 3 (2015): 366–390.

Chenoweth, Erica, and Jeremy Pressman. "This Is What We Learned by Counting the Women's Marches." *Washington Post*, February 7, 2017. www.washingtonpost.com.

Chenoweth, Erica, and Maria J. Stephan. *Why Civil Resistance Works: The Strategic Logic of Nonviolent Conflict*. New York: Columbia University Press, 2011.

Cherian, Finney. "'Tikkun Olam'—to Repair and Perfect the World: The Importance of Teaching Social Justice Pedagogy." *International Journal of Learning* 15, no. 2 (2008): 287–294.

Cohen, Mari. "Avodah Considers Stepping Out on Israel/Palestine." July 22, 2021. www.jewishcurrents.org.

Cohen, Naomi W. *The Americanization of Zionism, 1897–1948*. Hanover, NH: Brandeis University Press, 2003.

Cohen, Shaul Ephraim. *The Politics of Planting: Israeli-Palestinian Competition for Control and Land in the Jerusalem Periphery*. Chicago: University of Chicago Press, 1993.

———. *"We Refuse to Be Enemies": Political Geographies of Violence and Resistance in Palestine*. Chicago: University of Chicago Press, 1993.

Cohen, Steven M., and Ari Y. Kelman. *Beyond Distancing: Young Adult American Jews and Their Alienation from Israel*. New York: Andrea and Charles Bronfman Philanthropies, 2007.

———. "Thinking about Distancing from Israel." *Contemporary Jewry* 30, no. 2/3 (2010): 287–296.

Cohen, Steven M., and Charles S. Liebman. "Israel and American Jewry in the Twenty-First Century: A Search for New Relationships." In *Beyond Survival and Philanthropy: American Jewry and Israel*, edited by Allon Gal and Alfred Gottschalk, 3–24. Cincinnati: Hebrew Union College Press, 2000.

Cohn-Sherbok, Dan. *Messianic Judaism*. London: Continuum, 2000.

Collins-Kreiner, Noga, Yoel Mansfeld, and Nurit Kliot. "The Reflection of a Political Conflict in Mapping: The Case of Israel's Borders and Frontiers." *Middle Eastern Studies* 42, no. 3 (2006): 381–408.

Cook, Jonathan. *Disappearing Palestine: Israel's Experiments in Human Despair*. London: Zed Books, 2008.

Cooper, Adina. "What They Didn't Teach Me at Solomon Schechter." *Jewschool*, September 7, 2017. www.jewschool.com.

Cortellessa, Eric. "How IfNotNow Is Getting 2020 Democrats to Talk Occupation." *Times of Israel*, July 30, 2019. www.timesofisrael.com.

Corwin Berman, Lila. *The American Jewish Philanthropic Complex: The History of a Multibillion-Dollar Institution*. Princeton, NJ: Princeton University Press, 2020.

Cramer, Philissa. "Dozens of US Rabbinical Students Sign Letter Calling for American Jews to Hold Israel Accountable for Its Human Rights Abuses." *Jewish Telegraphic Agency*, May 14, 2021. www.jta.org.

Crenshaw, Kimberlé Williams. "Mapping the Margins: Intersectionality, Identity Politics, and Violence Against Women of Color." *Stanford Law Review* 43, no. 6 (1989): 1241–1299.

Cruger-Zaken, Ilana. "Questioning Zionism Is Not Allowed within the Mainstream Jewish Community." *Mondoweiss*, January 15, 2021. www.mondoweiss.net.

Cunningham, Jonathan. "BDS Victory at TIAA-CREF." *Socialist Worker*, July 22, 2013. www.socialistworker.org.

Curcie, Corrine. "Why Walking Off My Birthright Trip Was the Jewish Thing to Do." *Medium*, July 24, 2018. www.medium.com.

Dana, Karam. "The West Bank Apartheid/Separation Wall: Space, Punishment and the Disruption of Social Continuity." *Geopolitics* 22, no. 4 (2017): 887–910.

Daniele, Giulia. "Mizrahi Jews and the Zionist Settler Colonial Context: Between Inclusion and Struggle." *Settler Colonial Studies* 10, no. 4 (2020): 461–480.

———. *Women, Reconciliation, and the Israeli-Palestinian Conflict*. London: Routledge, 2014.

Dash Moore, Deborah, ed. *American Jewish Identity Politics*. Ann Arbor: University of Michigan Press, 2008.

———. "Bonding Images: Miami Jews and the Campaign for Israel Bonds." In *Envisioning Israel: The Changing Ideals and Images of North American Jews*, edited by Allon Gal, 254–267. Detroit: Wayne State University Press, 1996.

———. *To the Golden Cities: Pursuing the American Jewish Dream in Miami and LA.* Cambridge, MA: Harvard University Press, 1994.

Davis, Angela. *Freedom Is a Constant Struggle: Ferguson, Palestine, and the Foundations of a Movement.* Chicago: Haymarket Books, 2016.

Davis, Uri. *Apartheid Israel: Possibilities for the Struggle Within.* London: Zed Books, 2003.

Delamont, Sara, and Paul Atkinson. *Ethnographic Engagements: Encounters with the Familiar and the Strange.* London: Routledge, 2021.

Dias, Elizabeth, and Ruth Graham. "Gaza Conflict Stokes 'Identity Crisis' for Young American Jews." *New York Times*, May 19, 2021. www.nytimes.com.

Diller Teen Foundation Alumni. "We Alumni of the Diller Teen Foundation Call on the Federation to Do Teshuva." *Forward*, October 10, 2018. www.forward.com.

Dimock, Michael. "Defining Generations: Where Millennials End and Generation Z Begins." Pew Research Center, January 17, 2019.

Dinas, Elias, Vassiliki Georgiadou, Iannis Konstantinidis, and Lamprini Rori. "From Dawn to Dusk: Local Party Organization and Party Success of Right-Wing Extremism." *Party Politics* 22, no. 1 (2016): 80–92.

Di Stefano, Paul, and Mostafa Henaway. "Boycotting Apartheid from South Africa to Palestine." *Peace Review* 26, no. 1 (2014): 19–27.

Dixon, John, Kevin Durrheim, and Colin Tredoux. "Beyond the Optimal Contact Strategy: A Reality Check for the Contact Hypothesis." *American Psychologist* 60, no. 7 (2005): 697–711.

Dollinger, Marc. *Black Power, Jewish Politics: Reinventing the Alliance in the 1960s.* Waltham, MA: Brandeis University Press, 2018.

Dolphin, Ray. *The West Bank Wall: Unmaking Palestine.* London: Pluto Press, 2006.

Dolsten, Josefin. "Jewish Currents, a 72-Year-Old Left-Wing Magazine, Wants to Appeal to Millennials." *Jewish Telegraphic Agency*, April 17, 2018. www.jta.org.

Donitsa-Schmidt, Smadar, and Maggie Vadish. "American Students in Israel: An Evaluation of a Study Abroad Experience." *Frontiers* 11, no. 1 (2005): 33–56.

Eilberg-Schwartz, Penina, and Sulaiman Khatib. *In This Place Together: A Palestinian's Journey to Collective Liberation.* Boston: Beacon, 2021.

Einhorn, Alon. "Democratic Presidential Candidates Will Not Attend AIPAC." *Jerusalem Post*, March 22, 2019. www.jpost.com.

Eisner, Oriel. "I Was Arrested for a Crime I Didn't Commit. The Palestinians I Work with Suffer Far Worse." *Forward*, December 21, 2021. www.forward.com.

Elia-Shalev, Asaf. *Israel's Black Panthers: The Radicals Who Punctured a Nation's Founding Myth.* Oakland: University of California Press, 2024.

Ellis, Carolyn. "Telling Secrets, Revealing Lives: Relational Ethics in Research with Intimate Others." *Qualitative Inquiry* 13, no. 1 (January 2007): 3–29.

Elman, Miriam F. "Antisemitism and BDS on US Campuses: The Role of Jewish Voice for Peace." *Journal of Contemporary Antisemitism* 3, no. 2 (2020): 91–102.

Engler, Mark, and Paul Engler. *This Is an Uprising: How Nonviolent Revolt Is Shaping the Twenty-First Century.* New York: Bold Type Books, 2016.

Engler, Paul, and Sophie Lasoff. *The Resistance Guide: How to Sustain the Movement to Win*. Self-published, 2017.

Epstein, Ramon. "#IfNotNow Is Not Jewish Virtue, but Typical Progressive Craptivism." *Times of Israel*, August 22, 2018. www.timesofisrael.com.

Erakat, Noura. "Geographies of Intimacy: Contemporary Renewals of Black–Palestinian Solidarity." *American Quarterly* 72, no. 2 (2020): 471–496.

———. *Justice for Some: Law and the Question of Palestine*. Stanford, CA: Stanford University Press, 2019.

Essa, Azad. "The New Faces of Jewish-American Resistance to Israel." *Middle East Eye*, March 18, 2019. www.middleeasteye.net.

Farb, Sarah. "Israel Will Lose My Entire Generation if It Goes Ahead with Annexation." *Forward*, June 22, 2020. www.forward.com.

Farber, Seth. *Radicals, Rabbis, and Peacemakers: Conversations with Jewish Critics of Israel*. Monroe, ME: Common Courage Press, 2005.

Feld, Marjorie N. *Nations Divided: American Jews and the Struggle over Apartheid*. New York: Palgrave Macmillan, 2014.

Feldman, Ari. "After Getting Kicked Off Birthright, Trio Regroups in West Bank." *Forward*, December 24, 2018. www.forward.com.

Feldman, David, ed. *Boycotts Past and Present: From the American Revolution to the Campaign to Boycott Israel*. London: Palgrave Macmillan, 2019.

Finkelstein, Maura. "May Your Classroom Be a Sea Change: Further Thoughts on Teaching about Palestine." *Anthropology Now* 13, no. 2 (2021): 98–110.

Fischbach, Michael R. *Black Power and Palestine: Transnational Countries of Color*. Stanford, CA: Stanford University Press, 2018.

———. *The Movement and the Middle East: How the Arab-Israeli Conflict Divided the American Left*. Stanford, CA: Stanford University Press, 2019.

Fisher, Robert, and Sally Tamarkin. "Right-Wing Organizers Do This Too: The Case of the Christian Coalition." *Journal of Community Practice* 19, no. 4 (2011): 403–421.

Fishman, Eliana. "Why Young Jews Don't Trust What Their Institutions Say about Israel." *+972 Magazine*, September 14, 2017. www.972mag.com.

Fishman, Joel S. "The BDS Message of Anti-Zionism, Anti-Semitism, and Incitement to Discrimination." *Israel Affairs* 18, no. 3 (2012): 412–425.

———. "'A Disaster of Another Kind': Zionism=Racism, Its Beginning, and the War of Delegitimization Against Israel." *Israel Journal of Foreign Affairs* 5, no. 3 (2011): 75–92.

Fleischmann, Leonie. *The Israeli Peace Movement: Anti-Occupation Activism and Human Rights since the Al-Aqsa Intifada*. London: I.B. Tauris, 2019.

Freedman, Aaron. "What Happened to IfNotNow?" *Jewish Currents*, April 26, 2021. www.jewishcurrents.org.

Freedman, Asher. *The Battle over BDS: Trends, Lessons and Future Trajectories*. Jerusalem: Jerusalem Center for Public Affairs, 2020.

Freedman, Max. "The Birthday Party, Part 3: Lilly." *Unsettled*, April 13, 2022. www.unsettledpod.com.

Freire, Paulo. *Pedagogy of the Oppressed*. 30th Anniversary ed. New York: Continuum, 2007.

Friedman, Hershey Harry, and Dov Fischer. "Learning about Leadership, Trust and Benevolence from Ethics of the Fathers (Avot)." *Journal of Religion and Business Ethics* 3, no. 1 (2015): 1–20.

Gale, Leanne. "'The Coloniser Who Refuses': Co-resistance and the Paradoxical Reality of Israeli Solidarity Activists." *Journal of Peacebuilding & Development* 9, no. 2 (2014): 49–64.

Ganin, Zvi. *An Uneasy Relationship: American Jewish Leadership and Israel, 1948–1957*. Syracuse, NY: Syracuse University Press, 2005.

Garcia, Matt. "A Moveable Feast: The UFW Grape Boycott and Farm Worker Justice." *International Labor and Working Class History* 83 (2013): 146–153.

Gawerc, Michelle I. "Building Solidarity across Asymmetrical Risks: Israeli and Palestinian Peace Activists." *Research in Social Movements, Conflicts and Change* 42 (2018): 87–112.

———. "Solidarity Is in the Heart, Not in the Field: Joint Israeli-Palestinian Peace Movement Organizations during the 2014 Gaza War." *Social Movement Studies* 16, no. 5 (2017): 520–534.

Gelvin, James. *The Israel-Palestine Conflict: One Hundred Years of War*. Cambridge: Cambridge University Press, 2005.

Gerbaudo, Paolo. *Tweets and the Streets: Social Media and Contemporary Activism*. London: Pluto Press, 2012.

Gerber, Karen Abrams, and Aliza Mazor. *Mapping Israel Education: An Overview of Trends and Issues in North America*. San Mateo, CA: Gilo Family Foundation, 2003.

Ghanayem, Eman, Jennifer Mogannam, and Rana Sharif. "Locating Palestinians at the Intersections: Indigeneity, Critical Refugee Studies, and Decolonization." *Amerasia Journal* 47, no. 1 (2021): 9–19.

Ghanem, As'ad, and Tariq Khateeb. "Israel in One Century—From a Colonial Project to a Complex Reality." In Hahn Tapper and Sucharov, *Social Justice and Israel/Palestine*, 79–92.

Glick, Emily, and Maya Rosen. "Portraits of Resistance in Masafer Yatta." *Jewish Currents*, November 10, 2021. www.jewishcurrents.org.

Goldberg, Elisheva. "Why Don't Young Diaspora Jews Like Naftali Bennett?" *Daily Beast*, May 20, 2013. www.thedailybeast.com.

Goldberg, J. J. *Jewish Power: Inside the Jewish American Establishment*. New York: Perseus, 1996.

Goldstein, Eric L. *The Price of Whiteness: Jews, Race, and American Identity*. Princeton, NJ: Princeton University Press, 2006.

Goodstein, Laurie. "Presbyterians Vote to Divest Holdings to Pressure Israel." *New York Times*, June 20, 2014. www.nytimes.com.

Gordon, Neve. *Israel's Occupation*. Berkeley: University of California Press, 2008.

Gordon, Uri. "Against the Wall: Anarchist Mobilization in the Israeli-Palestinian Conflict." *Peace and Change* 35, no. 3 (2010): 412–433.

———. "Israel's 'Tent Protests': The Chilling Effect of Nationalism." *Social Movement Studies* 11, no. 3–4 (2012): 349–355.

Gordon, Uri, and Ohad Grietzer, eds. *Anarchists Against the Wall: Direct Action and Solidarity with the Palestinian Popular Struggle.* Oakland, CA: AK Press, 2013.

Graizbord, David L. *The New Zionists: Young American Jews, Jewish National Identity, and Israel.* London: Lexington Books, 2020.

Grant, Lisa D., and Ezra Kopelowitz. *Israel Education Matters: A Twenty-First Century Paradigm for Jewish Education.* Jerusalem: Center for Jewish Peoplehood Education, 2012.

Greenberg, Erik. "The Jewish Pass: The Growth of Jewish Institutions in Los Angeles' Sepulveda Pass." Mapping Jewish LA, 2019. www.mappingjewishla.com.

Griffiths, Mark. "Hope in Hebron: The Political Affects of Activism in a Strangled City." *Antipode* 49, no. 3 (2017): 617–635.

Groesberg, Sholom. *Jewish Renewal: A Journey, the Movement's History, Ideology, and Future.* New York: iUniverse, 2007.

Gross, Rachel B. *Beyond the Synagogue: Jewish Nostalgia as Religious Practice.* New York: New York University Press, 2021.

Gross, Zehavit, and Rotem Maor. "Is Contact Theory Still Valid in Acute Asymmetrical Violent Conflict? A Case Study of Israeli Jewish and Arab Students in Higher Education." *Peace and Conflict* (2020): 1–5.

Haaretz. "Young U.S. Jews Aim 'Occupy' Movement at Birthright Israel." November 10, 2011. www.haaretz.com.

Habash, Dalia. "The Unmaking of Palestinian Neighborhoods in Jerusalem: 'French Hill' in Focus." *Jerusalem Quarterly*, no. 3 (1999): 35–39.

Habeeb, Noah. "Denial." In Karcher, *Reclaiming Judaism from Zionism*, 178–186.

Habib, Jasmin. *Israel, Diaspora, and the Routes of National Belonging.* 2nd ed. Toronto: University of Toronto Press, 2019.

Hafsa, Lanouar Ben. "The Role of Arab American Advocacy Groups in Shaping American Foreign Policy." *Society* 51, no. 5 (2014): 513–523.

Hahn Tapper, Aaron J. *Judaisms: A Twenty-First-Century Introduction to Jews and Jewish Identities.* Oakland: University of California Press, 2016.

———. "A Pedagogy of Social Justice Education: Social Identity Theory, Intersectionality, and Empowerment." *Conflict Resolution Quarterly* 30, no. 4 (2013): 411–445.

Hahn Tapper, Aaron J., and Mira Sucharov, eds. *Social Justice and Israel/Palestine: Foundational and Contemporary Debates.* Toronto: University of Toronto Press, 2019.

Hallward, Maia Carter. "Creative Responses to Separation: Israeli and Palestinian Joint Activism in Bil'in." *Journal of Peace Research* 46, no. 4 (2009): 541–558.

———. *Struggling for a Just Peace: Israeli and Palestinian Activism in the Second Intifada.* Gainesville: University of Florida Press, 2011.

———. *Transnational Activism and the Israeli-Palestinian Conflict.* New York: Palgrave Macmillan, 2013.

Hammack, Phillip L. "Exploring the Reproduction of Conflict through Narrative: Israeli Youth Motivated to Participate in a Coexistence Program." *Peace and Conflict* 15, no. 1 (2009): 49–74.

———. "Identity, Conflict, and Coexistence." *Journal of Adolescent Research* 21, no. 4 (2006): 323–369.

Hammack, Phillip L., and Andrew Pilecki. "Power in History: Contrasting Theoretical Approaches to Intergroup Dialogue." *Journal of Social Issues* 71, no. 2 (2015): 371–385.

Hancock, Ange-Marie. *Intersectionality: An Intellectual History*. New York: Oxford University Press, 2016.

Hantzopoulos, Maria. "Encountering Peace: The Politics of Participation When Educating for Co-existence." In *Critical Issues in Peace and Education*, edited by Peter Pericles Trifonas and Bryan Wright, 21–39. New York: Routledge, 2011.

Hass, Amira. "Israel Pushing to Legalize West Bank Outpost Slated for Demolition." *Haaretz*, February 23, 2014. www.haaretz.com.

Hassenfeld, Jonah. "Negotiating Critical Analysis and Collective Belonging: Jewish American Students Write the History of Israel." *Contemporary Jewry* 36, no. 1 (2016): 55–84.

Hasson, Nir. "For Second Time in Two Weeks: U.S. Jews Walk Off Birthright Trip to Join Anti-Occupation Activity." *Haaretz*, July 15, 2018. www.haaretz.com.

———. "Israeli Court Clears the Way to Evict Palestinian Family from East Jerusalem Home." *Haaretz*, July 1, 2020. www.haaretz.com.

———. "Jerusalem Police Raided Pro-Palestinian Activists' Apartment Twice over Graffiti." *Haaretz*, December 1, 2021. www.haaretz.com.

Head, Naomi. "A Politics of Empathy: Encounters with Empathy in Israel and Palestine." *Review of International Studies* 42, no. 1 (2016): 95–113.

Hemmings, Clare. "Affective Solidarity: Feminist Reflexivity and Political Transformation." *Feminist Theory* 13, no. 2 (2012): 147–161.

Higgins-Desbiolles, Freya. "Justifying Tourism: Justice through Tourism." In *Tourism and Inequality: Problems and Prospects*, edited by Stroma Cole and Nigel Morgan, 194–211. Cambridge: CABI Press, 2010.

Hill, Lauryn. *The Miseducation of Lauryn Hill*. Columbia Records, 1998.

Hill, Marc Lamont, and Mitchell Plitnick. *Except for Palestine: The Limits of Progressive Politics*. New York: New Press, 2021.

Hill, Sophia, Ella Ben Hagai, and Eileen L. Zurbriggen. "Intersecting Alliances: Non-Palestinian Activists in Support of Palestine." *Journal of Diversity in Higher Education* 11, no. 3 (September 2018): 239–253.

Hillel International. "Hillel Israel Guidelines." 2023. www.hillel.org.

Hilton, Em. "Palestinian Freedom Isn't a Threat to Jews." *Tribune*, May 23, 2021. www.tribunemag.co.uk.

Hodgson, Marshall G. S. *Rethinking World History: Essays on Europe, Islam, and World History*. New York: Cambridge University Press, 1993.

hooks, bell. *Teaching to Transgress: Education as the Practice of Freedom*. New York: Routledge, 1994.

Horowitz, Bethamie. *Defining Israel Education*. Chicago: iCenter, 2012.

Horowitz, Dan, and Baruch Kimmerling. "Some Implications of Military Service and the Reserve System in Israel." *European Journal of Sociology* 15, no. 2 (1974): 262–276.

Horowitz, Yael. "Moving Away from Zionism." In Karcher, *Reclaiming Judaism from Zionism*, 164–165.

Human Rights Watch. "A Threshold Crossed: Israeli Authorities and the Crimes of Apartheid and Persecution." 2021.

Hyslop, Jonathan. "The South African Boycott Experience." *Academe* 92, no. 5 (2006): 59–70.

IfNotNow. "Beyond Talk: Five Ways the American Jewish Establishment Supports the Occupation." 2018.

———. "IfNotNow DNA Guide: Our Story, Strategy, Principles, Structure." Unpublished report, 2015.

"Israeli Government OKs $72 Million Anti-BDS Project." *Jewish Telegraphic Agency*, December 29, 2017. www.jta.org.

Jacobs, Jill. *Where Justice Dwells: A Hands-On Guide to Doing Social Justice in Your Jewish Community*. Woodstock, VT: Jewish Lights, 2011.

Jasper, James M. *The Art of Moral Protest: Culture, Biography, and Creativity in Social Movements*. Chicago: University of Chicago Press, 2008.

Jewish Voice for Peace, NYC. *Confronting Zionism*. Self-published, 2017.

Johnston, Hank, Enrique Laraña, and Joseph R. Gusfield. "Identities, Grievances, and New Social Movements." In *New Social Movements: From Ideology to Identity*, edited by Enrique Larana, Hank Johnston, and Joseph R. Gusfield, 3–35. Philadelphia: Temple University Press, 2009.

JStreet. "Anti-BDS, Anti-occupation: A JStreet U Statement of Principles." 2017.

———. "Boycott, Divestment, and Sanctions Movement." 2010. www.jstreet.org.

———. "National Jewish Survey Results." November 2020. www.jstreet.org.

Juris, Jeffrey S., and Alex Khasnabish. *Insurgent Encounters: Transnational Activism, Ethnography, and the Political*. Durham, NC: Duke University Press, 2013.

Kabas, Marisa. "Young American Jews Have Reached a Tipping Point with Israel." *Rolling Stone*, May 21, 2021. www.rollingstone.com.

Kampeas, Ron. "The Fallout from Eliot Engel's Likely Defeat and a Look at Other Primaries." *Jewish Telegraphic Agency*, June 25, 2020. www.jta.org.

———. "With History in Mind, Jews across US Join Airport Protests of Trump Refugee Ban." *Jewish Telegraphic Agency*, January 29, 2017. www.jta.org.

Kane, Alex. "'It's Killing the Student Movement': Canary Mission's Blacklist of Pro-Palestine Activists Is Taking a Toll." *Intercept*, November 22, 2018. www.theintercept.com.

———. "States Are Cracking Down on the Movement for Palestinian Rights—but Cities Are Pushing Back." *Nation*, December 21, 2018. www.thenation.com.

Kaplan, Amy. *Our American Israel: The Story of an Entangled Alliance*. Cambridge, MA: Harvard University Press, 2018.

Kaplan, Daniel. "Three Reasons to #ReturnTheBirthright." *Jewschool*, November 27, 2017. www.jewschool.com.

Kaplan, Elaine Bell. "The Millennial/Gen Z Leftists Are Emerging: Are Sociologists Ready for Them?" *Sociological Perspectives* 63, no. 3 (2020): 408–427.

Karcher, Carolyn L. "Afterword: American Jews' Changing Attitudes toward Israel, 1948–2018." In Karcher, *Reclaiming Judaism from Zionism*, 349–371.

———, ed. *Reclaiming Judaism from Zionism: Stories of Personal Transformation.* Northampton, MA: Olive Branch Press, 2019.

Karni, Annie, and Luke Broadwater. "Biden Signs Law Making Juneteenth a Federal Holiday." *New York Times*, June 17, 2021. www.nytimes.com.

Karpf, Anne, Brian Klug, Jacqueline Rose, and Barbara Rosenbaum, eds. *A Time to Speak Out: Independent Jewish Voices on Israel, Zionism, and Jewish Identity.* London: Verso, 2008.

Katz, Emily Alice. *Bringing Zion Home: Israel in American Culture, 1948–1967.* Albany: State University of New York Press, 2015.

Katz, Sheila. *Connecting with the Enemy: A Century of Palestinian-Israeli Joint Nonviolence.* Austin: University of Texas Press, 2016.

Kaufman, Ami. "Best Day of My Life: Making It to the Jewish S.H.I.T. List." *+972 Magazine*, July 4, 2013. www.972mag.com.

Kaufman, Edy, Walid Salem, and Juliette Verhoeven, eds. *Bridging the Divide: Peacebuilding in the Israeli-Palestinian Conflict.* Boulder, CO: Lynne Rienner, 2006.

Kaye/Kantrowitz, Melanie. *The Colors of Jews: Racial Politics and Radical Diasporism.* Bloomington: Indiana University Press, 2007.

Kelly, Jennifer Lynn. *Invited to Witness: Solidarity Tourism across Occupied Palestine.* Durham, NC: Duke University Press, 2023.

Kelman, Ari Y., Abiya Ahmed, Ilana Horwitz, Jeremiah Lockwood, Marva Shalev Marom, and Maja Zuckerman. "Safe and on the Sidelines: Jewish Students and the Israel-Palestine Conflict on Campus." Research Group of the Concentration in Education and Jewish Studies, 2017.

Kelner, Shaul. "The Impact of Israel Experience Programs on Israel's Symbolic Meaning." *Contemporary Jewry* 24, no. 1 (2003): 124–155.

———. *Tours That Bind: Diaspora, Pilgrimage, and Israeli Birthright Tourism.* New York: New York University Press, 2010.

Kershner, Isabel. "U.S. Student, Barred from Israel over Boycott, Goes to Court." *New York Times*, October 9, 2018. www.nytimes.com.

Kerstein, Benjamin. "Tufts University Group Condemns Passage of 'Modern-Day Antisemitic Blood Libel' by Student Government." *Algemeiner*, December 20, 2020. www.algemeiner.com.

Keshet, Yehudit Kirstein. *Checkpoint Watch: Testimonies from Occupied Palestine.* London: Zed Books, 2005.

Kimmerling, Baruch. "Some Social Implications of Military Service and the Reserves System in Israel." *European Journal of Sociology* 15, no. 2 (1974): 262–276.

King, Martin Luther, Jr. *Letter from a Birmingham Jail.* San Francisco: Harper, 1994.

Kingkade, Tyler. "These Activists Are Training Every Movement That Matters." *Vice*, November 18, 2019. www.vice.com.

Kingsley, Patrick. "Evictions in Jerusalem Become Focus of Israeli-Palestinian Conflict." *New York Times*, May 7, 2021. www.nytimes.com.

Kirk, Mimi. "Open Hillel: A New Campus Politics on Israel." *Middle East Report* 280 (2016): 30–34.

Klapper, Melissa R. *Ballots, Babies, and Banners of Peace: American Jewish Women's Activism, 1890–1940*. New York: New York University Press, 2013.

Klein, Naomi. *On Fire: The Burning Case for a Green New Deal*. New York: Simon & Schuster, 2019.

Knesset. "Jerusalem Day: A Historical Introduction." 2014. www.knesset.gov.il.

Knopf-Newman, Marcy Jane. *The Politics of Teaching Palestine to Americans*. New York: Palgrave Macmillan, 2011.

Knox, Liam. "Tufts Police Chief Travels to Israel for Counterterrorism Seminar." *Tufts Daily*, January 26, 2018. www.tuftsdaily.com.

Kober, Avi. "The Israel Defense Forces in the Second Lebanon War: Why the Poor Performance?" *Journal of Strategic Studies* 31, no. 1 (2008): 3–40.

Kolsky, Thomas. *Jews Against Zionism: The American Council for Judaism, 1942–1948*. Philadelphia: Temple University Press, 1990.

Kranson, Rachel. *Ambivalent Embrace: Jewish Upward Mobility in Postwar America*. Chapel Hill: University of North Carolina Press, 2017.

Krasner, Jonathan B. "The Place of Tikkun Olam in American Jewish Life." *Jewish Political Studies Review* 25, no. 3/4 (October 1, 2013): 59–98.

Kroll-Zeldin, Oren. "Activists Reclaimed a Water Source for Palestinians, Showing Co-resistance Works." *Truthout*, January 10, 2020. www.truthout.org.

———. "Does Israel Function as an Apartheid State? Critically Engaging the Complexities of the Apartheid Debate in Palestine/Israel." In Hahn Tapper and Sucharov, *Social Justice and Israel/Palestine*, 175–187.

———. "Ethnography of Exclusion: Israeli Policies and Palestinian Resistance in Jerusalem." PhD dissertation, California Institute of Integral Studies, 2014.

———. "Institutionalized Separation and Sumud in Jerusalem's Periphery: Survival and Resistance in Shaykh Sa'd." *Jerusalem Quarterly* 73 (2018): 101–116.

———. "Jewish Students Feel Unsafe on Campus? A New Study Says Otherwise." *+972 Magazine*, October 6, 2017. www.972mag.com.

———. "Separate, Excluded, Unequal: Struggle and Resistance for Palestinian Permanent Residents in East Jerusalem." In *Citizenship and Place: Case Studies on the Borders of Citizenship*, edited by Cherstin M. Lyon and Allison F. Goebel, 143–168. London: Rowman & Littlefield, 2018.

———. "U.S. Jews Are Standing Up for Black Lives. Why Aren't We Doing So for Palestinians?" *+972 Magazine*, June 4, 2020. www.972mag.com.

Kushner, Tony, and Alisa Solomon, eds. *Wrestling with Zion: Progressive Jewish-American Responses to the Israeli-Palestinian Conflict*. New York: Grove Press, 2003.

Landau, Noa. "Official Documents Prove: Israel Bans Young Americans Based on Canary Mission Website." *Haaretz*, October 18, 2020. www.haaretz.com.

Landau, Noa, and Yotam Berger. "Israel Denies Entry to U.S. Jewish BDS Activist." *Haaretz*, July 2, 2018. www.haaretz.com.

Landy, David. *Jewish Identity and Palestinian Rights: Diaspora Jewish Opposition to Israel*. London: Zed Books, 2011.

———. "The Place of Palestinians in Tourist and Zionist Discourses in the 'City of David,' Occupied East Jerusalem." *Critical Discourse Studies* 14, no. 3 (2017): 309–323.

Laor, Yitzhak. *The Myths of Liberal Zionism*. London: Verso, 2009.

Lawson, Steven F. "Freedom Then, Freedom Now: The Historiography of the Civil Rights Movement." *American Historical Review* 96, no. 2 (1991): 456–471.

Lederach, John Paul. *Preparing for Peace: Conflict Transformation across Cultures*. Syracuse, NY: Syracuse University Press, 1995.

Lentin, Ronit. "Palestinian Lives Matter: Racialising Israeli Settler-Colonialism." *Journal of Holy Land and Palestine Studies* 19, no. 2 (2020): 133–149.

Levit, Daphna. *Wrestling with Zion*. Northampton, MA: Olive, 2020.

Levitan, Michael. *Generation Occupy: Reawakening American Democracy*. Berkeley, CA: Counterpoint, 2021.

Liebman, Charles S. "Israel and American Jewry in the Twenty-First Century: A Search for New Relationships." In *Beyond Survival and Philanthropy: American Jewry and Israel*, edited by Allon Gal and Alfred Gottschalk, 3–24. Cincinnati, OH: Hebrew Union College Press, 2000.

Liebman, Charles S., and Steven M. Cohen. *Two Worlds of Judaism: The Israeli and American Experiences*. New Haven, CT: Yale University Press, 1990.

Liew, Jonathan. "Sportswashing Is Associated with Certain Countries—Why Not Israel?" *Guardian*, January 24, 2022. www.theguardian.com.

Lloyd, David. "Settler Colonialism and the State of Exception: The Example of Palestine/Israel." *Settler Colonial Studies* 2, no. 1 (2012): 59–80.

Lough, Benjamin J., and Margaret M. C. Thomas. "Building a Community of Young Leaders: Experiential Learning in Jewish Social Justice." *Journal of Experiential Education* 37, no. 3 (September 2014): 248–264.

Lowery, Wesley. *They Can't Kill Us All: Ferguson, Baltimore, and a New Era in America's Racial Justice Movement*. New York: Little, Brown, 2016.

Lustick, Ian S. "Reinventing Jerusalem." *Foreign Policy* 93 (1993): 41–59.

Mackey, Robert. "Pete Buttigieg and Joe Biden Condemn Israeli Occupation, as Young American Jews Urge Democrats to Press Israel." *Intercept*, July 13, 2019. www.theintercept.com.

MacLean, Malcolm. "Revisiting (and Revising?) Sports Boycotts: From Rugby Against South Africa to Soccer in Israel." *International Journal of the History of Sport* 31, no. 15 (2014): 1832–1851.

Madmoni-Gerber, Shoshana. *Israeli Media and the Framing of Internal Conflict: The Yemenite Babies Affair*. New York: Palgrave Macmillan, 2009.

Magarik, Raphael. "Birthright Is Chasing Away Engaged Jews to Please Pro-Israel Hardliners." *Forward*, December 23, 2018. www.forward.com.

Magid, Shaul. *American Post-Judaism: Identity and Renewal in a Postethnic Society.* Bloomington: Indiana University Press, 2013.

Magid, Yehuda. "The Jewish American Peace Camp: New Expressions of the Jewish Diaspora." In *Non-state Actors in the Middle East: Factors for Peace and Democracy,* edited by Galia Golan and Walid Salem, 156–175. London: Routledge, 2014.

Makdisi, Saree. "The Architecture of Erasure." *Critical Inquiry* 36, no. 3 (2010): 519–559.

Maltz, Judy. "After Summer Walkouts, New Birthright Contract Bans Efforts to Hijack Discussion." *Haaretz,* December 20, 2019. www.haaretz.com.

———. "Israel's New Travel Ban: A Survival Kit for Activists Stopped at Israel's Airport." *Haaretz,* March 9, 2017. www.haaretz.com.

———. "Jewish Group Releases Blacklist of U.S. Professors Who Back Academic Boycott of Israel." *Haaretz,* March 30, 2017. www.haaretz.com.

———. "J Street Launches Birthright Alternative, Featuring 'Occupation 101.'" *Forward,* July 1, 2019. www.forward.com.

———. "Sharp Decline in Number of American Jews on Birthright Trips." *Haaretz,* December 11, 2018. www.haaretz.com.

Maoz, Ifat. "Does Contact Work in Protracted Asymmetrical Conflict? Appraising 20 Years of Reconciliation-Aimed Encounters between Israeli Jews and Palestinians." *Journal of Peace Research* 48, no. 1 (2011): 115–125.

———. "Peace Building in Violent Conflict: Israeli-Palestinian Post-Oslo People-to-People Activities." *International Journal of Politics, Culture, and Society* 17, no. 3 (2004): 563–574.

Masalha, Nur. "Remembering the Palestinian Nakba: Commemoration, Oral History and Narratives of Memory." *Holy Land Studies* 7, no. 2 (2008): 123–156.

Mason, Moriah Ella. "An Epiphany in Slow Motion: Solidarity in Seven Parts." In Karcher, *Reclaiming Judaism from Zionism,* 168–177.

Massad, Joseph. "The Ends of Zionism: Racism and the Palestinian Struggle." *Interventions* 5, no. 3 (2003): 440–451.

———. "Zionism's Internal Others: Israel and the Oriental Jews." *Journal of Palestine Studies* 25, no. 4 (1996): 53–68.

Matar, Haggai. "Israel Chooses Violence." *+972 Magazine,* May 10, 2021. www.972mag.com.

McAdam, Doug, John D. McCarth, and Mayer N. Zald, eds. *Comparative Perspectives on Social Movements: Political Opportunities, Mobilizing Structures, and Cultural Framings.* Cambridge: Cambridge University Press, 1996.

McAdam, Doug, Sydney Tarrow, and Charles Tilley. *Dynamics of Contention.* Cambridge: Cambridge University Press, 2001.

McCarthy, John D., and Mayer N. Zald. "Resource Mobilization and Social Movements: A Partial Theory." *American Journal of Sociology* 82, no. 6 (1977): 1212–1241.

Meyer, David S. *The Politics of Protest: Social Movements in America.* 2nd ed. Oxford: Oxford University Press, 2015.

———. "Protest and Political Opportunities." *Annual Review of Sociology* 30 (2004): 125–145.

Meyer, David S., and Sydney Tarrow. *The Social Movement Society: Contentious Politics for a New Century*. Oxford: Rowman & Littlefield, 1998.

Mi'Ari, Mahmoud. "Attitudes of Palestinians toward Normalization with Israel." *Journal of Peace Research* 36, no. 3 (1999): 339–348.

Minkin, Sarah Anne. "Fear, Fantasy, and Family: Israel's Significance to American Jews." PhD dissertation, University of California, Berkeley, 2014.

———. "An Invitation to Belong: Challenging the Systemic Exclusion of Palestinians as Present Absentees." *Journal of Palestine Studies* 51, no. 1 (2022): 62–67.

Mitchell, Alexis. "Building Home/Land: Jewish Summer Camps as Architecture of Zionism in America." PhD dissertation, University of Toronto, 2018.

Mitchell, Christopher. "Beyond Resolution: What Does Conflict Transformation Actually Transform?" *Peace and Conflict Studies* 9, no. 1 (2002): 1–23.

Mitelpunkt, Shaul. *Israel in the American Mind: The Cultural Politics of U.S.-Israeli Relations, 1958–1988*. Cambridge: Cambridge University Press, 2018.

Mlyn, Noah. "Why I Refuse to Go on Birthright—and You Should, Too." *Forward*, October 17, 2017. www.forward.com.

Moynihan, Colin. "About 20 Rabbis Arrested during Protest over Trump Travel Ban." *New York Times*, February 6, 2017. www.nytimes.com.

Naaman, Dorit. "The Silenced Outcry: A Feminist Perspective from the Israeli Checkpoints in Palestine." *NWSA Journal* 18, no. 3 (2006): 168–180.

Nabulsi, Mira. "'Hungry for Freedom': Palestine Youth Activism in the Era of Social Media." In *Wired Citizenship: Youth Learning and Activism in the Era of Social Media*, edited by Linda Herrera and Rehab Sakr, 117–132. London: Routledge, 2014.

Nagel, Risa. "Why I Walked Off My Birthright Israel Trip." *HuffPost*, July 23, 2018. www.huffpost.com.

Nardini, Gia, Tracy Rank-Christman, Melissa G. Bublitz, Samantha N. N. Cross, and Laura A. Peracchio. "Together We Rise: How Social Movements Succeed." *Journal of Consumer Psychology* 31, no. 1 (2021): 112–145.

Nathan-Kazis, Josh. "Canary Mission Dumped by Diller Foundation, but Critics Say It Doesn't Go Far Enough." *Forward*, October 26, 2018. www.forward.com.

———. "REVEALED: Canary Mission Blacklist Is Secretly Bankrolled by Major Jewish Federation." *Forward*, October 3, 2018. www.forward.com.

Neuman, Jenny. "Return the Birthright." *Times of Israel*, December 5, 2017. www.timesofisrael.com.

Neumann, Boaz. *Land and Desire in Early Zionism*. Translated by Haim Watzman. Waltham, MA: Brandeis University Press, 2011.

Newstrom, John W. "The Management of Unlearning: Exploding the 'Clean Slate' Fallacy." *Training and Development Journal* 37, no. 8 (1983): 36–39.

Now This News. "Birthright Participant Questions Israel Map That Erases Palestine." www.nowthisnews.com.

Noy, Chaim. "The Political Ends of Tourism: Voices and Narratives of Silwan / the City of David." In *Critical Thinking in Tourism Studies*, edited by Irena Ateljevic, Nigel Morgan, and Annette Pritchard, 69–83. London: Routledge, 2012.

Ofer, Dalia. *Escaping the Holocaust: Illegal Immigration to the Land of Israel, 1939–1944.* New York: Oxford University Press, 1990.

Olesker, Ronnie. "Delegitimization as a National Security Threat." *Israel Studies Review* 34, no. 2 (2019): 33–54.

Omer, Atalia. *Days of Awe: Reimagining Jewishness in Solidarity with Palestinians.* Chicago: University of Chicago Press, 2019.

Omer-Man, Michael Schaeffer. "Diaspora Jews Bring Solidarity to South Hebron Hills." *+972 Magazine,* June 15, 2015. www.972mag.com.

———. "JVP Just Declared Itself Anti-Zionist and It's Already Shifting the Conversation." *+972 Magazine,* January 30, 2019. www.972mag.com.

Onishi, Bradley. *Preparing for War: The Extremist History of White Christian Nationalism—And What Comes Next.* Minneapolis: Broadleaf Books, 2023.

Palestinian BDS National Committee. "Palestinians Salute the Movement for Black Lives Emphasizing Common Struggle Against Racial Oppression." August 9, 2016. www.bdsmovement.net.

Pallister-Wilkins, Polly. "Radical Ground: Israeli and Palestinian Activists and Joint Protest Against the Wall." *Social Movement Studies* 8, no. 4 (2009): 393–407.

———. "The Separation Wall: A Symbol of Power and a Site of Resistance?" *Antipode* 43, no. 5 (2011): 1851–1882.

Pappe, Ilan. *The Ethnic Cleansing of Palestine.* Oxford: OneWorld, 2006.

———. *Ten Myths about Israel.* London: Verso, 2017.

———. "What Is Left of the Israeli Left? (1948–2015)." *Brown Journal of World Affairs* 22, no. 1 (2015): 351–367.

Passy, Florence, and Marco Giugni. "Social Networks and Individual Perceptions: Explaining Differential Participation in Social Movements." *Sociological Forum* 16, no. 1 (2001): 123–153.

Peace Now. "Return of the Outpost Method: 32 New Unauthorized Settlements under the Netanyahu Government." 2019.

Pegues, Juliana. "Empire, Race, and Settler Colonialism: BDS and Contingent Solidarities." *Theory & Event* 19, no. 4 (2016).

Penslar, Derek J. "What's Love Got to Do with It? The Emotional Language of Early Zionism." *Journal of Israeli History* 38, no. 1 (2020): 25–52.

Perea, Juan F. *Immigrants Out! The New Nativism and the Anti-immigrant Pulse in America.* New York: New York University Press, 1997.

Pessin, Andrew, and Doron S. Ben-Atar, eds. *Anti-Zionism on Campus: The University, Free Speech, and BDS.* Bloomington: Indiana University Press, 2018.

Pettigrew, Thomas F. "Intergroup Contact Theory." *Annual Review of Psychology* 49, no. 1 (1998): 65–85.

Pew Research Center. "Jewish Americans in 2020." 2021. www.pewresearch.org.

———. "A Portrait of Jewish Americans." 2013. www.pewresearch.org.

———. "U.S. Public Has Favorable View of Israel's People, but Is Less Positive toward Its Government." April 24, 2019. www.pewresearch.org.

Pfeffer, Anshel. *Bibi: The Turbulent Life and Times of Benjamin Netanyahu*. Oxford: Oxford University Press, 2018.

Pink, Aiden. "New Independent Jewish Student Network Seeks 'Judaism on Our Own Terms.'" *Forward*, May 19, 2019. www.forward.com.

Piterberg, Gabriel. *The Returns of Zionism: Myths, Politics and Scholarship in Israel*. London: Verso, 2008.

Plitnick, Mitchell. "More Than 100 Progressive Groups Push Biden to Support Palestinian Rights." *Responsible Statecraft*, June 22, 2020. www.responsiblestatecraft.com.

Polletta, Francesca. "Culture and Movements." *Annals of the American Academy of Political and Social Science* 619, no. 1 (2008): 78–96.

Pollock, Mica. "Using and Disputing Privilege: Young U.S. Activists Struggling to Wield 'International Privilege' in Solidarity." *Race/Ethnicity: Multidisciplinary Global Contexts* 1, no. 2 (2008): 227–251.

Pomson, Alex, Jack Wertheimer, and Hagit Hacohen Wolf. *Hearts and Minds: Israel in North American Jewish Day Schools*. New York: Avi Chai Foundation, 2014.

Prescod-Weinstein, Chanda. "Black and Palestinian Lives Matter: Black and Jewish American in the Twenty-First Century." In *On Antisemitism: Solidarity and the Struggle for Justice*, edited by Jewish Voice for Peace, 31–41. Chicago: Haymarket Books, 2017.

Prusher, Ilene. "The Tree Uprooting Heard around the World." *Haaretz*, June 12, 2014. www.haaretz.com.

Rabkin, Yakov M. *A Threat from Within: A Century of Jewish Opposition to Zionism*. London: Zed Books, 2006.

Rahman, Omar H. "Co-existence vs. Co-resistance: A Case Against Normalization." *+972 Magazine*, January 3, 2012. www.972mag.com.

Raider, Mark A. *The Emergence of American Zionism*. New York: New York University Press, 1998.

Raider, Mark A., Jonathan D. Sarna, and Ronald W. Zweig. *Abba Hillel Silver and American Zionism*. New York: Routledge, 1997.

Raskin, Danielle. "We Had to Meet Our Peers Where They Were." *Jewish Currents*, November 21, 2019. www.jewishcurrents.org.

Reingold, Matt. "Not the Israel of My Elementary School: An Exploration of Jewish-Canadian Secondary Students' Attempts to Process Morally Complex Israeli Narratives." *Social Studies* 108, no. 3 (2017): 87–98.

Researching the American-Israeli Alliance and Jewish Voice for Peace. "Deadly Exchange: The Dangerous Consequences of American Law Enforcement Trainings in Israel." 2018.

Reut Institute. "The Delegitimization Challenge: Creating a Political Firewall." 2010.

Riemer, Matthew, and Leighton Brown. *We Are Everywhere: Protest, Power, and Pride in the History of Queer Liberation*. Berkeley, CA: Ten Speed Press, 2019.

Riesman, Abraham. "The Jewish Revolt." *New York Magazine*, July 12, 2018. www.nymag.com.

Rise Up. "Rise Up Grantees." 2021. www.riseupinitiative.org.

Roberts, Samuel J. *Party and Policy in Israel: The Battle between Hawks and Doves*. New York: Routledge, 2019.

Rose, John. *The Myths of Zionism*. London: Pluto, 2004.

Rose, Liz. "Generational Shift: Young Jews Come Out as Anti-Zionist without Fearing Parents' Wrath." *Mondoweiss*, July 23, 2019. www.mondoweiss.net.

Rosen, Maya, and A. Daniel Roth. "A Progressive Jewish Response to the Discriminatory Policies of KKL-JNF." Breaking the Silence, 2022.

Rosenfeld, Arno. "As Conflict in Gaza Rages Again, a Shift in the American Jewish Response." *Forward*, May 15, 2021. www.forward.com.

———. "Roadblocks Ahead as Activists Push for Jewish Fossil Fuel Divestment." *Forward*, January 12, 2022. www.forward.com.

———. "What Does Annexation Mean for American Jews?" *Washington Jewish Week*, June 24, 2020. www.washingtonjewishweek.com.

Rosner, Shmuel, and Inbal Hakman. *The Challenge of Peoplehood: Strengthening the Attachment of Young American Jews to Israel in the Time of the Distancing Discourse*. Jerusalem: Jewish People Policy Institute, 2011.

Ross, Jack. *Rabbi Outcast: Elmer Berger and American Jewish Anti-Zionism*. Washington, DC: Potomac Books, 2011.

Rothman, Moriel. "10 Reasons the 'City of David' Is Not the Wholesome Tourist Site You Thought It Was." *Times of Israel*, February 9, 2014. www.timesofisrael.com.

Roth-Rowland, Natasha. "U.S. Jewish Activist to Undergo Surgery on Arm Broken by Israeli Cops." *+972 Magazine*, May 28, 2017. www.972mag.com.

Roy, Sara. "Why Peace Failed: An Oslo Autopsy." *Current History* 651 (2002): 8–16.

Rudow, Zoe. "'Camp Is Life, the Rest Is Just Details': Jewish Nationalism and Israeli Militarism in an American Jewish Summer Camp." BA thesis, University of California, Berkeley, 2012.

Saʿdi, Ahmad H., and Lila Abu-Lughod, eds. *Nakba: Palestine, 1948, and the Claims of Memory*. New York: Columbia University Press, 2007.

Said, Edward. *Orientalism*. New York: Vintage, 1978.

———. "Zionism from the Standpoint of Its Victims." *Social Text* 1 (1979): 7–58.

Salaita, Steven. *Uncivil Rights: Palestine and the Limits of Academic Freedom*. Chicago: Haymarket Books, 2015.

Salem, Walid. "The Anti-normalization Discourse in the Context of Israeli-Palestinian Peace-Building." *Palestine-Israel Journal of Politics, Economics, and Culture* 12, no. 1 (2005): 100–109.

Sales, Amy L., and Leonard Saxe. *"How Goodly Are Thy Tents": Summer Camps as Jewish Socializing Experiences*. Hanover, NH: University Press of New England, 2004.

Sales, Ben. "15 Jewish Anti-occupation Activists Arrested while Protesting Outside Birthright Offices in New York." *Haaretz*, April 5, 2019. www.haaretz.com.

Sasson, Theodore. "Mass Mobilization to Direct Engagement: American Jews' Changing Relationship to Israel." *Israel Studies* 15, no. 2 (2010): 173–195.

———. *The New American Zionism*. New York: New York University Press, 2014.

Sasson, Theodore, Bruce Phillips, Charles Kadushin, and Leonard Saxe. *Still Connected: American Jewish Attitudes about Israel*. Waltham, MA: Brandeis University, Cohen Center for Modern Jewish Studies, 2010.

Sasson, Theodore, Michelle Shain, Shahar Hecht, Graham Wright, and Leonard Saxe. "Does Taglit-Birthright Israel Foster Long-Distance Nationalism?" *Nationalism and Ethnic Politics* 20, no. 4 (2014): 438–454.

Saxe, Leonard, et al. *Beyond 10 Days: Parents, Gender, Marriage, and the Long Term Impact of Birthright Israel*. Waltham, MA: Brandeis University, Cohen Center for Modern Jewish Studies, 2017.

———. *Generation Birthright Israel: The Impact of an Israel Experience on Jewish Identity and Choices*. Waltham, MA: Brandeis University, Cohen Center for Modern Jewish Studies, 2009.

———. *Israel, Politics, and Birthright Israel: Findings from the Summer 2017 Cohort*. Waltham, MA: Brandeis University, Cohen Center for Modern Jewish Studies, 2019.

———. *Young Adults and Jewish Engagement: The Impact of Taglit-Birthright Israel*. Waltham, MA: Brandeis University, Cohen Center for Modern Jewish Studies, 2013.

Saxe, Leonard, Benjamin Phillips, Theodore Sasson, Shahar Hecht, Michelle Shain, Graham Wright, and Charles Kadushin. "Intermarriage: The Impact and Lessons of Taglit-Birthright Israel." *Contemporary Jewry* 31, no. 2 (2011): 151–172.

Saxe, Leonard, Theodore Sasson, and Shahar Hecht. *Taglit-Birthright Israel: Impact on Jewish Identity, Peoplehood, and Connection to Israel*. Waltham, MA: Brandeis University, Cohen Center for Modern Jewish Studies, 2006.

Saxe, Leonard, Theodore Sasson, Graham Wright, and Shahar Hecht. *Antisemitism and the College Campus: Perceptions and Realities*. Waltham, MA: Brandeis University, Cohen Center for Modern Jewish Studies, 2015.

Saxe, Leonard, Graham Wright, Shahar Hecht, Michelle Shain, Theodore Sasson, and Fern Chertok. *Hotspots of Antisemitism and Anti-Israel Sentiment on US Campuses*. Waltham, MA: Brandeis University, Cohen Center for Modern Jewish Studies, 2016.

Schiff, Alvin I. "Towards a Mission Statement on Jewish Zionist Education." *Journal of Jewish Education* 61, no. 2 (1994): 17–19.

Schindler, Max. "What's Shabbat Like in a Palestinian Village." *Jerusalem Post*, July 18, 2016. www.jpost.com.

Schleifer, Ron. "Jewish and Contemporary Origins of Israeli 'Hasbara.'" *Jewish Political Studies Review* 15, no. 1/2 (2003a): 123–153.

Schneider, Emily M. "It Changed My Sympathy, Not My Opinion: Alternative Jewish Tourism to the Occupied Palestinian Territories." *Sociological Focus* 53, no. 4 (2020): 378–398.

———. "Pathways to Global Justice: Turning Points, Media, and Palestine Solidarity among Diaspora Jews." *Arab Media and Society* 32 (2021): 1–20.

———. "Touring for Peace: The Role of Dual-Narrative Tours in Creating Transnational Activists." *International Journal of Tourism Cities* 5, no. 2 (2019): 200–218.

Schock, Kurt. *Unarmed Insurrections: People Power Movements in Nondemocracies*. Minneapolis: University of Minnesota Press, 2005.

Schorr, Rebecca Einstein, and Alysa Mendelson Graf, eds. *The Sacred Calling: Four Decades of Women in the Rabbinate*. New York: CCAR Press, 2016.

Schroeder, Juliana, and Jane L. Risen. "Befriending the Enemy: Outgroup Friendship Longitudinally Predicts Intergroup Attitudes in a Coexistence Program for Israelis and Palestinians." *Group Processes & Intergroup Relations* 19, no. 1 (2016): 72–93.

Schultz, Debra L. *Going South: Jewish Women in the Civil Rights Movement*. New York: New York University Press, 2001.

Seidel, Timothy. "'We Refuse to Be Enemies': Political Geographies of Violence and Resistance in Palestine." *Journal of Peacebuilding & Development* 12, no. 3 (2017): 25–38.

Seliktar, Ofira. *Divided We Stand: American Jews, Israel, and the Peace Process*. Westport, CT: Praeger, 2002.

Sfard, Michael. *The Wall and the Gate: Israel, Palestine, and the Legal Battle for Human Rights*. New York: Metropolitan Books, 2018.

Shafir, Gershon. *Land, Labor, and the Origins of the Israeli-Palestinian Conflict, 1882–1914*. Berkeley: University of California Press, 1996.

Shahak, Israel. "Israeli Apartheid and the *Intifada*." *Race and Class* 30, no. 1 (1988): 1–12.

Sharansky, Natan. "3D Test of Anti-Semitism: Demonization, Double Standards, Delegitimization." *Jewish Political Studies Review* 16, no. 3–4 (2004): 3.

Sharp, Gene. *The Politics of Nonviolent Action*. Boston: Porter Sargent, 1973.

Shatz, Adam, ed. *Prophets Outcast: A Century of Dissident Jewish Writing about Zionism and Israel*. New York: Nation Books, 2004.

Shaul Bar Nissim, Hanna. "'New Diaspora Philanthropy'? The Philanthropy of the UJA-Federation of New York toward Israel." *Nonprofit and Voluntary Sector Quarterly* 48, no. 4 (2019): 839–858.

"Sheldon Adelson: Palestinians Are Made-Up Nation That Exists Only to Destroy Israel." *Haaretz*, November 9, 2014. www.haaretz.com.

Sheskin, Ira M., and Ethan Felson. "Is the Boycott, Divestment, and Sanctions Movement Tainted by Anti-Semitism?" *Geographical Review* 106, no. 2 (2016): 270–275.

Shohat, Ella. "Sephardim in Israel: Zionism from the Standpoint of Its Jewish Victims." *Social Text* 19/20 (1988): 1–35.

Shtern, Marik, and Haim Yacobi. "The Urban Geopolitics of Neighboring: Conflict, Encounter and Class in Jerusalem's Settlement/Neighborhood." *Urban Geography* 40, no. 4 (2019): 467–487.

Shulman, David. *Freedom and Despair: Notes from the South Hebron Hills*. Chicago: University of Chicago Press, 2018.

Shuman, Amy. *Other People's Stories: Entitlement Claims and the Critique of Empathy*. Urbana: University of Illinois Press, 2005.

Siapera, Eugenia. "Tweeting #Palestine: Twitter and the Mediation of Palestine." *International Journal of Cultural Studies* 17, no. 6 (2014): 539–555.

Silver, M. M. *Our Exodus: Leon Uris and the Americanization of Israel's Founding Story*. Detroit: Wayne State University Press, 2010.

Simons, Jon. "Fields and Facebook: Ta'ayush's Grassroots Activism and Archiving the Peace That Will Have Come in Israel/Palestine." *Media and Communication* 4, no. 1 (2016): 27–38.

Simpson, Katie. "Why Didn't They Teach Me about the Occupation? It's Time for NFTY to Speak Out." *J Weekly*, April 26, 2018. www.jweekly.com.

Sirri, Omar. "BDS in a Time of Precarity: Graduate Students, Untenured Faculty and Solidarity with Palestine." *Middle East Report* 281 (2016): 44–48.

Sokol, Sam. "Israel Demolished Tower Blocks in Gaza. Here's What They Housed." *Haaretz*, May 18, 2021. www.haaretz.com.

Solomon, Daniel J. "IfNotNow Launches #YouNeverToldMe Anti-Occupation Campaign." *Forward*, September 11, 2017. www.forward.com.

Sommer, Allison Kaplan. "Jewish Voice for Peace Urges Young Jews to Boycott Birthright Israel." *Haaretz*, September 2, 2017. www.haaretz.com.

———. "Principled Activists or Entitled Brats? What's Wrong with the Birthright Walk-Outs." *Haaretz*, July 16, 2018. www.haaretz.com.

Sommer, Allison Kaplan, and Steve Silber. "Jewish-American Protestor Hurt by Israeli Cops: I'm Proud to Be Jewish, but Occupation Is Not My Judaism." *Haaretz*, May 25, 2017. www.haaretz.com.

Staggenborg, Suzanne. *Social Movements.* Oxford: Oxford University Press, 2015.

Staub, Michael E. *Torn at the Roots: The Crisis of Jewish Liberalism in Postwar America.* New York: Columbia University Press, 2002.

Stern, Kenneth. *The Conflict over the Conflict: The Israel/Palestine Campus Debate.* Toronto: New Jewish Press, 2020.

Stewart, Emily. "We Are (Still) the 99 Percent." *Vox*, April 30, 2019. www.vox.com.

Sucharov, Mira. "Values, Identity, and Israel Advocacy." *Foreign Policy Analysis* 7, no. 4 (2011): 361–380.

Suh, Doowon. "How Do Political Opportunities Matter for Social Movements? Political Opportunity, Misframing, Pseudosuccess, and Pseudofailure." *Sociological Quarterly* 42, no. 3 (2001): 437–460.

Sumka, Ilana. "It's Time to Put Our Privileged Jewish Bodies on the Line." *Tikkun* 32, no. 2 (2017): 33.

Sunshine, Spencer. "Get Ready for the New Wave: Young, Passionately Jewish—and Anti-Zionist." *Jewish Telegraphic Agency*, July 8, 2019. www.jta.org.

Sutherland, Neil, Christopher Land, and Steffen Böhm. "Anti-leaders(hip) in Social Movement Organizations: The Case of Autonomous Grassroots Groups." *Organization* 21, no. 6 (2014): 759–781.

Svirsky, Marcelo. *Arab-Jewish Activism in Israel-Palestine.* Burlington, VT: Ashgate, 2012.

———. "BDS as a Mediator." *Concentric: Literary and Cultural Studies* 41, no. 2 (2015): 45–74.

Svirsky, Marcelo, and Ronnen Ben-Arie. *From Shared Life to Co-resistance in Historic Palestine.* London: Rowman & Littlefield, 2018.

Swartz, Michael. "Ritual about Myth about Ritual: Towards an Understanding of the Avodah in the Rabbinic Period." *Journal of Jewish Thought & Philosophy* 6, no. 1 (1997): 135–155.

Tamimi, Abdelrahman A. "Socioeconomic and Environmental Impacts of the Israeli Separation Wall." *International Journal of Environmental Studies* 68, no. 4 (2011): 557–564.

Tarlau, Rebecca. "'We Do Not Need Outsiders to Study Us': Reflections on Activism and Social Movement Research." *Postcolonial Directions in Education* 3, no. 1 (2014): 63–87.

Tarrow, Sidney. *The New Transnational Activism*. Cambridge: Cambridge University Press, 2005.

———. *Power in Movement: Social Movements and Contentious Politics*. New York: Cambridge University Press, 1998.

Tatour, Lana. "The 'Unity Intifada' and '48 Palestinians: Between the Liberal and the Decolonial." *Journal of Palestine Studies* 50, no. 4 (2021): 84–89.

Tatum, Beverly Daniel. "The Complexity of Identity: Who Am I?" In *Readings for Diversity and Social Justice: An Anthology on Racism, Antisemitism, Sexism, Heterosexism, Ableism, and Classism*, edited by Maurianne Adams et al., 9–14. New York: Routledge, 2000.

———. "Teaching White Students about Racism: The Search for White Allies and the Restoration of Hope." *Teachers College Record* 95, no. 4 (1994): 462–476.

Telhami, Shibley. "What Do Americans Think of the BDS Movement, Aimed at Israel?" *Brookings*, January 8, 2020. www.brookings.edu.

Thiessen, Chuck, and Marwan Darweish. "Conflict Resolution and Asymmetric Conflict: The Contradictions of Planned Contact Interventions in Israel and Palestine." *International Journal of Intercultural Relations* 66 (2018): 73–84.

Thrall, Nathan. "BDS: How a Controversial Non-violent Movement Has Transformed the Israeli-Palestinian Debate." *Guardian*, August 14, 2018. www.theguardian.com.

Ticktin, Miriam. *Casualties of Care: Immigration and the Politics of Humanitarianism in France*. Berkeley: University of California Press, 2011.

Tighe, Elizabeth, et al. *American Jewish Population Project*. Waltham, MA: Brandeis University, Steinhardt Social Research Institute, 2019.

Tilley, Charles, and Sydney Tarrow. *Contentious Politics*. 2nd ed. Oxford: Oxford University Press, 2015.

Tobin, Gary A. *The Transition of Communal Values and Behavior in Jewish Philanthropy*. San Francisco: Institute for Jewish and Community Research, 2001.

Todorova, Teodora. "Vulnerability as a Politics of Decolonial Solidarity: The Case of the Anarchists Against the Wall." *Identities: Global Studies in Culture and Power* 27, no. 3 (2020): 321–338.

Torstrick, Rebecca L. *The Limits of Coexistence: Identity Politics in Israel*. Ann Arbor: University of Michigan Press, 2000.

Tracy, Marc. "Inside the Unraveling of American Zionism." *New York Times Magazine*, November 2, 2021. www.nytimes.com.

T'ruah. "Freedom of Speech in Jewish Tradition: Upholding It Even When We Disagree." 2019.

Tufts University Students for Justice in Palestine. "Op-Ed: Vote YES to End the Deadly Exchange at Tufts." *Tufts Daily*, November 23, 2020. www.tuftsdaily.com.

———. "Tufts Students Pass Referendum Demanding University End the Deadly Exchange." *Mondoweiss*, December 22, 2020. www.mondoweiss.net.

Tunis, Molly, and Parker Breza. "Boycott Birthright—Unconditionally." *New Voices*, April 16, 2019. www.newvoices.org.

Union for Reform Judaism. *Speak Truth to Power: A Guide for Congregations Taking Public Policy Positions*. Washington, DC: Union for Reform Judaism, 2007.

United Nations Human Rights Council. "Report of the Independent Commission of Inquiry Established Pursuant to Human Rights Council Resolution S-21/1." 2015.

United Nations Office for the Coordination of Humanitarian Affairs Occupied Palestinian Territories. "The Humanitarian Impact of Israeli-Declared 'Firing Zones' in the West Bank." 2012.

———. "Response to the Escalation in the oPt Situation Report No 1: 21–27 May 2021." 2021.

Uri, Renad, and Omri Evron. "Forget about Dialogue Groups, It's Time to Switch to Co-resistance." *+972 Magazine*, February 12, 2019. www.972mag.com.

Urofsky, Melvin I. *Louis D. Brandeis*. New York: Schocken Books, 2009.

———. *A Voice That Spoke for Justice: The Life and Times of Stephen S. Wise*. Albany: State University of New York Press, 1982.

Usher, Graham. "Unmaking Palestine: On Israel, the Palestinians, and the Wall." *Journal of Palestine Studies* 35, no. 1 (2005): 25–43.

Veracini, Lorenzo. "The Other Shift: Settler Colonialism, Israel, and the Occupation." *Journal of Palestine Studies* 42, no. 2 (2013): 26–42.

Wagner, Noah. "Why I Walked Off a Birthright Trip." *Dig Boston*, July 24, 2018. www.digboston.com.

Waxman, Dov. *Trouble in the Tribe: The American Jewish Conflict over Israel*. Princeton, NJ: Princeton University Press, 2016.

———. "Young American Jews and Israel: Beyond Birthright and BDS." *Israel Studies* 22, no. 3 (2017): 177–199.

Weiner, Katie A., and Allen S. Weiner. "When My Daughter Called Israel an Apartheid State, I Objected. Now I'm Not So Sure." *Haaretz*, July 5, 2020. www.haaretz.com.

Weinthal, Benjamin. "Ilhan Omar, Rashida Tlaib, Jeremy Corbyn Top List of Worst Anti-Semites." *Jerusalem Post*, December 20, 2019. www.jpost.com.

Weiss, Erica. *Conscientious Objectors in Israel: Citizenship, Sacrifice, Trials of Fealty*. Philadelphia: University of Pennsylvania Press, 2014.

Wermenbol, Grace. *A Tale of Two Narratives: The Holocaust, the Nakba, and the Israeli-Palestinian Battle of Memories*. Cambridge: Cambridge University Press, 2021.

Wertheimer, Jack. "American Jews and Israel: A 60-Year Retrospective." *American Jewish Year Book* 108 (2008): 3–79.

———. *Generation of Change: How Leaders in Their Twenties and Thirties Are Reshaping American Jewish Life*. New York: Avi Chai Foundation, 2010.

Wilmer, Franke. *Breaking Cycles of Violence in Israel and Palestine: Empathy and Peacemaking in the Middle East*. Lanham, MD: Lexington Books, 2021.

Wilner, Michael. "Ocasio-Cortez, Tlaib and Other Star Freshmen Crash into Congress." *Jerusalem Post*, January 5, 2019. www.jpost.com.

Wise, Alissa. "I'm the First Jew Banned from Israel for Supporting BDS." *Forward*, July 26, 2017. www.forward.com.

Wright, Fiona. *The Israeli Radical Left: An Ethics of Complicity*. 2018. Philadelphia: University of Pennsylvania Press.

———. "Palestine, My Love: The Ethico-politics of Love and Mourning in Jewish Israeli Solidarity Activism." *American Ethnologist* 43, no. 1 (2016): 130–143.

Yiftachel, Oren. *Ethnocracy: Land and Politics in Israel/Palestine*. Philadelphia: University of Pennsylvania Press, 2006.

Zaiman, Bethany. "Of Birthright Transgressions." *Protocols*, no. 3 (2018). www.prtcls.com.

Zakai, Sivan. "'Bad Things Happened': How Children of the Digital Age Make Sense of Violent Current Events." *Social Studies* 110, no. 2 (2019): 67–85.

———. *My Second Favorite Country: How American Jewish Children Think about Israel*. New York: New York University Press, 2022.

———. "Values in Tension: Israel Education at a U.S. Jewish Day School." *Journal of Jewish Education* 77, no. 3 (2011): 239–265.

Zald, Mayer N., Doug McAdam, and John D. McCarthy. *Comparative Perspectives on Social Movements: Political Opportunities, Mobilizing Structures, and Cultural Framings*. Cambridge: Cambridge University Press, 1996.

Zborowski, Mark, and Elizabeth Herzog. *Life Is with People: The Culture of the Shtetl*. New York: Schocken Books, 1952.

Zibechi, Raúl. *Dispersing Power: Social Movements as Anti-state Forces*. Oakland, CA: AK Press, 2010.

Zimmerman, Simone, and Yonah Lieberman. "Which Side Are You On, My People? Ending American Jewish Support for the Occupation." *Tikkun* 32, no. 2 (2017): 36–37.

Zink, Valerie. "A Quiet Transfer: The Judaization of Jerusalem." *Contemporary Arab Affairs* 2, no. 1 (2009): 122–133.

Ziv, Amalia. "Performative Politics in Israeli Queer Anti-occupation Activism." *GLQ: A Journal of Lesbian and Gay Studies* 16, no. 4 (2010): 537–556.

Ziv, Oren. "Palestinian, Israeli, and Diaspora Jewish Activists Reclaim Spring Seized by Settlers." *+972 Magazine*, January 3, 2020. www.972mag.com.

Zonszein, Mairav. "Breaking the Silence: Inside the Israeli Right's Campaign to Silence an Anti-occupation Group." *Intercept*, March 3, 2019. www.theintercept.com.

———. "IDF Maps Village of Susya as Forced Displacement Looms." *+972 Magazine*, May 10, 2015. www.972mag.com.

Zreik, Raef. "Palestine, Apartheid, and the Rights Discourse." *Journal of Palestine Studies* 34, no. 1 (2004): 68–80.

Zunes, Stephen. "The Israel Lobby: How Powerful Is It Really?" *Mother Jones*, May 18, 2006. www.motherjones.com.

———. "Reflections on BDS." *Tikkun* 33, no. 4 (2018): 30.

INDEX

Numbers in *italics* denote figures

Umm al-Khair, 123, 149
Unity Intifada, 49
University of Illinois, 184
University of Maryland Critical Issues
  Poll, 173
unlearning: as coming out, 91; author's
  experiences with, 62–70; as emancipatory Jewish identity, 65, 69, 94–96;
  emotional response to, 91; interpola-
  tion, 73; as intervention, 71–79; and the
  miseducation of Jewish Youth, 29–30,
  83–90; and personal transformation,
  30, 79–83; and righteous indignation,
  91–94. *See also* Zionism
Uri, Renad, 133
Uris, Leon, 11

Vilkomerson, Rebecca, 175–76
violence: airstrikes, 1; bombs, 1, 66–67,
  133; rockets, 1, 33, 66; systemic, 74–75;
  weapons manufacturing, 174

water, 4, 89–90, 126–27, 199–202
Weiner, Allen and Katie, 92

whites, 91, 137, 153, 171, 192: whiteness, 11;
  white supremacy, 51–54, 74
Wise, Alissa, 191
Wise, Stephen S., 62

Ya'aseh Mishpat, 59
Yemenite Babies Affair, 71
Youth Against Settlements, 146

Zeldin, Isaiah, 18, 62–63
Zionism: America as Zion for American
  Jews, 10; American Zionism, 11, 21;
  anti-Zionism, 10, 22, 27, 91, 95, 161,
  169, 174–77; "checking" their Zionism,
  14–15, 99; defined, 72–73; International
  Jewish Anti-Zionist Network, 174; land
  without a people for a people without
  a land, 85–86; as liberation for Jews,
  69; and liberals, 20–21, 27, 56, 73, 99,
  102, 175; myths of, 12, 29–30, 64–65,
  68–75, 83, 86–91, 136; NFTY-EIE program, 63; as political ideology, 14, 73,
  198; Zionist Organization of America
  (ZOA), 183

ABOUT THE AUTHOR

OREN KROLL-ZELDIN is Assistant Professor in the Department of Theology and Religious Studies as well as Assistant Director of the Swig Program in Jewish Studies and Social Justice at the University of San Francisco. He is the co-editor of *This Is Your Song Too: Phish and Contemporary Jewish Identity*.

www.ingramcontent.com/pod-product-compliance
Ingram Content Group UK Ltd.
Pitfield, Milton Keynes, MK11 3LW, UK
UKHW040505200225
455270UK00012B/134/J